RACHEL ALLEN

Home Cooking

RACHEL ALLEN

Home Cooking

Collins

HarperCollins*Publishers*
77–85 Fulham Palace Road
London W6 8JB
www.harpercollins.co.uk

First published in 2009 by Collins

ISBN 978-0-00-725971-7

Editorial Director: Jenny Heller
Senior Development Editor: Lizzy Gray
Editors: Emma Callery, Kate Parker
and Ione Walder
Design: Smith & Gilmour, London
Calligraphy: Peter Horridge
Styling: Liz Belton and Abigail Fawcett

Colour reproduction by ButlerTanner
& Dennis, Frome, Somerset
Printed and bound by Lego, Italy

Contents

Introduction

Home cooking is not about recreating fancy restaurant meals — although that is obviously great fun too — it's more a way of life. It's about food that anyone can achieve for friends and family, and taking great pleasure in the preparation as much as in the sharing, and of course the eating! The value of cooking at home goes beyond merely having control over your ingredients (though this is profoundly important for health, wellbeing, and your wallet ...), it's also about gathering your loved ones together to share and enjoy the most fundamental part of life; it's about teaching your children how to appreciate a home-cooked meal and showing them how much fun cooking can be; it's about slowing down the busy pace of your life when you can, but also knowing that when there isn't much time you can still put a loving meal on the table, made by you.

Home cooking is also about the joy of learning old skills and kitchen crafts such as making home-made sweets. It's about feeling proud as a parent when making by hand your child's very first foods. It's about the wonderful kitchen smells and sounds and flavours that you just can't get any other way.

In this book, you'll not only find recipes for many occasions from breakfasts to dinners, you'll also find trusted kitchen tips, such as home freezing, which not only saves time, but money too. You'll also find hints on menu planning and how to encourage healthy eating habits.

I hope you and your loved ones enjoy every meal together, that you eat well, that you take a moment to appreciate one another's company around the table, and above all, have fun cooking at home!

Rachel x

p.s. The oven temperatures in this book are for a conventional oven, but if I am using a fan oven, then I usually reduce the temperature by 10 per cent.

Breakfast

Homemade yoghurt

MAKES ABOUT 425ML (15FL OZ) · VEGETARIAN

Making your own yoghurt is very satisfying as well as being a good way to encourage children to eat it, as they can add their own flavours. It is crucial to use sugar-free yoghurt for the recipe to work. It is also important that the milk and yoghurt mixture stays in a warm, draught-free place like an airing cupboard or beside an Aga or radiator. Pouring into a flask will also help if you have one. Remember to keep 1 teaspoon of the yoghurt back to make the next batch!

1 litre (1¾ pints) whole milk
25g (1oz) skimmed milk powder
1 tsp natural probiotic yoghurt

1 Pour the milk into a large, heavy-based or cast-iron saucepan on a gentle heat. As the milk is beginning to warm up, add the milk powder, stirring to dissolve. Heat the milk until it reads 90°C (194°F) on a cooking thermometer (if judging by eye, the milk will be sweet smelling and just coming to the boil – steaming heavily and frothing around the edges).

2 Remove from the heat and leave to stand for about 15 minutes to cool until it reads 40°C (104°F) on the thermometer (or the milk has stopped steaming and feels just tepid when you dip your finger in and leave it there for a few seconds).

3 Stir in the yoghurt and cover with a double layer of foil. Wrap with a tea towel and leave in a warm place (or in a flask) until the mixture thickens, which will take 4–5 hours. Remove the towel, transfer to a bowl, cover and place in the fridge to cool overnight.

Variations

Apple and sweet geranium yoghurt: Cook 600g (1⅓lb) (about 2) peeled, cored and roughly chopped cooking apples with 50g (2oz) caster or granulated sugar, 1 tablespoon of water and 2 sweet geranium (or mint) leaves for 6–8 minutes until soft. Leave to cool completely and remove the leaves before stirring into the set yoghurt.

Raspberry yoghurt: Make a raspberry coulis (see page 337) and stir into or drizzle over the yoghurt to serve.

Orange curd yoghurt: Ripple a spoonful of orange curd (see page 336) through the yoghurt.

Natural yoghurt with fresh fruits: Serve the yoghurt with one of the fresh fruit salads on page 14.

Natural yoghurt with poached fruits: Serve the yoghurt with some poached fruits (dried or fresh, see pages 44 and 212) or chop them up and stir them into the yoghurt.

Porridge

SERVES 2 · VEGETARIAN

My dad always used to make us eat porridge before going to school, and now I appreciate why. Oats are a great slow-release carbohydrate and so porridge makes a good, hearty breakfast. It can be slightly sinful, depending on what you serve it with, but if you choose healthy toppings it's a lot more healthy and nutritious than many breakfast cereals.

100g (3½oz) porridge oats
Pinch of salt (optional)
225ml (8fl oz) milk
   (optional)

1 Place the oats in a medium saucepan, add a pinch of salt (if you wish) and pour over 500ml (18fl oz) water, or a mixture of water and milk.

2 Cook on a low–medium heat, stirring regularly, for 7–10 minutes or until the oats are tender and the porridge creamy and thick. (Feel free to add more liquid if you prefer a thinner consistency.)

3 Serve in warm bowls and make more interesting with one of the tasty additions suggested below.

Additions
* Sweeten with soft brown sugar, honey or maple or golden syrup.
* Add a dash of cream or milk, or drizzle over a little natural yoghurt.
* Try adding dried fruit such as raisins, sultanas, apricots or prunes before cooking the oats.
* Top your porridge with your favourite nuts or seeds for a crunchier texture.
* Try flavouring your porridge with added ground cinnamon, cardamom or nutmeg, either during or after cooking.
* For a serious weekend brunch for grown-ups, you could even go so far as to add a splash of whiskey and cream over your porridge … now *that* is pure indulgence.

Rachel's tip
If using pinhead oatmeal, it needs to be soaked overnight in water and then cooked as above, but it may take about 20 minutes.

Crunchy granola

MAKES ABOUT 1.5KG (3LB 5OZ) · VEGETARIAN

A bowl of granola, bursting with different textures and flavours, is a fantastic way to start the day. Serve it either with milk or natural yoghurt and feel free to mix and match the ingredients; you could use rye or barley flakes instead of some of the oat flakes, for instance, or add chocolate chips or dried cranberries. Whatever takes your fancy.

125g (4½oz) butter
150ml (5fl oz) honey
1 tsp vanilla extract
500g (1lb 2oz) rolled oats
50g (2oz) pecan nuts, roughly chopped
150g (5oz) hazelnuts, roughly chopped
75g (3oz) pumpkin seeds
75g (3oz) sunflower seeds
50g (2oz) golden linseeds
100g (3½oz) desiccated coconut
300g (11oz) mixed dried fruit, such as dates, figs, apricots, raisins or sultanas, the larger fruit chopped

1 Preheat the oven to 170°C (325°F), Gas mark 3.

2 Place the butter, honey and vanilla extract in a small saucepan on a low heat and gently melt together. Mix the oats, nuts, seeds and desiccated coconut together in a large bowl. Pour over the melted butter and honey mixture and stir really well to ensure all the dry ingredients are evenly coated.

3 Divide the mixture between two large baking trays and spread in an even layer. Bake in the oven for 20–25 minutes, tossing every 5 minutes, until golden brown. Remove from the oven and leave to cool on the trays, stirring every now and then. (If you transfer it into a deep bowl at this stage, while it is still warm, it will go soggy.)

4 Once completely cool, transfer to a large bowl and stir in your choice of dried fruits. Pour into an airtight container and store at room temperature for up to two months.

Fresh fruit salads

There's nothing like a fresh fruit salad to make you feel healthy and invigorated. Eat for breakfast or serve as a starter, simple snack or dessert, either on its own or with natural yoghurt (see page 10 for making your own). First make the fruit juice dressing, then mix with your choice of fruit salad.

Fruit juice dressing

1 tbsp freshly squeezed orange juice
1 tbsp freshly squeezed lemon juice
1 tsp caster sugar or runny honey
2 tbsp finely chopped mint (optional)

Mix the orange juice and lemon juice together in a bowl and stir in the sugar or honey to dissolve. Pour this over your choice of fruit salad below (adding finely chopped mint, if you wish). Stir to combine and serve immediately.

Grape, melon and grapefruit

110g (4oz) seedless red or green grapes (or a mixture), halved
250g (9oz) peeled and deseeded melon, diced
1 grapefruit, peeled and segmented
1 tbsp very finely chopped celery (optional)

Mix the red or green grapes with the melon, grapefruit and celery (if using). Stir in the dressing (see left) and serve.

Pink grapefruit and pomegranate

2 pink grapefruit, peeled and segmented
Seeds from ½ pomegranate

Mix the pink grapefruit segments and pomegranate seeds together. Stir in the dressing (see above) and serve.

Tropical fruit mix

1 large orange, peeled and segmented
200g (7oz) peeled and stoned mango, roughly chopped
125g (4½oz) peeled and cored pineapple, roughly chopped
110g (4oz) peeled and deseeded papaya, diced
Seeds and pulp from 1 large passion fruit

Mix the orange, mango, pineapple and diced papaya with the passion fruit. Stir in the dressing (see above left) and serve.

American buttermilk pancakes

My children and I love making these thick and spongy pancakes (see picture on page 18). The basic recipe is delicious, but the pancakes also taste great with other ingredients added to the batter to flavour them (see the variations opposite). Once cooked and cooled, the pancakes can be kept in the fridge and then warmed through for a few minutes in a hot oven. Spread with a little butter and jam or apple jelly or try one of the toppings suggested below.

150g (5oz) plain flour
2 tsp baking powder
¼ tsp bicarbonate of soda
50g (2oz) caster sugar
2 eggs
150ml (5fl oz) buttermilk or soured milk (see tip on page 24)
25g (1oz) butter, melted and cooled
Sunflower oil, for frying
Icing sugar, for dusting

1 Sift the flour, baking powder and bicarbonate of soda into a large bowl, then stir in the sugar. Whisk the eggs, buttermilk or soured milk and melted butter together in another bowl, then pour into the dry ingredients, whisking all the time until you have a smooth batter. The batter is now ready to use or may be stored in the fridge overnight.

2 When you are ready to cook the pancakes, fold your chosen flavouring (if using – see opposite) into the batter. Place a large frying pan on a medium heat and oil it very lightly (I usually pour the oil onto a piece of kitchen paper and rub it on). Working in batches, drop large spoonfuls (about 50ml/2fl oz) of the pancake batter into the pan, spacing them apart to allow for spreading while cooking.

3 Cook on one side for 1–2 minutes until bubbles appear on the upper surface, then flip over with a fish slice or palette knife and cook on the other side for a further 1–2 minutes until golden brown on both sides. Repeat with any remaining mixture, keeping any cooked pancakes warm in a low oven (cover with foil) as you go.

4 Serve dredged with icing sugar and your choice of toppings from below.

Toppings
* Crème fraîche or Greek or natural yoghurt
* Slices of mango or strawberry, or pomegranate seeds
* Honey or maple or golden syrup
* Chopped nuts, such as pecans, hazelnuts or almonds
* Pumpkin or sunflower seeds
* Top with banana slices and toffee sauce (see page 337)

Variations

Choose one of the following to fold into the batter once it's made:

Banana pancakes: 1 large or 1½ small–medium bananas, mashed (giving 150g/5oz mashed weight)

Berry pancakes: 75g (3oz) fresh or frozen (and defrosted) berries of your choice

Chocolate chip pancakes: 75g (3oz) chocolate chips (dark or milk chocolate)

Dried fruit pancakes: 75g (3oz) dried fruit such as raisins, sultanas, apricots or cranberries (chopped if large)

Cinnamon pancakes: 1½ tsp ground cinnamon

Fresh apple muesli

SERVES 2 · VEGETARIAN

This delicious wet muesli is so easy to assemble and more nutritious than shop-bought dried muesli. You could use other fruit instead of apples — whatever is to hand.

4 tbsp oat flakes
2 eating apples
1 tsp honey
1 tbsp single or regular
   cream (optional)

1 Measure 3 tablespoons of water into a bowl and sprinkle in the oats. Leave for a few minutes to soak.

2 In the meantime, coarsely grate the apples with the skin still on and avoiding the core. Stir into the softened oats, along with the honey. Taste, adding a little more honey to sweeten, if necessary. Spoon into bowls and serve immediately, drizzled with cream, if you wish.

Variations

Apple and cinnamon muesli: Stir a pinch of cinnamon into the water before adding the oats.

Raspberry and orange muesli: Substitute the apples with 50g (2oz) crushed raspberries and stir into the oats with the finely grated zest of 1 small orange.

Apple, blackberry and pecan nut muesli: In addition to the apple, stir 25g (1oz) blackberries into the oats with 2 teaspoons of finely chopped pecan nuts.

Waffles

MAKES 16—20 WAFFLES · VEGETARIAN
(WITH NON-VEGETARIAN VARIATIONS)

Waffles are a perfect weekend breakfast, but they can make an excellent snack at any time of day. They go well with so many different toppings, sweet or savoury. I've listed some of my favourites below.

400g (14oz) plain flour
2 tsp baking powder
2 tsp salt
100g (3½oz) caster sugar
4 eggs
200g (7oz) butter, melted and cooled
600ml (1 pint) milk
Icing sugar, for dusting (optional)

1 Sift the flour and baking powder into a large bowl. Add the salt and sugar and mix well together. Whisk the eggs in another bowl, then stir in the melted butter and milk. Pour the wet ingredients into the centre of the dry ingredients, whisking all the time until you have a smooth batter.

2 Heat the waffle machine. Using a ladle, pour some batter into the machine – don't fill it too full. Close the lid and cook for 4–5 minutes or following the manufacturer's instructions, or until the waffles are golden brown and cooked through. Remove the waffles, dredge with icing sugar (if using) and add your choice of topping to serve.

Toppings

The quantities are for 1 waffle.

Bacon and maple syrup: Serve each waffle with 1–2 pieces of back or streaky bacon, a drizzle of maple syrup and a dollop of soured cream.

Peanut butter and jam: Spread 1 tablespoon of peanut butter or homemade nut butter (see page 252) over the waffle and blob 1 tablespoon of raspberry or strawberry jam on top.

Kiwi fruit and raspberries: Scatter over 1 chopped kiwi fruit and a small handful of raspberries. Drizzle with a little runny honey and add a dollop of Greek or natural yoghurt.

Classic French omelette

The ultimate fast food, an omelette is perfect at any time of day,
either on its own or with a crisp green salad. It is incredibly
versatile, too. Try the variations listed here.

2 eggs
2 tsp milk
Salt and freshly ground
    black pepper
2 tsp butter
1 tbsp olive oil

1 Place a 23cm (9in) non-stick or cast-iron frying pan on a high
heat until very hot. (The omelette should take only about 40–45
seconds to cook if the pan is hot enough.) Place the eggs in a bowl,
add the milk, season with salt and pepper and beat together until
thoroughly mixed.

2 Add the butter and olive oil to the pan and as soon as the butter
sizzles and starts to turn brown, pour in the egg mixture. It will
start to cook immediately, so using a plastic fish slice or wooden
spatula, quickly pull the edges of the omelette towards the centre,
tilting the pan so that the uncooked egg runs to the sides.
Continue until most of the egg is set and will not run any more –
the omelette may need to cook for a further 5 seconds to slightly
brown the bottom. The centre should still be soft and moist. If
you are using a filling (see below), then add it in a line along the
centre now (except for those added to the egg mixture at the start).

3 To fold the omelette, flip the edge closest to the handle into
the centre, then tilt the pan so that it is almost perpendicular
to the plate so that the opposite edge of the omelette folds in
and the omelette flips over. As you do this, slide the omelette
out of the pan and onto the plate, and serve immediately.

Variations

Alpine breakfast omelette: To the egg mixture add 25g (1oz)
grated Emmental and Gruyère cheese, 25g (1oz) soft and creamy
goat's cheese and 1 teaspoon of finely chopped chives and beat
all the ingredients together.

Courgette and herb omelette: Sauté 50g (2oz) finely diced
courgette with 1 finely chopped clove of garlic and a small pinch of
salt and pepper in 15g (½oz) of butter or 2 tablespoons of olive oil
for about 5 minutes until soft and golden. Drain on kitchen paper
and leave to cool. Stir into the egg mixture along with 2 tablespoons
of finely chopped herbs (such as mint, marjoram or basil).

Bacon and mushroom omelette: Stir 1 teaspoon of finely chopped chives into the egg mixture before cooking. Place 2 rashers of grilled bacon and 1 fried or roasted flat mushroom in the middle of the omelette before folding over. (This is a great way of using up leftover ingredients from a fried breakfast.)

Smoked salmon and goat's cheese omelette: Add 25g (1oz) finely diced smoked salmon and 25g (1oz) soft, mild goat's cheese (or cream cheese for an even milder flavour) to the middle of the omelette before folding over.

French toast

SERVES 4 · VEGETARIAN

The French call this *pain perdu* ('lost bread'). It is made with slightly stale, leftover bread that you would otherwise throw out, but if you have only fresh bread to hand, leave it out overnight to dry out.

25g (1oz) butter
2 eggs
2 tbsp single or regular cream (or milk)
Pinch of salt
4 slices of white or brown bread
Icing sugar, for dusting
Honey or golden or maple syrup, to serve

1 Place a large, non-stick or cast-iron frying pan on a medium heat and add the butter. While it is melting, whisk the eggs with the cream or milk and salt in a wide, shallow bowl. Soak the bread in the egg mixture for a few seconds on each side and place in the hot pan.

2 Cook for 1–2 minutes on each side until deep golden in colour, then place on warm plates, dredge generously with icing sugar and serve with honey or golden or maple syrup drizzled over.

Variations

Spicy French toast: Add ground spices such as cinnamon, nutmeg or mixed spice to the egg mix before soaking the bread.

Fruity French toast: Add 1 small mashed banana or 50g (2oz) mashed raspberries or strawberries to the egg mix.

Rhubarb muffins

These are great for breakfast or as a snack at any time of the day.
Use fresh rhubarb when it's in season in spring or frozen rhubarb
at other times. If it is already sliced, it needn't be defrosted.

150g (5oz) soft light
    brown sugar
1 tbsp sunflower oil
1 egg
1 tsp vanilla extract
100ml (3½fl oz)
    buttermilk or soured
    milk (see tip on page 24)
100g (3½oz) rhubarb,
    finely diced
175g (6oz) plain flour
1 tsp baking powder
1 tsp bicarbonate of soda
Pinch of salt

12-hole muffin tin

1 Preheat the oven to 200°C (400°F), Gas mark 6. Line the muffin tin with paper cases.

2 Place 125g (4½oz) of the sugar, the sunflower oil, egg, vanilla extract and buttermilk or soured milk in a large bowl. Beat until well mixed, then stir in the rhubarb. Sift in the flour, baking powder, bicarbonate of soda and salt, and stir until all the ingredients are combined. Try to avoid over-mixing or the muffins will become tough.

3 Divide the mixture between the muffin cases, filling them three-quarters full with batter and then sprinkle the remaining sugar on top of the batter in each muffin case.

4 Bake on the centre shelf of the oven for 18–20 minutes or until golden brown and firm to the touch. Allow to stand in the tin for a few minutes before placing on a wire rack to cool.

Spicy prune and apple muffins

MAKES 12 MUFFINS · VEGETARIAN

These are really delicious and filling first thing in the morning.
They are also great for a snack or as a lunchbox treat.

275g (10oz) plain
wholemeal flour
50g (2oz) rolled oats
125g (4½oz) soft light
brown sugar
1 tbsp baking powder
1 tsp bicarbonate of soda
2 tsp ground mixed spice
175g (6oz) pitted prunes,
roughly chopped
1 eating or cooking apple,
peeled, cored and
finely diced
250ml (9fl oz) buttermilk
or soured milk (see tip
below right)
50g (2oz) butter, melted
and cooled
2 eggs

12-hole muffin tin

1 Preheat the oven to 200°C (400°F), Gas mark 6. Line the muffin tin with paper cases.

2 Mix the flour, oats and sugar together in a large bowl and sift in the baking powder, bicarbonate of soda and mixed spice. Stir in the prunes and apple.

3 Beat the buttermilk or soured milk, butter and eggs together and pour into the dry ingredients, stirring to combine and to give a smooth batter. Try to avoid over-mixing or the muffins will become tough.

4 Divide the batter between the muffin cases, filling them almost to the top. Bake on the centre shelf of the oven for about 20 minutes or until golden and firm to the touch. Allow to stand in the tin for a few minutes before placing on a wire rack to cool.

Rachel's tip
To make your own soured milk, gently heat some standard milk (to the quantity required for the recipe) until warm, then remove from the heat, add the juice of ½ lemon and leave at room temperature overnight. If you are allergic to dairy products, this recipe works well with soya or rice milk soured in the same way.

Boiled eggs with soldiers

SERVES 2 · VEGETARIAN

This is the simplest recipe in the world but definitely one of my favourite things to eat. I love boiled eggs either for breakfast or for a simple supper when there's nothing else in the house — the perfect standby! Use the freshest eggs possible and ones cooked from room temperature rather than from the fridge, so they are less likely to crack.

2 eggs, at room
   temperature
4 slices of white or
   brown bread
25g (1oz) butter, softened
Salt and freshly ground
   black pepper

1 Bring a small saucepan of water to a rolling boil. Carefully lower the eggs into the water with a slotted spoon (dropping the eggs may cause the shells to crack). Bring back up to the boil and begin timing from the point at which the water starts to boil. For soft-boiled eggs, cook for 4–5 minutes; 8 minutes for hard-boiled.

2 While the eggs are cooking, pop the bread in a toaster or under a preheated grill and toast until it is golden brown. Remove and spread with butter immediately so that it melts. Cut each piece into 4–5 fingers.

3 Carefully remove each egg with a slotted spoon and place it in an egg cup. When the eggs are cool enough to handle, either crack the tops with the back of a teaspoon (and peel the shell away) or slice them off with a knife. Season with salt and pepper.

4 Dip the buttered soldiers into the soft yolk (unless it's hard-boiled, of course) and enjoy!

Variation
For a romantic, elegant, or Mother's Day breakfast: serve with asparagus tips (blanched for 2–3 minutes in boiling water) for dipping rather than the soldiers. You can also use duck eggs.

Scrambled eggs

SERVES 2 · VEGETARIAN

As with omelettes and boiled eggs (see pages 20 and 25), scrambled eggs make the perfect quick meal. And just as with omelettes, they can be served in a huge number of delicious combinations. Mexican scrambled eggs are perfect for getting rid of a hangover: the chopped fresh coriander and chilli are just what you need to wake you up! Use the best free-range eggs for their lovely rich, yellow yolks and great flavour.

Basic scrambled eggs

SERVES 2 · VEGETARIAN

4 eggs
1 tbsp milk
Salt and freshly ground black pepper
25–40g (1–1½oz) butter
2–4 slices of white or brown bread

1 Crack the eggs into a bowl, add the milk, season with salt and pepper and beat together. Add 15g (½oz) of the butter to a small saucepan on a low heat, then immediately pour in the eggs and cook for 2–3 minutes, stirring continuously (I find a wooden spatula best for this), until the butter has melted and they are softly scrambled. Remove from the heat immediately so that the eggs don't become overcooked.

2 Meanwhile, pop the slices of bread into a toaster or under a preheated grill and toast until golden brown. Remove and spread with the remaining butter, then place on plates, spoon over the cooked eggs and serve immediately.

Scrambled eggs with smoked mackerel, chives and parsley

SERVES 2

1 smoked mackerel fillet
    (about 110g/4oz in weight)
4 eggs
1 tbsp milk
Salt and freshly ground black pepper
15g (½oz) butter
1 tsp finely chopped chives
1 tsp finely chopped parsley

1 Remove the skin from the mackerel fillet, scraping off any dark residue left behind, then flake the flesh into small pieces.

2 Crack the eggs into a bowl, add the milk, season with salt and pepper and beat together. Add the butter to a small saucepan on a low heat, pour in the eggs and cook as in the basic recipe left.

3 Stir the flaked mackerel into the scrambled eggs, along with the chives and parsley. Check the seasoning and serve immediately.

Scrambled eggs with sautéed mushrooms and chives

SERVES 2 · VEGETARIAN

1 tbsp sunflower oil
25g (1oz) butter
75g (3oz) mushrooms, quartered
Squeeze of lemon juice
Salt and freshly ground black pepper
4 eggs
1 tbsp milk
1 tbsp finely chopped chives

1 Heat the sunflower oil with half the butter in a medium-sized frying pan on a gentle heat and sauté the mushrooms for 4–5 minutes or until softened and turning golden. Squeeze over the lemon juice and season well with salt and pepper before removing from the heat with a slotted spoon.

2 Meanwhile, crack the eggs into a bowl, add the milk, season with salt and pepper and beat together. Add the remaining butter to a small saucepan on a low heat, pour in the eggs and cook as in the basic recipe opposite.

3 Stir in the chives and sautéed mushrooms and check the seasoning. Divide between plates and serve immediately.

Scrambled eggs with crispy bacon and Gruyère cheese

SERVES 2

1 tbsp olive oil
3 rashers of streaky bacon, cut into slices
4 eggs
1 tbsp milk
Salt and freshly ground black pepper
15g (½oz) butter
25g (1oz) Gruyère cheese, finely grated
1 tbsp finely chopped parsley

1 Heat the olive oil in a small frying pan and sauté the bacon for 2–3 minutes or until crisp and golden. Remove from the pan with a slotted spoon and drain on kitchen paper.

2 Meanwhile, crack the eggs into a bowl, add the milk, season with salt and pepper and beat together. Add the butter to a small saucepan on a low heat, pour in the eggs and cook as in the basic recipe opposite.

3 Stir in the cooked bacon, Gruyère and parsley. Check the seasoning, adding more salt and pepper if necessary, and serve immediately.

Mexican scrambled eggs: huevos revueltos

SERVES 2 · VEGETARIAN

15g (½oz) butter
6 cherry tomatoes, quartered
1 tsp finely chopped red or green chilli
4 eggs
1 tbsp milk
Salt and freshly ground black pepper
1 tbsp finely chopped red onion
1 tbsp roughly chopped coriander

1 Melt the butter in a small saucepan on a medium heat, add the tomatoes and chilli and cook for 2–3 minutes, covered with a lid, until they are soft.

2 Crack the eggs into a bowl, add the milk, season with a good pinch of salt and some pepper and beat together. Pour into the tomato and chilli mixture, reduce the heat and cook for 2–3 minutes, stirring continuously, until the eggs are softly scrambled.

3 Stir in the onion and coriander and check the seasoning. Divide between plates and serve the eggs either on their own or on top of warm tortillas or buttered toast.

Eggs Benedict

The secret of poaching eggs is to use the freshest, highest-quality eggs you can find. These eggs are seriously dolled up, but you can of course serve them more simply on toast. Prepare the hollandaise sauce first and keep warm while you cook everything else.

Salt and freshly ground
 black pepper
4 eggs
2 English muffins,
 sliced in half
25g (1oz) butter
4 slices (about 110g/4oz)
 of ham or grilled
 rashers of bacon
150ml (5fl oz) hollandaise
 sauce (see page 331)
1 tbsp finely chopped
 chives

1 Fill a saucepan with water, add a pinch of salt and bring to a gentle simmer. Crack the eggs one by one into a small cup and slide it into the water. The water should not boil, but remain bubbling gently. Cook the eggs for 2—3 minutes or until the whites are set and the yolks still runny. Lift out carefully with a slotted spoon and drain well on kitchen paper.

2 Meanwhile, lightly toast the muffins in a toaster or under a preheated grill and butter the cut side. Put the muffin halves on plates and arrange a folded ham slice or grilled bacon rasher on top of each. Place a poached egg on top and spoon over the hollandaise sauce. Scatter with the chopped chives, grind some black pepper over the top and serve immediately.

Variation

Vegetarian eggs Benedict: Try this take on eggs Florentine (eggs served with spinach) by melting 25g (1oz) butter in a frying pan and sautéing 200g (7oz) spinach leaves, seasoned with salt and pepper, for 2—3 minutes or until wilted. Drain on kitchen paper and arrange on the muffin halves in place of the ham. Top with the poached egg, hollandaise sauce and chives, to serve.

Spotted dog

MAKES 1 LOAF · VEGETARIAN

This is a rich white soda bread with dried fruit added to make it 'spotted'.
It is also called 'railway cake' in some parts of Ireland, dating from the time
when people took the train everywhere, with a currant for each station. A real
family favourite of ours, it's divine served straight from the oven, cut into
slices and smothered in butter and jam or toasted and topped with cheese.

450g (1lb) plain flour,
    plus extra for dusting
1 level tsp bicarbonate
    of soda
1 tsp salt
1 tbsp caster sugar
110g (4oz) sultanas,
    raisins or currants
    (or a mixture)
1 egg
400ml (14fl oz) buttermilk
    or soured milk (see tip
    on page 24)

1 Preheat the oven to 220°C (425°F), Gas mark 7.

2 Sift the flour, bicarbonate of soda and salt into a large bowl,
stir in the sugar and dried fruit and make a well in the centre.
Beat the egg and buttermilk or soured milk together and pour
most of it in (leaving about 50ml/2fl oz in the measuring jug).

3 Using one hand with your fingers outstretched like a claw,
bring the flour and liquid together moving your hand in circles
around the bowl, adding a little more buttermilk if necessary.
Don't knead the mixture or it will become too heavy. The dough
should be softish but not too wet and sticky.

4 Once it comes together, turn onto a floured work surface and
bring together a little more. Pat the dough into a round, about
6cm (2½in) in height, and cut a deep cross in it, from one side
of the loaf to the other. Place on a baking tray lightly dusted
with flour.

5 Bake in the oven for 10 minutes, then reduce the oven
temperature to 200°C (400°F), Gas mark 6 and bake for
a further 30–35 minutes. I often turn the loaf upside down
for the last 5 minutes of cooking to help crisp the bottom.
When cooked the bread will be golden and sound hollow
when tapped on the base. Allow to cool on a wire rack before
cutting into thick slices to serve.

Variation
Spotted dog scones: Make the spotted dog dough as above
but flatten into a round about 2.5cm (1in) deep. Cut into
scones using a cookie cutter or knife and bake for 15–20
minutes at 230°C (450°F), Gas mark 8.

Potato and onion frittata with Gruyère and thyme

SERVES 6—8 · VEGETARIAN

Frittata is a thick Italian omelette that can be made with a variety of different cheeses, vegetables and herbs. It's a great way of using up leftover cooked potatoes, and is equally delicious served hot straight from the pan for breakfast or at room temperature for a picnic.

300g (11oz) (about
    1 large or 2 small) waxy
    potatoes, peeled (and
    halved if large)
Salt and freshly ground
    black pepper
4 tbsp olive oil
1 onion, peeled and sliced
8 eggs
50g (2oz) Gruyère cheese,
    finely grated
110ml (4fl oz) single
    or regular cream
1 tbsp thyme leaves
Bunch of spring onions,
    sliced

*25cm (10in) diameter ovenproof
frying pan with a lid*

1 Preheat the oven to 180°C (350°F), Gas mark 4.

2 Place the potatoes in a large saucepan, cover with water and add 1 teaspoon of salt. Bring to the boil and cook for 20—25 minutes or until tender. Drain the potatoes well and return to the pan on a very low heat to dry out for a minute or so. Remove from the heat, tip out onto a plate to cool a little and roughly dice.

3 Meanwhile, pour half the olive oil into the ovenproof frying pan on a gentle heat. Add the onion, cover with a lid and cook gently for 6—8 minutes, stirring regularly, until soft and slightly golden. Remove from the pan, spread out on a large plate and set aside to cool a little.

4 Next, whisk the eggs in a large bowl, then add the remaining ingredients and the cooked onions and potatoes, season with salt and pepper and gently stir together.

5 Place the remaining olive oil in the ovenproof pan and pour in the egg mixture, stirring briefly to distribute the ingredients evenly. Cook on a gentle heat for a few minutes until the mixture begins to set on the bottom, then bake in the oven for 15—20 minutes or until the mixture is set in the centre.

6 Remove the pan from the oven and allow the frittata to cool for a couple of minutes before sliding it onto a large serving plate. Cut into wedges to serve.

Kedgeree

This classic dish is perfect for entertaining, whether for breakfast, brunch, lunch or dinner. It's so easy to increase the quantities to feed lots of people. I love the addition of wild rice in this recipe, but it's fine to use just basmati rice (white or brown) if you prefer. There are quite a few different elements to cook in this recipe, but then it's just a matter of assembling all the individual ingredients. Serve this simply on its own, or with some mango chutney and a green salad.

150g (5oz) wild rice
Salt and freshly ground
    black pepper
350g (12oz) white or
    brown basmati rice
500g (1lb 2oz) smoked
    haddock (about 2
    medium fillets)
25g (1oz) butter
350ml (12fl oz) milk
2 tsp cumin seeds
2 tsp coriander seeds
4 tbsp olive oil
2 large onions, peeled
    and thinly sliced
½ tsp cayenne pepper
½ tsp garam masala
10 eggs, at room
    temperature
225g (8oz) fresh or
    frozen peas
2 tbsp chopped coriander
    or parsley
2 tbsp chopped chives
50ml (2fl oz) single
    or regular cream

1 Tip the wild rice and a pinch of salt into a saucepan of boiling water and cook on a medium heat for about 45 minutes until the rice is cooked but with a tiny bite still left. Add the basmati rice and a pinch of salt to another saucepan of boiling water and cook until tender. (White basmati rice will take 10–12 minutes to cook and brown basmati rice 25–30 minutes.) Drain well and return both to one pan to keep warm.

2 Meanwhile, place the smoked haddock in a wide saucepan and add the butter, milk and a pinch of black pepper. Bring slowly to the boil, then reduce the heat and simmer gently for 10–12 minutes or until the fish is cooked. When it is ready it will begin to fall apart in chunks. Remove from the heat and set aside to cool slightly.

3 Place a very large frying pan on a high heat and toast the cumin and coriander seeds for a few seconds until just a shade darker, then remove the seeds and roughly crush them. (If you don't have a pestle and mortar, simply tip them out onto a chopping board and crush them with a rolling pin or the base of a pan.)

4 Return the pan to a medium heat and add the olive oil. Tip in the onions and sauté for 4–5 minutes or until just turning golden. Add the crushed cumin and coriander seeds, along with the cayenne pepper and garam masala. Turn the heat down to low, cover the pan with a lid and continue to cook the onions for 12–15 minutes, stirring occasionally, until completely soft.

5 While the onions are cooking, bring a large saucepan of water to the boil, gently lower the eggs into the water with a slotted spoon and boil for just 6 minutes until semi-hard boiled. Drain the eggs and run cold water over them to stop them cooking. Peel them once they are cool enough to handle and cut into quarters.

6 Tip the peas into a saucepan of boiling water and cook for 1–2 minutes or until tender, then drain. Meanwhile, the haddock should now be cool enough to handle, so remove from the milk (reserving the milk for later), peel away the skin, remove any bones and flake the fish into chunks of about 1cm (½in).

7 Now that everything is cooked and prepared, you are ready to assemble the dish. Remove the lid covering the onions and, leaving the pan on a low heat, add the drained wild and basmati rice, the peas and half of each of the coriander or parsley and chives, stirring to mix. Pour over the cream, along with 50ml (2fl oz) of the milk the fish was cooked in, and gently stir to loosen the whole mixture slightly. Add the flaked haddock pieces, season with salt and pepper, to taste, and stir gently together.

8 Transfer the kedgeree to a wide, shallow serving dish or plate and arrange the quartered eggs on top and around the sides, then sprinkle with the remaining chopped herbs and serve.

Weekend fry-up

Not something for breakfast every morning, of course, but there are times when this is just what you need to keep you going for the rest of the day. A fry-up is great when friends are staying — simply multiply the ingredients given below by however many people you are feeding. Source the best local ingredients you can and follow up with a big walk. If you prefer your eggs boiled or poached, see pages 25 and 30.

Vegetable, sunflower
   or olive oil, for frying
2 sausages
2 rashers of thick, dry-
   cured, smoked or
   unsmoked, back or
   streaky bacon, rind
   removed
2–3 slices of black and/
   or white pudding
Butter, for frying and
   spreading on toast
50g (2oz) button
   mushrooms, sliced, or
   1 large flat mushroom,
   any stalk removed
Salt and freshly ground
   black pepper
1 ripe tomato, halved
Pinch of caster sugar
   (if roasting the tomato
   in the oven)
1–2 eggs
1 tbsp milk
   (for scrambled eggs)
2 slices of white or
   brown bread

1 Add 1 tablespoon of oil to a large frying pan on a medium heat and begin by frying the sausages. Cook gently for 10–15 minutes or until golden and cooked through. Add the bacon rashers to the same pan with the sausages and fry for 3–4 minutes on each side or until crisp and golden, dabbing off any milky liquid with kitchen paper. Add the black and/or white pudding slices to the pan and fry for 2–3 minutes on each side or until beginning to crisp and the white pudding (if using) turns golden. Remove the sausages, bacon and pudding slices from the pan and drain on kitchen paper. Place in an ovenproof dish and keep warm in a low oven if necessary.

2 Meanwhile, add a dash of oil and knob of butter to another frying pan on a medium heat, and sauté the mushrooms for 3–4 minutes or until softened and turning golden. Season with salt and pepper, then remove from the pan and keep warm (adding to the dish with the cooked sausages and bacon). If cooking a large flat mushroom, then add the oil and butter to the pan and fry the mushrooms for 8–10 minutes, turning halfway through, until softened and browned.

3 Season the cut side of the tomato halves and drizzle over 1 tablespoon of oil. Gently fry them, cut side down first, for 2–3 minutes, then turn over and fry for a further 2–3 minutes or until just softened.

4 Alternatively, cook the large flat mushroom and/or the tomatoes in the oven. Preheat the oven to 200°C (400°F), Gas mark 6. Drizzle 2 teaspoons of olive oil or add a knob of butter over the mushroom and season with salt and

pepper before roasting for 12–15 minutes until tender. Put a knob of butter on the cut side of each tomato half, add the sugar and season with a little salt and pepper before roasting for 12–15 minutes or until softened. If using the oven, begin roasting the mushroom and tomatoes a few minutes before frying the sausages and bacon. Once cooked, reduce the oven temperature to low for keeping everything warm as it is cooked.

5 To fry an egg, melt a knob of butter in a small, clean frying pan on a low heat. Carefully crack the egg into the pan and allow to fry gently. For an over-easy egg, fry for 1–2 minutes until beginning to set, then flip over with a fish slice and fry for a further 1–2 minutes. If you prefer your egg sunny side up, then fry gently for 4–5 minutes until the yolk has filmed over. Remove from the pan and serve immediately with the other cooked ingredients.

6 For scrambled egg, follow the method for Basic Scrambled Eggs on page 28. Serve at once with the other cooked ingredients.

7 While the egg is cooking, put the slices of bread in a toaster or under a preheated grill and toast for a few minutes (and on both sides, if using the grill) until golden. Butter the toast and cut the slices in half.

8 To serve, arrange everything on a warm serving plate, with the hot buttered toast on the side and with some tomato ketchup (see page 329) or relish.

Variation

Fried bananas: We sometimes like to add a fried banana to a full breakfast. It goes particularly well with bacon. Allowing 1 small banana per person, peel and cut in half across and then halve lengthways to give four pieces. Melt a knob of butter in a small frying pan on a medium heat and fry the banana pieces for 2–3 minutes on each side until softened and turning golden.

Pan-fried kippers with dill butter

SERVES 2

Some people love them, others hate them, but kippers are a favourite of mine because of their smoky saltiness, which I really enjoy first thing in the morning. I particularly like them with dill butter because the herb complements fish perfectly.

4 kipper fillets
Freshly ground black
   pepper
1 tbsp sunflower oil
Dill butter (see page 327),
   to serve
½ lemon, to serve

1 Prepare the kippers by removing the head and any fins and wiping the fish clean with kitchen paper. Season with a little pepper. Add the sunflower oil to a large frying pan on a medium–high heat and fry the kippers, flesh side down first, for 2–3 minutes, then turn the fish over and fry for a further 2–3 minutes. The skin should be crispy and the flesh hot and cooked through.

2 Place the kippers on plates, flesh side up, with a spoonful of dill butter on top, and serve with lemon and some thin slices of brown bread.

Rachel's tip
These can easily be grilled rather than fried, if you prefer. Preheat the grill to medium–high, rub the sunflower oil over the kippers and grill for 2–3 minutes, flesh side up, then turn the fish over and grill for a further 2–3 minutes.

Smoothies and Juices

Smoothies and juices are quick and easy to make. They are so nutritious and often the easiest way of getting the family to eat lots of fruit. Make up your own variations using whatever fruit you have to hand. The juices can be stored in the fridge for a day but are at their best (both taste-wise and nutritionally) if drunk immediately. If you don't have a juicing machine, then blitz the fruit in a blender and push it through a sieve to get rid of any seeds or stringy or rough pieces.

Pear, apple and ginger smoothie

Place 2 peeled, cored and roughly chopped pears and ½ teaspoon of finely grated root ginger in a blender, pour in 200ml (7fl oz) apple juice and 50ml (2fl oz) natural yoghurt and blitz until smooth. Pour into glasses and serve immediately.

Mixed berry smoothie

Place 225g (8oz) fresh or frozen (and defrosted) mixed berries and 1 peeled and chopped banana in a blender, pour in 300ml (½ pint) cranberry juice and add 1–2 tablespoons of honey (optional), then whiz until smooth. Pour into glasses and serve immediately.

Strawberry, banana and yoghurt smoothie

Place 225g (8oz) hulled strawberries and 2 peeled chopped bananas in a blender, pour in 100ml (3½fl oz) freshly squeezed orange juice and 150ml (5fl oz) natural yoghurt, add 1 tablespoon of honey (optional) and whiz until completely smooth. Pour into glasses to serve, and drink immediately.

Pineapple, coconut and lime smoothie

Place 4 rings (about 500g/1lb 2oz) of fresh, peeled and cored pineapple and 2 peeled and chopped bananas in a blender. Pour in 100ml (3½fl oz) orange juice, 200ml (7fl oz) coconut milk and the juice of 1 lime and blitz until smooth. Pour into glasses and serve immediately.

Raspberry nectar

Put 175g (6oz) fresh or frozen (and
defrosted) raspberries, 1 large peeled and
segmented orange, and 1 halved and stoned
nectarine through a juicer, or whiz in a
blender and then push through a sieve.

Four fruits juice

Put 125g (4½oz) (about a 2cm/¾in slice)
of peeled pineapple through a juicer, followed
by 1 small peeled and segmented orange,
75g (3oz) hulled strawberries and 50g (2oz)
seedless red or green grapes, or blitz all the
fruit in a blender and push through a sieve.

Blueberry blush

Pass 125g (4½oz) blueberries and 75g (3oz)
stoned cherries through a juicer, followed
by 2 quartered (peeled and cored if using a
blender) eating apples, or whiz in a blender
and push through a sieve.

Peach and pear juice

Pass 2 halved and stoned peaches and
1 large quartered (peeled and cored if using
a blender) pear through a juicer, or blitz
in a blender and push through a sieve.

Kiwi fruit and apple juice

Put 2 quartered (peeled and cored if using
a blender) eating apples through a juicer,
followed by 3 halved (peeled if using a
blender) kiwi fruit, or whiz both fruit
in a blender and push through a sieve.

Poached dried fruits

SERVES 8 · VEGETARIAN

These poached fruits are great on their own or served with yoghurt, or in porridge (see pages 10 and 11). They can be made in advance and they keep well in an airtight container in the fridge for up to two weeks.

200g (7oz) pitted prunes
175g (6oz) dried apricots
25g (1oz) raisins
1 vanilla pod, split
Strip of orange zest
1–2 tbsp honey
4 tbsp warm water
225ml (8fl oz) freshly
   squeezed orange juice
50g (2oz) dried coconut
   shavings (optional),
   to serve

1 Place the prunes and apricots in a bowl, pour over enough boiling water to cover and leave to soak overnight.

2 The next day, drain the dried fruits, reserving the liquid, and place them in a saucepan. Add the raisins, vanilla pod, orange zest and honey and pour over the warm water. Top with enough of the reserved soaking liquid to just cover and then bring to the boil before reducing the heat and simmering for about 35 minutes.

3 Remove from the heat and leave to cool completely. The fruits can be refrigerated at this point until needed. Just before serving, stir the orange juice into the mixture (or about 2 tablespoons per serving if not serving the whole amount) and scatter with the coconut shavings (if using).

Additions
* Slice 3–4 bananas. Put a few pieces into each bowl of poached fruits when serving.
* Serve with a dollop of Greek or natural yoghurt.

Variations
Almond topping: Substitute the coconut shavings with 50g (2oz) toasted flaked almonds (see tip on page 50).

Different dried fruits: Try substituting the prunes with dried figs or pitted dates, and the raisins with sultanas.

Lunch

Roast tomato soup

SERVES 4–6 · VEGETARIAN (IF MADE WITH VEGETABLE STOCK)

I adore this soup because it tastes of summer to me. It's delicious
served as it is, or drizzled with pesto. To make it more of a meal,
try serving with the cheese and basil quesadillas on page 259.

900g (2lb) ripe tomatoes
(about 8), halved
1 red onion, peeled and
thickly sliced
6 large cloves of garlic,
peeled
Leaves from 4 sprigs
of thyme
1 tsp caster sugar
2 tbsp extra-virgin olive oil
1 tbsp balsamic vinegar
Sea salt and freshly ground
black pepper
600ml (1 pint) chicken
or vegetable stock
(see page 326)
50ml (2fl oz) double
or regular cream
Basil leaves, to serve

1 Preheat the oven to 200°C (400°F), Gas mark 6.

2 Arrange the tomato halves, cut side up, in a single layer on
a baking tray and scatter over the onion, garlic, thyme and
sugar. Drizzle over the olive oil and balsamic vinegar and season
well with salt and pepper. Roast in the oven for 35–40 minutes
or until softened.

3 Once cooked, tip the entire contents of the baking tray,
including any juices, into a blender. Add the stock and blend
until smooth, then pour into a large saucepan. Alternatively,
place the cooked tomatoes in the saucepan, pour in the stock
and purée using a hand-held blender. Bring the soup to the
boil, add the cream, reduce the heat and simmer for a few
minutes to heat through.

4 Ladle the soup into bowls and sprinkle with basil leaves.

Mushroom soup with stuffed mushrooms

SERVES 6 · VEGETARIAN (IF MADE WITH VEGETABLE STOCK)

An ideal dish if you are entertaining friends for lunch and need something that little bit special, or as a starter for a dinner party.

For the soup
1 onion, peeled and quartered
2 cloves of garlic, peeled and roughly chopped
25g (1oz) butter
350g (12oz) large flat mushrooms, quartered
Salt and freshly ground black pepper
600ml (1 pint) chicken or vegetable stock (see page 326)
150ml (5fl oz) double or regular cream

For the stuffed mushrooms
6 large flat mushrooms, stalks removed and retained
3 slices of white bread (stale is best), roughly torn
2 cloves of garlic, peeled and roughly chopped
150g (5oz) Gruyère cheese, grated
75g (3oz) Parmesan cheese, finely grated
1 tbsp finely chopped marjoram, plus extra to serve
75g (3oz) butter, melted
Salt and freshly ground black pepper
Truffle oil, for drizzling (optional)
Marjoram leaves, to serve

1 Blend the onion and garlic in a food processor for a few seconds until finely chopped, or finely chop by hand using a sharp knife. Melt the butter in a large saucepan on a medium heat and sauté the onion and garlic for 2–3 minutes to soften a little, but not brown.

2 Blend the mushrooms in the food processor until finely chopped, or finely chop by hand. Add the mushrooms to the saucepan and sweat for 1–2 minutes or until softened. Season with salt and pepper, pour over the stock and bring slowly to the boil, then reduce the heat and simmer gently for 20–25 minutes.

3 Preheat the oven to 200°C (400°F), Gas mark 6.

4 To make the stuffed mushrooms, place the mushroom stalks in the food processor along with the torn bread and garlic. Blend to fine crumbs and tip the mixture into a bowl. Alternatively, finely chop by hand and transfer to a bowl. Add the cheeses and the marjoram and then drizzle with the melted butter. Season with salt and pepper and toss everything together to combine.

5 Arrange the mushrooms on a baking tray, flat side down, and pile the stuffing mixture on top of each one. Bake in the oven for 15–20 minutes or until the mushrooms are soft and the topping crisp and golden.

6 Once the soup has finished cooking, check the seasoning, then pour in the cream and simmer gently for a few minutes to warm through. Ladle the soup into wide soup bowls to a depth of no more than 2cm (¾in). Carefully place a stuffed mushroom in the centre of each bowl, drizzle over the truffle oil (if using) and decorate with the marjoram leaves.

Rachel's tip
You can prepare the mushroom soup in advance (freezing it, if you wish) and then prepare the stuffed mushrooms on the day.

Gazpacho

Gazpacho is a classic chilled summer soup from Spain. It reminds
me of the many happy holidays I've had in Mallorca.

800g (1¾lb) ripe tomatoes
(about 3–4), quartered
1 red pepper, deseeded and
roughly chopped
½ large cucumber, peeled
and roughly chopped
8 spring onions, trimmed
and roughly chopped
8 tbsp extra-virgin olive
oil, plus extra for
drizzling
2 tbsp sherry vinegar
or red wine vinegar
Squeeze of lemon juice
2 cloves of garlic, peeled
2 tsp caster sugar
Salt and freshly ground
black pepper

1 Place all of the ingredients in a blender and blitz until
smooth. Check the seasoning and add a little more sugar
if necessary. Push the soup through a fine sieve over a large
bowl, cover and place in the fridge to chill before serving.

2 Ladle into bowls and drizzle over a little olive oil. Serve with
your choice of toppings from below, placing little bowls of
them on the table for each person to add to their own soup.

Toppings

* Mix ½ red or yellow pepper, deseeded and finely chopped,
with 4 teaspoons of finely chopped red onion and 4 tablespoons
of golden croutons (2 thick slices of white or brown bread cut
into 5mm/¼in cubes, brushed with olive oil and baked in the
oven, preheated to 200°C/400°F/Gas mark 6, for 10 minutes).
* Mix 2 tablespoons of fresh white crab meat with ¼ avocado,
finely chopped.
* Push 1 cold hard-boiled egg through a sieve and mix with
25g (1oz) finely chopped cooked ham.
* Vodka ice cubes – 1 teaspoon of vodka mixed with 1 teaspoon
of water per ice cube and frozen overnight. Add to the soup,
with or without the other toppings.

Brussels sprout soup with toasted almonds and chive cream

SERVES 4—6 · VEGETARIAN (IF MADE WITH VEGETABLE STOCK)

A perfect winter dish and particularly lovely at Christmas, this delicious and nourishing soup uses up leftover Brussels sprouts, or you can use raw sprouts instead — just give them an extra minute or two to cook in the soup. Like many children, mine aren't too keen on Brussels sprouts on their own, but they lap them up in this soup!

15g (½oz) butter

1 onion, peeled and chopped

1 large potato (about 250g/9oz), peeled and chopped

Salt and freshly ground black pepper

1 litre (1¾ pints) chicken or vegetable stock (see page 326)

450g (1lb) cooked or raw (and peeled) Brussels sprouts, halved

100ml (3½fl oz) double or regular cream

1 tbsp finely chopped chives

25g (1oz) flaked almonds, lightly toasted (see tip below right)

1 Melt the butter in a saucepan on a low heat, add the onion and potato and season lightly with salt and pepper. Cover with a lid and leave to cook very gently for about 8–10 minutes, stirring every now and then, until the potatoes are just soft but not browned.

2 Add the stock, bring to a rolling boil and cook for 1 minute before tipping in the sprouts. With the lid off this time, boil the cooked sprouts for 1–2 minutes only (enough time to warm through but not to overcook) or 3–4 minutes for raw sprouts.

3 Remove the saucepan from the heat and whiz the soup in a blender until smooth. Return the soup to the pan and stir in half the cream. Check the seasoning and simmer for a few minutes to warm through.

4 Finally, lightly whip the remaining cream to soft peaks and stir in the chives. Divide the soup between warm bowls, spoon a dollop of chive cream on top, scatter over the toasted almonds and serve immediately.

Rachel's tip

To toast the almonds (or any other kind of nuts or seeds), toss them in a dry pan for 2–3 minutes on a medium–high heat. Remove from the heat as soon as they start to turn golden as they can quickly burn.

Asian noodle broth with chicken dumplings

SERVES 6

This is a fragrant and light soup, with noodles and chicken dumplings poached in the broth to make it more substantial. The sweet element in the broth makes it popular with children; if the chilli is too spicy for them (or you), then leave it out. Likewise, the nuts in the dumplings can be omitted.

500g (1lb 2oz) chicken dumpling mixture (see page 155)
1.8 litres (3 pints) chicken stock (see page 326)
100g (3½oz) medium egg noodles
200g (7oz) Savoy cabbage, finely shredded
1 red chilli, deseeded (optional) and finely chopped
Juice of 1 lime
Salt and freshly ground black pepper
Large handful of mint leaves, roughly chopped

To serve
Lime wedges
Fish sauce (nam pla)

1 Divide the chicken dumpling mixture into 36 walnut-sized pieces and shape each one into a small ball.

2 Pour the chicken stock into a large saucepan and bring just to the boil. Reduce the heat so the stock is simmering gently and add the chicken dumplings. Cook for 4–5 minutes, then add the noodles, cabbage and chilli. Simmer for 3–4 minutes or until the noodles are tender and the chicken dumplings cooked through. Stir in the lime juice and season to taste with salt and pepper.

3 Ladle into serving bowls (serving six dumplings per bowl), scatter with the mint and serve with the lime wedges and fish sauce for people to add themselves.

Molly Malone's cockle and mussel chowder

SERVES 4—6

A little more work is involved in making this soup, but it's definitely well worth the effort. It makes a decent meal in its own right, especially with chunks of crusty bread, or you can serve it as a starter. Cockles and mussels are a classic combination but if you can only get one or the other, you can use them singly in this soup.

2 tbsp sunflower oil
110g (4oz) smoked
  bacon, diced
25g (1oz) butter
110g (4oz) leek, trimmed
  and very finely diced
110g (4oz) carrot, peeled
  and very finely diced
275g (10oz) potato (about
  1 medium), peeled
  and finely diced
1kg (2lb 3oz) mixed
  cockles and mussels
300ml (½ pint) dry
  white wine
200ml (7fl oz) milk
200ml (7fl oz) single
  or regular cream
Salt and freshly ground
  black pepper
4 tbsp roughly chopped
  parsley

1 Heat the sunflower oil in a saucepan on a medium—high heat and sauté the bacon for about 1 minute until crisp and golden. Melt the butter in the pan and add the leek, carrot and potato. Sauté gently on a low heat for 4—5 minutes or until soft but not browned.

2 Meanwhile, prepare the cockles and mussels. Scrub the shells clean and discard any that remain open when you tap them against a hard surface. Remove the beard — the little fibrous tuft — from each mussel. Bring the wine to the boil in a large saucepan and add the cockles and mussels. Cover with a tight-fitting lid and leave to cook for 3—4 minutes, shaking the pan occasionally, until the shells have opened.

3 Remove from the heat, drain the shellfish in a colander, retaining the cooking juices, and discard any shells that remain closed. Once drained, return the shellfish to the empty pan to keep warm. Place a fine sieve over a measuring jug and strain the cooking liquid. If the juices caught in the jug measure less than 600ml (1 pint), add water to make up to that quantity.

4 Add the pan juices and the milk to the bacon and vegetable mixture and bring to the boil. Reduce the heat and simmer for 6—8 minutes or until the potato is tender. Add the cream and simmer for a further 2—3 minutes or until reduced and thickened slightly. Season with salt and pepper.

5 Meanwhile, remove half of the cockles and mussels from their shells and add them with the remaining cockles and mussels still in their shells to the chowder. Stir in the parsley and serve at once with some crusty bread.

Nettle soup with smoked mackerel crostini

SERVES 6 · VEGETARIAN (IF MADE WITH VEGETABLE STOCK)

This is a tasty and highly nutritious soup that freezes very well. Feel free to substitute the nettles with other greens such as spinach, watercress or sorrel. For the best flavour, pick young new nettles that haven't been sprayed. Don't forget to wear gloves while picking and chopping! The sting goes out of the nettles as soon as they hit the hot stock. Like all green soups, this should not be left to simmer for a long time or it will lose its fresh green colour and flavour.

25g (1oz) butter or
   2 tbsp olive oil
110g (4oz) peeled and
   chopped onions
150g (5oz) peeled and
   chopped potatoes
Sea salt and freshly ground
   black pepper
600ml (1 pint) chicken
   or vegetable stock
   (see page 326)
600ml (1 pint) milk
350g (12oz) nettles,
   destalked and chopped

For the crostini
2 demi baguettes or 1 thin
   baguette, cut in half
1 tbsp extra-virgin olive oil
2 smoked mackerel fillets
   (about 150g/5oz
   in weight)
4 tbsp crème fraîche
Juice of 1 lemon
1 tbsp dill
1 tbsp sweet chilli sauce
   (optional)

1 Add the butter or olive oil to a large saucepan on a very low heat and when the butter has melted, tip in the onions and potatoes and season with salt and pepper. Cover with a lid and cook for 8–10 minutes, stirring occasionally, until soft but not browned.

2 Pour the stock and milk into the pan, bring to the boil and add the nettles. Cook, uncovered, on a high heat for about 1 minute until the nettles are just cooked – don't heat them for too long or they will lose their fresh green colour. Remove from the heat and purée until smooth in a blender or using a hand-held blender. Check the seasoning, adding more salt and pepper if necessary.

3 Meanwhile, preheat the oven to 180°C (350°F), Gas mark 4, and prepare the crostini.

4 With the baguettes running lengthways away from you, trim the ends of each loaf and then cut the remaining bread into six long thin slices. Arrange the slices on a baking tray crust side down and brush the olive oil over evenly. Bake in the oven for 6–8 minutes or until crisp and golden. Remove and allow to cool.

5 Peel the skin from the mackerel and chop the flesh. Place in a blender with the crème fraîche, lemon juice, most of the dill, chilli sauce (if using) and a little pepper. Blend for a few seconds until smooth. Taste and season with a little salt, if necessary.

6 When ready to serve, divide the mackerel pâté between the cooled crostini, spread evenly and sprinkle with the remaining dill. Ladle the soup into warm bowls, arrange two pieces of mackerel crostini on the side and serve.

Chicken and garlic soup

SERVES 6—8

This is a wonderfully easy, warming soup with deliciously sweet garlic. As well as normal garlic, you could use wild garlic leaves in this soup, which are in season in April and May. Simply substitute for the chives and spring onions.

50g (2oz) butter
1 onion, peeled and diced
10 cloves of garlic, peeled and finely chopped
1 skinless, boneless chicken breast (about 200g/ 7oz), finely diced
Salt and freshly ground black pepper
600ml (1 pint) chicken stock (see page 326)
300ml (½ pint) milk
300ml (½ pint) double or regular cream
1 tbsp finely chopped chives
4 spring onions, trimmed and finely chopped

1 Melt the butter in a large saucepan on a medium heat and fry the onion and garlic for 3—4 minutes or until soft but not browned. Add the chicken, season with salt and pepper and cook for a further 4—5 minutes.

2 Pour in the stock, the milk and cream and bring to the boil. Stir in the chives and spring onions and simmer for about 5 minutes or until the spring onions have softened. Check the seasoning, adjusting it if necessary, and ladle into warm bowls to serve.

Oxtail soup

SERVES 10–12

This old-fashioned, rustic and hearty soup has been popular since
the 18th century and makes good use of a cheaper cut of beef. It is ideal
for warming up friends and family on a cold day.

1 tbsp plain flour
Salt and freshly ground
　　black pepper
1.5kg (3lb 5oz) oxtail,
　　cut into 3cm (1¼in)
　　pieces and trimmed
　　of excess fat
2–3 tbsp vegetable oil
1 large onion, peeled
　　and finely chopped
2 carrots, peeled and
　　finely chopped
3 sticks of celery, trimmed
　　and finely sliced
1 bay leaf
1 sprig of thyme
6 peppercorns
2 cloves
1 tbsp tomato purée
1 tbsp Worcestershire sauce
2 litres (3½ pints) beef
　　stock (see page 326)

1 Sift the flour onto a large plate, season with salt and pepper
and toss the oxtail pieces in the flour to coat evenly. Place a large
saucepan or casserole dish on a high heat, add 1–2 tablespoons
of the oil and fry the oxtail pieces in batches, adding more oil
if necessary, for 4–5 minutes in total, or until they are well
browned all over. Remove from the pan and set aside.

2 Add the onion, carrots and celery, cover with a tight-fitting
lid and cook on a gentle heat for 8–10 minutes, stirring
occasionally, until the vegetables are soft but not browned.

3 Return the oxtail to the pan and add the bay leaf, thyme,
peppercorns, cloves, tomato purée and Worcestershire sauce.
Season with salt and pepper, pour in the stock and bring
slowly to the boil, skimming off any frothy impurities that
rise to the surface. Reduce the heat to very low, cover with
the lid and gently simmer for about 3 hours or until the meat
is falling off the bone. Continue to occasionally skim off any
impurities as well as any melted fat.

4 Remove from the heat and strain through a colander over a
large bowl to catch the liquid. Tip the meat and vegetables into
a large, shallow bowl and leave to cool a little. Add a few ice cubes
to the liquid and wait for the fat to solidify and rise to the top,
before removing and discarding it. Once the meat and vegetables
are cool enough to handle, discard the bay leaf and thyme stalks
(the cloves will be blended into the soup later) and remove the
meat from the oxtail bones.

5 Pour the liquid into a blender with the reserved vegetables
and two-thirds of the meat (you may have to do this in batches)
and blitz to a smooth soup, then return to the pan. Add the
remaining chunks of meat and bring slowly to the boil. Check
the seasoning and serve immediately.

Alphabet soup

Alphabet pasta is available in larger supermarkets, but use what other little shapes you can get hold of, such as small rings, tiny shells, little bows, wheels, stars or moons — they are fun additions to soup, amusing adults just as much as children. You can use raw chorizo or chicken instead of the bacon, if you prefer.

1 tbsp olive oil
150g (5oz) streaky bacon, thinly sliced
1 onion, peeled and diced
4 cloves of garlic, peeled and crushed
1 x 400g tin of chopped tomatoes
1 litre (1¾ pints) chicken or vegetable stock (see page 326)
Salt and freshly ground black pepper
½–1 tsp caster sugar
100g (3½oz) alphabet pasta or other small pasta shapes
2 tbsp finely shredded basil (optional)

1 Add the olive oil to a large saucepan on a high heat and fry the bacon for 3–4 minutes or until crisp and golden. Tip in the onion and garlic, reduce the heat and gently cook for 8–10 minutes or until soft but not browned. Add the tomatoes and stock and season to taste with salt, pepper and sugar.

2 Increase the heat a little and simmer for about 15 minutes or until slightly reduced. Add the pasta shapes and continue to simmer for a further 5 minutes or until the pasta is cooked.

3 Remove from the heat and stir in the basil (if using). Check the seasoning, adding more salt, pepper or sugar if necessary, and ladle into warm bowls.

Zac's chicken and sweetcorn soup

SERVES 4

Ideal for a light lunch, this is a quick and easy meal in a bowl — something
the whole family will enjoy. Use leftover chicken or even the leftover Christmas
turkey, adding it to the soup later in the method, as described below.

25g (1oz) butter
200g (7oz) skinless,
  boneless chicken
  breast, cut into 2cm
  (¾in) cubes
1 large onion, peeled
  and finely chopped
3–4 large cloves of garlic,
  peeled and finely
  chopped
600ml (1 pint) chicken
  stock (see page 326)
125ml (4½fl oz) milk
125ml (4½fl oz) single
  or regular cream
1 x 340g tin of sweetcorn,
  drained
Salt and freshly ground
  black pepper
2 tbsp roughly chopped
  parsley
1 spring onion, trimmed
  and finely chopped
Squeeze of lemon juice

1 Melt the butter in a large saucepan on a medium heat and
add the chicken, onion and garlic. Cook gently for 8–10
minutes, stirring occasionally, until the chicken and onion
start turning light golden around the edges. If you are using
pre-cooked chicken, just cook the onion and garlic and
then add the meat.

2 Place the stock, milk, cream and sweetcorn in a blender,
season with salt and pepper and whiz for a few seconds to
a rough purée. Alternatively, place in a large bowl and blitz
with a hand-held blender. Pour the purée over the cooked
chicken and onion mixture and bring slowly to the boil.
Reduce the heat and simmer for 4–5 minutes.

3 Stir in the parsley and spring onion and squeeze in a little
lemon juice to taste. Check the seasoning, adjusting if
necessary, and serve the soup immediately.

Potato, leek and smoked bacon soup with parsley pesto

SERVES 6

The rich wintry flavours of this soup are made even more delicious with a drizzle of parsley pesto.

1 tbsp sunflower or olive oil
4 rashers of smoked streaky bacon, diced
25g (1oz) butter
1 onion, peeled and roughly chopped
1 large leek, trimmed and diced
500g (1lb 2oz) potatoes (about 2 large), peeled and diced
Salt and freshly ground black pepper
1.2 litres (2 pints) chicken or vegetable stock (see page 326)

For the parsley pesto
15g (½oz) flat-leaf parsley
1 clove of garlic, peeled and roughly chopped
1 tbsp pine nuts, lightly toasted (see tip on page 50)
1 tbsp finely grated Parmesan cheese
4 tbsp extra-virgin olive oil
Salt and freshly ground black pepper

1 Add the oil to a large saucepan on a high heat and sauté the bacon pieces quickly for about 1 minute or until crisp and golden. Remove from the pan and drain on kitchen paper.

2 Reduce the heat a little and add the butter to the oil in the pan. When it has melted, add the onion, leek and potatoes, season with salt and pepper and cook gently for 8–10 minutes without browning. Pour the stock over and simmer gently for 5 minutes or until the potatoes are completely cooked through.

3 Meanwhile, make the parsley pesto. Discard the stalks from the parsley and place in a bowl with the garlic, pine nuts, Parmesan and olive oil. Using a hand-held blender, purée to a fairly smooth paste, adding a little more oil if necessary so that it is a thick but drizzling consistency. Alternatively, crush the parsley, garlic and pine nuts using a pestle and mortar and stir in the Parmesan and olive oil. Season to taste with salt and pepper and set aside.

4 Purée the soup until smooth in a blender or using a hand-held blender. Return to the pan and stir in all but 1 tablespoon of the reserved bacon pieces. Check the seasoning, adjusting if necessary, and heat for a minute more before serving.

5 Ladle the soup into warm bowls. Drizzle over the parsley pesto and scatter the remaining bacon pieces on top.

Rachel's tip
Use the leek trimmings and parsley stalks for making a delicious stock (see stock recipes on page 326).

Salad with goat's cheese toast and walnuts

SERVES 2 · VEGETARIAN

This is the kind of simple salad that so many little brasseries in Paris have on their menus. In France the goat's cheese served for this dish is usually the type with a rind, but you can also use a soft goat's cheese for this salad. Make sure the walnuts are good and fresh; if stored for too long they can become bitter and rancid.

2 slices of white bread or 4–6 baguette slices
1 x 150g mini goat's cheese log, cut into twelve 1cm (½in) slices
4 shelled walnuts, roughly chopped
2 handfuls (about 50g/2oz) of salad leaves

For the dressing
2 tbsp walnut oil or extra-virgin olive oil
2 tsp white wine vinegar
1 tsp Dijon mustard
1 tsp runny honey
Salt and freshly ground black pepper

1 Preheat the grill to high and lightly toast the bread on both sides. Arrange the goat's cheese slices on top to cover evenly. Return to the grill for a few minutes until just molten.

2 Meanwhile, toast the walnuts in a dry pan for a few minutes until just turning brown, then remove. Make the dressing by whisking all the ingredients together and seasoning with salt and pepper to taste. (This will keep in the fridge for a week or two.) Dress the salad leaves with enough dressing to just lightly coat.

3 Place the dressed salad in the centre of two plates and arrange the goat's cheese toast on top or to the side. Sprinkle over the toasted walnuts and serve.

Variation
Cranberry sauce: For a change, mix together equal quantities of cranberry sauce and boiling water (1 teaspoon of each per person) and drizzle over the goat's cheese toast before serving.

Fragrant sugar snap and beansprout noodle laksa

SERVES 6–8 · VEGETARIAN (IF MADE WITH SOY SAUCE)

Laksa is an Southeast Asian dish consisting of noodles either in a coconut-based curry soup (as here) or in a 'sour' fish-based soup. The vegetables add a bit of crunch, so it's important that they remain as fresh-tasting as possible and are not overcooked. For a completely vegetarian dish, substitute the fish sauce with soy sauce.

150g (5oz) fine rice noodles
2 red chillies, deseeded and roughly chopped
4 cloves of garlic, peeled and finely chopped
2.5cm (1in) piece of root ginger, peeled and roughly chopped
1 stick of lemongrass, outer leaves removed, roughly chopped
50g (2oz) coriander, leaves and stalks torn
Juice of 1–2 limes
2 tbsp toasted sesame oil
2 x 400ml tins of coconut milk
700ml (1¼ pints) vegetable stock (see page 326)
1–2 tbsp fish sauce (nam pla) or soy sauce
250g (9oz) sugar snap peas, halved lengthways
150g (5oz) beansprouts
8 spring onions, trimmed and finely sliced at an angle

1 Place the noodles in a large bowl, pour over boiling water to cover, so that it comes up to about 2.5cm (1in) above the noodles, and leave to soak for 3–4 minutes or until soft. Drain well.

2 Meanwhile, place the chillies, garlic, ginger, lemongrass, coriander (reserving a few leaves for scattering over the dish) and juice of one of the limes in a food processor (or use a pestle and mortar) and blend to a paste. Heat the sesame oil in a large saucepan on a medium heat and fry the chilli paste for 3 minutes. Add the coconut milk, stock and 1 tablespoon of fish sauce or soy sauce. Bring to the boil, then reduce the heat and simmer for 10 minutes.

3 Add the sugar snap peas and beansprouts and simmer for a further 2–3 minutes or until almost cooked but still a bit crunchy. Check the taste and add more lime juice or fish/soy sauce if necessary.

4 Divide the noodles between warm bowls, ladle the hot soup over and scatter the sliced spring onions and reserved coriander leaves on top.

Variation

Chicken noodle laksa: Use chicken stock rather than vegetable stock and substitute the sugar snap peas and beansprouts with 550g (1lb 3oz) thinly sliced raw chicken breast, legs or thighs, cooking for 5 rather than 3 minutes.

Broccoli, olive and Parmesan salad

SERVES 2 · VEGETARIAN

This is a really easy dish to prepare, highly nutritious and perfect for a quick lunch. It's unusual to have broccoli in a salad of this style, but it combines beautifully with the olives and Parmesan. Serve the salad as a side dish with barbecued food or with toasted or grilled bread drizzled with olive oil, bruschetta style.

Salt and freshly ground black pepper
225g (8oz) broccoli or purple sprouting broccoli, cut into florets
1–2 tbsp extra-virgin olive oil
½ lemon, for squeezing
8–10 black olives, stoned and chopped
2 tbsp grated Parmesan or Parmesan shavings

1 Bring a large saucepan of salted water to the boil, add the broccoli and blanch for 3–4 minutes, so that it stays crunchy. Drain well.

2 While still warm, arrange on plates, drizzle over the olive oil and add a squeeze of lemon juice. Scatter over the olives and Parmesan, add a good twist of pepper and serve.

Summer garden salad

SERVES 4 · VEGETARIAN

A fabulously simple salad. The dressing is based on an
old-fashioned recipe and is wonderful served with fresh
ingredients plucked straight from the garden.

Salt and freshly ground
  black pepper
5 eggs
4 tbsp olive oil
2 cloves of garlic, peeled
  and crushed
2 tsp soft light brown sugar
2 tbsp lime or lemon juice
1 small cucumber,
  finely sliced
8 small plum tomatoes,
  halved
Small bunch of spring
  onions, trimmed
  and sliced
15g (½oz) bunch of
  mint, leaves only
75g (3oz) watercress
  leaves, any thick
  stalks removed

1 Bring a saucepan of salted water to a rolling boil and carefully
add the eggs, cooking them for 6–7 minutes or until semi-hard
boiled. Drain and immediately cool under cold running water
to stop them cooking. Peel off the shells and cut the eggs in half.

2 In the meantime, start making the dressing. Pour the olive oil
into a small frying pan on a medium heat, add the garlic and fry
for about 30 seconds until golden brown. Remove from the
heat and leave the oil to cool completely.

3 Place the sugar and lime or lemon juice in a large bowl and
stir until the sugar dissolves. Scoop out two halves of egg yolk
from the whites and add to the mixture, mashing them down
with the back of a spoon. Roughly chop the whites and reserve
for serving. Add the cooled oil and garlic, season with salt
and pepper and vigorously whisk everything together to form
a smooth, thick dressing. Check the seasoning, adding more
salt and pepper if necessary.

4 Put the cucumber, tomatoes and spring onions into a large
bowl and pour over the dressing. Add the mint and watercress
and toss all the ingredients together.

5 Pile the salad onto plates, arrange two egg halves on top of
each, scatter over the reserved chopped egg whites and serve.

Middle Eastern spiced lamb koftas with dips and spicy pittas

SERVES 4

Koftas are a type of meatball from the Middle East, but you can find variations (all with very similar names) in South Asia and the Balkans. They are lovely hot or cold, served as part of a meal or eaten as a snack or as canapés. Here I've served them meze-style with pitta bread and a variety of cooling dips. You could, of course, use minced pork or beef instead of lamb to make the koftas.

500g (1lb 2oz) minced lamb
½ onion, peeled and very finely chopped
2 cloves of garlic cloves, peeled and crushed
1 tsp ground cumin
1 tsp ground coriander
1 tsp ground turmeric
Pinch of ground cinnamon
¼ tsp cayenne pepper
2 tbsp chopped coriander
Salt and freshly ground black pepper
2 tbsp olive oil
2 tbsp chopped mint
1 lemon, cut into wedges

1 To make the koftas, mix the lamb in a large bowl with the onion, garlic, spices and coriander and season well with salt and pepper. (For checking the seasoning at this stage, see tip below.) Using wet hands, shape the rest of the mixture into 12 cigar shapes. These can be left in the fridge for up to 24 hours or frozen (so long as the mince hasn't been frozen beforehand) until ready to cook.

2 In the meantime, make your choice of accompaniments (see the recipes overleaf). If making them all, then start with the baba ghanouj (see page 72) as this takes the longest to prepare.

3 When you are ready to cook the koftas, add the olive oil to a large frying pan on a medium heat. Fry the koftas for 10–15 minutes or until they are brown on both sides and cooked through. Alternatively, sear the koftas quickly in a really hot ovenproof pan and transfer to the oven, preheated to 220°C (425°F), Gas mark 7 for about 10 minutes. Remove from the pan and leave to rest for a few minutes. When they are cool enough to handle, push a skewer through the length of each kofta to resemble an ice lolly on a stick.

4 Arrange three koftas on each plate. Scatter with the mint and serve with the lemon wedges and your choice of accompaniments.

Rachel's tips
* To check the seasoning before making up the koftas, shape a little of the mixture into a small patty and fry in a pan with a little olive for a few minutes until cooked through. Taste and add more salt and pepper to the mixture if necessary.
* To make sure that you end up with the correct number of evenly sized koftas, break off pieces of the mixture and weigh them, deducting or adding more of the mixture so that each piece weighs about 50g (2oz).

(dips and pittas continued overleaf)

Aubergine and tahini dip: baba ghanouj

MAKES ABOUT 550G (1LB 3OZ)
VEGETARIAN

There are many different versions of this popular Middle Eastern dip — sometimes it's made with ground cumin or chopped mint, for instance. It is delicious served with the lamb koftas or just as a snack with some toasted pitta bread.

3 tbsp extra-virgin olive oil
2 aubergines
Salt and freshly ground black pepper
2–4 cloves of garlic, peeled and left whole
3 tbsp light tahini paste (sesame paste)
Juice of 1 lemon
125ml (4½fl oz) Greek-style yoghurt
2 tbsp chopped parsley

1 Preheat the oven to 190°C (375°F), Gas mark 5.

2 Drizzle 1 tablespoon of the olive oil over a baking tray. Cut the aubergines in half lengthways and place skin side down on the tray. Drizzle with another tablespoon of the olive oil and season well with salt and pepper. Add the garlic to the tray and bake in the oven for 20–30 minutes or until the garlic and aubergines are soft.

3 Once cool enough to handle, use a spoon to scoop the flesh from the skin of the aubergine. Discard the skin and put the flesh into a food processor with the garlic, tahini, lemon juice and the remaining olive oil. Blend until smooth and transfer to a bowl. Alternatively, place all the ingredients in the bowl and purée using a hand-held blender. Allow to cool.

4 Once cool, fold in the yoghurt and almost all of the parsley. Check the seasoning, adjusting if necessary, then spoon into a serving bowl and scatter with the remaining parsley.

Coriander and mint salsa

MAKES ABOUT 200ML (7FL OZ)
VEGETARIAN

I love this sauce. It is rather like a pesto — great drizzled over barbecued lamb chops, for instance, or of course with the lamb koftas. It keeps really well in a jar in the fridge for up to a week. Just cover with a thin layer of olive oil to help preserve.

4 tbsp roughly chopped coriander,
    including soft stalks
2 tbsp roughly chopped mint
1 spring onion, trimmed and roughly chopped
2 cloves of garlic, peeled and roughly chopped
150ml (5fl oz) extra-virgin olive oil
Salt and freshly ground black pepper

Place all the ingredients in a food processor, season with salt and pepper and blend until fairly smooth, adding a little more oil if necessary. Alternatively, make by hand by finely chopping the herbs, spring onion and garlic and stirring into the oil. Adjust the seasoning if necessary, and place in a serving bowl.

Tzatziki

MAKES ABOUT 150ML (5FL OZ)
VEGETARIAN

150ml (5fl oz) natural yoghurt
3 tbsp roughly chopped mint
½ cucumber, diced
1 clove of garlic, peeled and crushed
Juice and finely grated zest of ½ lemon
Salt and freshly ground black pepper

Place the yoghurt in a small bowl and mix in the mint, cucumber, garlic and lemon juice and zest. Season to taste with salt and pepper.

Raita

MAKES ABOUT 400ML (14FL OZ)

This classic dip from India and South Asia is the perfect foil for spicy food, the yoghurt providing a welcome cooling touch.

1 x 250g tub of Greek-style yoghurt
½ cucumber, deseeded and diced
2 tbsp chopped mint
Salt and freshly ground black pepper

Simply stir all the ingredients together and season to taste with salt and pepper.

Hummus

MAKES ABOUT 400G (14OZ)
VEGETARIAN

Hummus is the Arabic word for chickpeas. Of course you can buy this in many shops now but it is quick and easy to make at home and so versatile. I often add chopped coriander or mint and sometimes a little chopped red chilli. It will keep in the fridge for 4–5 days.

1 x 400g (14oz) tin of chickpeas, drained, or 125g (4½oz) dried chickpeas, soaked and cooked (see page 329)
Juice of ½–1 lemon
2 cloves of garlic, peeled and crushed
2 heaped tbsp tahini paste (sesame paste)
3 tbsp extra-virgin olive oil
2 tbsp natural yoghurt
Salt and freshly ground black pepper

Place all the ingredients in a food processor, season with salt and pepper and blend until really smooth, adding a little more oil if necessary. Check the seasoning, adding more lemon juice and salt and pepper if needed, and place in a serving bowl.

Spicy pitta wedges

MAKES ABOUT 20 WEDGES

As well as serving with the lamb koftas, these could be used for dipping into and scooping up any of the dips on their own. They're best served straight away, slightly warm, but they will keep for a day or two in an airtight container, reheated when you need them.

2 tsp cumin seeds, toasted (see tip on page 50)
4 pitta breads, cut into wedges
2–3 tbsp olive oil
½ tsp finely chopped deseeded red chilli (optional)
¼ tsp sea salt

1 Preheat the oven to 220°C (425°F), Gas mark 7.

2 Crush the toasted cumin seeds using a pestle and mortar or spice grinder. Alternatively, once the seeds are cool, put them into a plastic bag and crush with a rolling pin. Place the pitta wedges in a large bowl, pour over the olive oil, add the crushed cumin seeds, chilli (if using) and salt and toss together to coat evenly.

3 Spread out flat on a baking tray and bake in the oven for 4–5 minutes until pale golden. Keep an eye on them as they can burn easily!

Food on the go

There's something special about a home-packed meal when you are out and about, on a train or car trip, out walking in the hills, enjoying a lazy afternoon at the beach or taking a break at work or school. My mother-in-law, Darina, is the snack queen when it comes to travelling. Once we all flew together to Mexico, and mid-flight she took out some lovely smoked salmon and brown bread sandwiches. I was so glad to be travelling with her! When we're travelling with the children, I'm always especially thankful that I've got packed food with me. It's not only practical and economical, but it can be a great distraction for restless young travellers. A bag of popcorn or some delicious homemade baked goods, such as the Squashed-fly Biscuits on page 277, are great for snacking.

Packed salads

Salads are great on-the-go foods and so many dishes are perfect served cold or at room temperature. They can easily be popped into a lidded plastic container for lunch on the hoof. Cold cooked pasta, rice, couscous and orzo are all wonderful as a base for salads. Try any of them with cut-up raw or roasted vegetables (peppers, tomato, broccoli, courgette), a drizzle of extra-virgin olive oil and a squeeze of lemon and other ingredients, such as chorizo, feta cheese, spring onion or a bit of crushed garlic for flavour. I love leftover cooked pasta or new potatoes mixed with tuna, hard-boiled egg, olives, tomatoes and cucumber. Beans, such as haricot or cannellini, chickpeas and lentils also work well as a base for a salad. Do avoid any kind of lettuce-based salad, though, as the leaves will go soggy.

Creative options

Not everyone loves sandwiches, but luckily there are so many delicious alternatives. For instance, pack a few flour or corn tortillas, some refried beans, shredded cooked chicken and tomato salsa and you can assemble portable tostadas on the spot (see pages 137–9). Chutney and crackers with cheese or cold meats are also perfectly portable. Leftover roast meat, meatloaf (see page 191) or nut loaf and pâté, not to mention the Pork and Egg Picnic Pie on page 80, are all great served cold and somehow taste even better when you're perched on a hillside or sitting on a train. These all make great finger foods, as do quesadillas (see page 259) or raw cut vegetables. I pack them with containers of sauces for dipping, such as pesto, mayonnaise or sweet chilli sauce. Indeed, why not try the Crudités and Dips on pages 250–2?

Antipasti from my local farmers' market also make excellent picnic fare — I might buy olives, artichoke hearts, cheese, salami or prosciutto, a focaccia loaf and a few cherry tomatoes. Hot or cold soup such as gazpacho (see page 48), brought in a flask, is so satisfying when you're out enjoying the view. See pages 46–62 for some wonderful soup-making ideas.

Packed lunches

Of course, all of the above make great packed lunches as well, whether for school or the office. For school lunches for the children, I always include cheese, raw vegetables like carrots, cauliflower, tomato and cucumber, a couple of homemade biscuits, some fresh fruit — an apple, tangerines or some grapes or strawberries, whatever is in season. Dried fruit such as apricots or figs are perfect for a child's lunchbox, too.

Sweet treats

A sweet 'fix' can be very welcome when you're out and about, especially if you've just been on a vigorous walk. Sweet things, whether biscuits or slices of cake, are ideal portable food and can easily be wrapped in foil or cling film and popped into a bag. Millionaire's Shortbread or the Coconut and Chocolate Flapjacks on pages 276 and 284 are perfect, as is fruitcake or gingerbread (see page 289). You can even take a small container of granola to munch on (see page 12) or, if you are out walking all day and don't want to overfill your backpack, just take some homemade fudge or toffees (see pages 308 and 300) with you.

Containers

When I pack everything up, I do try to create as little rubbish as possible. I like to keep an eye out for cute plastic boxes and any other type of small container with a lid, or vintage biscuit tins, which I line with greaseproof paper. The lid from the container can also serve as a plate. Darina puts sea salt and freshly ground pepper in old film canisters (if you can find them); they're the perfect size. I do like to use baskets whenever I can, but for travelling, a canvas bag that you can fold up when you've finished eating is much more practical. I keep all these supplies in one place in the kitchen so I'm never digging around for my containers or flasks when I'm packing meals.

Spiced chicken salad with tzatziki

SERVES 6

This is a perfect summer lunch. The spicy chicken is beautifully complemented by the cooling tzatziki. Chicken still warm from the oven is best, but this dish works equally well if you cook the chicken in advance and serve it cold.

800g (1¾lb) skinless, boneless chicken breasts or thighs
1 tbsp sunflower oil
150ml (5fl oz) tzatziki (see page 72)

For the marinade
2 tsp cumin seeds, toasted and ground (see tip on page 50)
2 tsp paprika
¼–½ tsp cayenne pepper
2 tsp ground turmeric
½ tsp caster sugar
½ tsp freshly ground black pepper
1 tsp salt
2 cloves of garlic, peeled and crushed
50ml (2fl oz) freshly squeezed lemon juice

For the salad
1 cos lettuce, halved across and leaves separated
3 tomatoes, each cut into 12 wedges
1 small red onion, peeled and thinly sliced in rings

1 Mix together all the ingredients for the marinade in a large bowl. Cut the chicken into long thin strips and toss in the marinade to evenly coat. Cover and leave in the fridge for at least 20 minutes, but preferably a couple of hours or even overnight.

2 Preheat the oven to 200°C (400°F), Gas mark 6.

3 Drizzle the sunflower oil on a large baking sheet and arrange the chicken pieces on it in a single layer. Bake in the oven for about 15 minutes until cooked through and golden.

4 Meanwhile, prepare the tzatziki as on page 72.

5 Toss the ingredients for the salad together in a bowl and pile onto a large serving platter or individual plates. Arrange the warm chicken pieces on top and drizzle with tzatziki. Serve immediately.

Aromatic crispy duck rolls

SERVES 4

These are fabulous for a party or for enjoying as a family meal.
They are also a great snack if everything is prepared and stored in small
containers in the fridge for people to help themselves whenever the
mood strikes. Chinese pancakes are available in Asian food stores,
some supermarkets or even from your local Chinese take-away.

2 duck breasts (about
   250g/9oz each), skin on
2 tsp salt
1 tsp Chinese five-spice
   powder
1.2 litres (2 pints) chicken
   stock (see page 326)
3 star anise
1 tsp Szechuan
   peppercorns or ½ tsp
   black peppercorns
6 cloves
1 cinnamon stick
4 spring onions, trimmed
   and very roughly
   chopped
2.5 cm (1in) piece of root
   ginger, peeled and sliced
100ml (3½fl oz) Chinese
   rice wine or dry sherry

To serve
16 Chinese pancakes
Bunch of spring onions,
   trimmed and cut into
   fine strips
2 x 6cm (2½in) pieces
   cucumber, cut into
   fine strips
200ml (7fl oz) Hoisin
   sauce

1 Preheat the oven to 220°C (425°F), Gas mark 7.

2 Remove the skin from the duck breasts and make three long
scores in each piece of skin with a sharp knife. Place the skins
in a small, non-stick roasting tin and rub the salt and five-spice
powder evenly over. Roast in the oven for 20–25 minutes until
crisp and golden.

3 Meanwhile, pour the stock into a saucepan and add all the
remaining ingredients. Bring slowly to the boil, reduce the
heat and simmer for 4–5 minutes.

4 Add the duck breasts to the stock, cover with a tight-fitting
lid and gently poach the duck for 15–20 minutes or until
cooked through. Remove the duck breasts from the pan and
allow to cool a little before shredding with two forks, pulling
the meat apart. Place on a plate or baking tray, cover with
foil and keep warm in a low oven.

5 Drain the crisp duck skins on kitchen paper and finely slice.
Scatter the slices back into the roasting tin (which should be
full of rendered duck fat) and return to the oven for 5 minutes.
Drain well on kitchen paper again and toss with the shredded
duck breast.

6 Warm the Chinese pancakes in a steamer or microwave,
then place the spring onions, cucumber and Hoisin sauce in
separate serving bowls and serve alongside the warmed pancakes
and shredded crispy duck. Allow people to assemble the rolls
themselves. Spread a little Hoisin sauce on a Chinese pancake,
scatter with some spring onions, cucumber and crispy duck
and roll up to enclose before eating with your fingers. Finger
bowls of warm water may come in handy, or lots of napkins!

Lamb, bean, olive and feta salad with redcurrant dressing

SERVES 4

I created this salad one day with some leftover lamb. It has delicious Greek flavours and works so well with the redcurrant jelly in the dressing. More of a meal in its own right than a starter, this dish is ideal for a midsummer lunch or supper.

300g (11oz) leftover, cooked lamb
1 x 200g tin of beans (such as butter beans, black eye or cannellini beans), drained, or 75g (3oz) dried beans, soaked and cooked (see page 329)
110g (4oz) salad leaves (about 4 large handfuls)
Small handful of mint leaves
About 24 black olives, pitted and halved
200g (7oz) feta cheese, crumbled

For the redcurrant dressing
4 tsp redcurrant jelly (see page 328)
2 tsp red wine vinegar
4 tbsp extra-virgin olive oil
Salt and freshly ground black pepper

1 First make the dressing. Place the redcurrant jelly in a small bowl, add the vinegar and olive oil, season with a little salt and pepper and whisk together until emulsified.

2 Carve or tear the lamb into thin slices and toss lightly with the beans, salad and mint leaves on one big serving platter or in individual bowls. Scatter the olives and crumbled bits of feta cheese on top. Drizzle over the dressing and serve.

Pork and egg picnic pie

SERVES 8–10

This is best served at room temperature and eaten with pickles and cheese on the side. It's also delicious served with a little chutney. The pie lasts for a few days in the fridge.

For the hot water crust pastry
75g (3oz) butter, cubed
225g (8oz) plain flour, plus extra for dusting
Pinch of salt
1 egg, beaten (plus another for glazing)

For the minced pork mixture
625g (1lb 6oz) minced pork
3 cloves of garlic, peeled and crushed or finely grated
1 tbsp chopped thyme and sage (a mixture)
1 egg, beaten
Pinch of freshly grated nutmeg
Salt and freshly ground black pepper

For the topping
10 rashers of back (not streaky) bacon, trimmed of fat
4 eggs

25cm (10in) diameter tart tin with 3cm (1¼in) sides

1 First, prepare the pastry. Place the butter and 100ml (3½fl oz) water in a saucepan and heat gently, stirring occasionally, until the butter melts, then allow the mixture to come to a rolling boil. Meanwhile, sift the flour and salt into a large bowl. Make a well in the centre and add the egg. Pour the hot liquid into the flour and quickly stir with a wooden spoon to mix to a dough. Use the wooden spoon to spread the dough out on a large plate and allow to cool for about 15 minutes. Knead the dough into a ball, flatten slightly, wrap in cling film and place in the fridge for about 30 minutes to firm up.

2 While the pastry is chilling, mix all ingredients for the minced pork mixture together in a large bowl. Season with salt and pepper, then fry a tiny bit to taste for seasoning (see tip on page 70).

3 Preheat the oven to 180°C (350°F), Gas mark 4.

4 Roll out half of the pastry on a lightly floured work surface until it is about 7mm (⅜in) thick and use to line the tart tin. Trim the edges and brush around them with some of the beaten egg.

5 Cover the base of the pastry with five of the trimmed bacon rashers. Place the minced pork mixture over the top, then make four 'dips' or 'wells' for the eggs to go into. Crack an egg into each of these 'wells', then cover the mixture with the remaining five rashers.

6 Roll out the second half of the pastry until it is also about 7mm (⅜in) thick and carefully place it on top of the pie. Trim the edges and brush the top with a little more of the beaten egg. If you wish, roll out the scraps until they are about 5mm (¼in) thick and cut into leaves or whatever shapes take your fancy! Place on top of the pie and brush the shapes with the remainder of the beaten egg to glaze.

7 Make a hole, about 5mm (¼in) wide in the centre of the pastry at the top of the pie and cook in the oven for approximately 1 hour and 10 minutes–1 hour and 20 minutes or until golden brown and a skewer inserted into the middle comes out hot (too hot to hold on the inside of your wrist). Allow to cool for at least 30 minutes before removing from the tin. When cooled, cut into slices to serve.

Linguini with shrimps, garlic and herbs

SERVES 4–6

A simple, classic Italian dish that is a particular favourite with my family. We try to get hold of shrimps (or small prawns) as often as possible. Use spaghetti if you don't have linguini or why not try making your own pasta (see page 130)?

Salt and freshly ground
   black pepper
300g (11oz) linguini
110g (4oz) butter
500g (18oz) cooked
   and peeled shrimps
   or small prawns
4 cloves of garlic, peeled
   and crushed
1 red chilli, deseeded
   and finely chopped
   (optional)
2 tbsp chopped mixed
   herbs, such as parsley,
   chives, dill, tarragon
   or chervil
Squeeze of lemon juice
Lemon slices, to serve

1 Fill a large saucepan with water, add 1 teaspoon of salt and bring to the boil. Add the linguini and cook for 10–12 minutes (or follow the instructions on the packet), stirring occasionally, until just tender.

2 Meanwhile, melt the butter in a frying pan on a medium heat and, once sizzling, add the shrimps (or prawns), garlic and chilli (if using) and season with salt and pepper. Cook for 4–5 minutes, tossing regularly until warmed through and becoming golden.

3 Drain the now cooked linguini (leaving a couple of tablespoons of the cooking liquid in the saucepan) and return it to the pan, removed from the heat. Stir in the herbs and tip the shrimp mixture onto the pasta.

4 Toss everything together and check the seasoning, adding enough lemon juice to taste and more salt and pepper if necessary. Serve immediately.

Rachel's tip
For a quick and easy snack or a simple starter, simply cook and serve the shrimps or prawns with crusty bread instead of the linguini.

Tagliatelle with smoked salmon, watercress and peas

SERVES 4

This is a really good pasta dish, great for all the family, and it makes a little bit of smoked salmon go a long way. Use rocket instead of watercress if you can't get hold of it. If you'd like to make your own pasta, try the recipe on page 130.

Salt and freshly ground
    black pepper
500g (1lb 2oz) tagliatelle
200g (7oz) crème fraîche
200g (7oz) smoked
    salmon, sliced into
    strips 1cm (½in) wide
50g (2oz) frozen peas
25g (1oz) finely grated
    Parmesan cheese
Good squeeze of
    lemon juice
2 tbsp chopped chives
50g (2oz) watercress leaves,
    roughly chopped

1 Fill a large saucepan with water, add 1 teaspoon of salt and bring to the boil. Add the tagliatelle and cook for 10–12 minutes (or follow the instructions on the packet), stirring occasionally, until just tender.

2 In the meantime, place the crème fraîche in a saucepan on a low heat and gently warm through for 1 minute. Add the smoked salmon strips and cook for 2–3 minutes, stirring occasionally.

3 Meanwhile, cook the peas in a small saucepan of boiling, salted water (I usually take some of the pasta cooking water from the large saucepan) for 1–2 minutes or until just cooked. Add the peas to the crème fraîche mixture along with three-quarters of the Parmesan cheese, the lemon juice and half of the chives, and stir together. Season to taste with salt and pepper and remove from the heat.

4 Drain the cooked pasta (leaving a couple of tablespoons of the cooking liquid in the saucepan) and return it to the saucepan, removed from the heat. Scatter with the watercress and pour over the crème fraîche mixture. Toss everything together so that all the ingredients are well combined and check the seasoning, adding more salt and pepper or lemon juice if necessary. Divide between plates or pasta bowls, scatter with the remaining chives and serve.

Fish cakes

Fish cakes are a great way of using up leftover cooked potato and fish and they go down well with children. You can also experiment with other ingredients like chilli, finely chopped cooked vegetables or different herbs to give a different flavour each time. Serve the fish cakes with a flavoured mayonnaise (see overleaf) or tomato relish.

600g (1lb 5oz) floury
    potatoes
Salt and freshly ground
    black pepper
400g (14oz) skinned
    white fish, such as cod,
    haddock or hake
150g (5oz) butter, diced
4 tbsp white wine
Juice of ¼ lemon
150g (5oz) button
    mushrooms, sliced
200g (7oz) cooked and
    peeled shrimps or
    small prawns, any
    larger ones chopped
2 egg yolks
3 tsp Dijon mustard
4 tbsp finely chopped
    herbs, such as parsley,
    tarragon, dill or chives
    (either one herb
    or a mixture)
3–4 tbsp olive oil

To serve
Salad leaves
Lemon wedges

1 Cook the potatoes as described in the mash recipe (see page 116). Peel and mash (but without adding any butter or milk) and transfer to a large bowl.

2 Meanwhile, place the fish in a wide, shallow saucepan and add 100g (3½oz) of the butter, the wine and the lemon juice. Season with salt and pepper, then cover with a lid and gently poach on a low heat for 10–15 minutes or until the fish is cooked through. Carefully remove the fish from the pan and set aside to cool a little. Turn up the heat to high and boil the poaching liquid until it has reduced by half.

3 In the meantime, melt 25g (1oz) of the butter in a small frying pan and sauté the mushrooms on a medium heat for 8–10 minutes or until soft and golden, seasoning with salt and pepper. Set aside and allow to cool a little.

4 Add the fish, reduced poaching liquid and cooked mushrooms to the mash along with the shrimps or prawns, egg yolks, mustard and herbs. Gently mix everything together, breaking the fish up as you go but being careful not to mash it up too much. Season to taste with salt and pepper.

5 Shape the mixture into eight patties (each about 8cm/3in wide and 2cm/¾in thick) and arrange on a baking sheet or large plate. Cover with cling film and place in the fridge for about 1 hour to firm up. (The fish cakes can be prepared to this stage in advance and either frozen or kept in the fridge for up to 24 hours.)

(continued overleaf)

6 Place the olive oil and remaining butter in a large, non-stick frying pan on a low–medium heat and very gently fry the fish cakes for about 5 minutes on each side or until golden and warmed through, adding a little more oil or butter to the pan during cooking if necessary.

7 Divide the fish cakes between plates, add some salad leaves to each plate and serve immediately with your choice of accompaniment from below.

Accompaniments

Flavoured mayonnaise: Serve with the tomato aioli or herb and garlic mayonnaise (see pages 175 and 330) or simply add the finely grated zest of 1 lemon to the homemade mayonnaise (see page 330).

Herb butter: Serve with the dill butter (see page 327) or make a different flavoured butter by stirring 1 heaped tablespoon of your favourite herb, chopped, into 75g (3oz) softened butter until it is well blended.

Poached salmon with hollandaise

When wild salmon is in season it's one of the best fish to serve —
quite unbeatable, and this is such an easy recipe. When poaching salmon,
or indeed any fish, be sure to use as little water as necessary to minimise
flavour loss. Use a saucepan that will just fit the fish. Also, I like to only add
salt to the cooking water and no other flavourings. Add 1 tablespoon of
salt to every 1.2 litres (2 pints) water. Salmon is delicious served with
asparagus and steamed or boiled new potatoes.

Salt
18–20cm (7–8in) piece
of salmon, still on the
bone, cut from a whole
fish that has been gutted
and descaled (ask your
fishmonger to do this
if necessary)
300ml (½ pint)
hollandaise sauce
(see page 331)

1 Bring a saucepan of salted water to the boil (see above for pan
size and quantity of salt to add). Slide in the salmon, bring back
up to the boil and then reduce the heat, cover with a lid and
gently simmer for 20 minutes. Remove from the heat and leave
the salmon to stand in the cooking liquid for 5 minutes, which
will continue cooking the fish.

2 Carefully remove the salmon from the water, and when cool
enough to handle, remove the skin and any brown sediment
by scraping gently with a small, sharp knife. You will see that
there are four segments of salmon on the bone. Run the knife
carefully down the seam of each segment to release the portions
away from the bone, giving four portions in total.

3 Serve immediately with the hollandaise sauce.

Rachel's tip
If you are feeding lots of people, poach a whole salmon in a
fish kettle. If you only want to poach one section of the salmon,
you can freeze the rest for another time.

Ivan Allen's dressed crab with tomato and basil salad

SERVES 6

Ivan Allen was Isaac's grandfather and this is his recipe. I remember him coming into the kitchens at Ballymaloe and checking the dressed crab to ensure it was just right. Try to find whole crabs so that that you can use both the white and flavourful brown meat. I've given instructions for cooking a crab from scratch, but if you can't get hold of a whole crab, you can use ready-cooked frozen crab meat instead. Try serving with a good-quality tomato relish.

How to cook a crab

1 First place the crab in the freezer for a couple of hours so that it is unconscious before boiling. To cook a crab, place it in a large saucepan, cover with warm water, add 1 tablespoon of salt for every 1.2 litres (2 pints) of water and bring to the boil. Simmer on a medium heat for 20 minutes per 450g (1lb) and then pour off about two-thirds of the water, cover with a lid and continue to cook for a further 6 minutes. To check to see if the crab is cooked, gently shake it quite close to your ear and you shouldn't hear liquid splashing around. Remove the crab and allow to cool.

2 First remove the large claws and crack these (using a heavy weight or nut crackers), then extract every bit of meat using the handle of a teaspoon. Retain the shell if making dressed crab (see overleaf), otherwise discard. Turn the body of the crab upside down and pull out the centre portion. Discard the gills, known as 'dead man's fingers', each about 4cm (1½in) long. Scoop out all the lovely brown meat and add it to the white meat from the claws. The meat can be used immediately or frozen for future use.

Rachel's tip

450g (1lb) of cooked crab in the shell yields approximately 175–225g (6–8oz) crab meat.

(continued overleaf)

425g (15oz) brown and
    white meat from 2–3
    cooked fresh crabs,
    reserving the crab shells
100g (3½oz) soft white
    breadcrumbs
150ml (5fl oz) white sauce
    (see page 327)
2 tbsp tomato chutney
    or tomato relish
2 tsp white wine vinegar
1 tsp Dijon mustard or a
    generous pinch of dry
    mustard powder
75g (3oz) butter, melted
Salt and freshly ground
    black pepper
100g (3½oz) white
    breadcrumbs

**For the tomato
and basil salad**
8 vine-ripened tomatoes
    (using one variety or
    a mixture)
Pinch of caster sugar
Good squeeze of lemon
    juice
2–3 tbsp extra-virgin
    olive oil
Small handful of basil
    leaves, larger leaves torn

*Two or three crab shells or
six 250ml (9fl oz) ramekins
or small dishes*

How to dress a crab

1 Preheat the oven to 180°C (350°F), Gas mark 4. If using the crab shells, scrub them clean, dry well and arrange upside down on a baking tray. Alternatively, place the ramekins or small dishes on the tray.

2 In a large bowl, mix together the crab meat, breadcrumbs, white sauce, chutney or relish, vinegar, mustard and 25g (1oz) of the melted butter and season to taste with salt and pepper. Spoon the mixture into the crab shells or ramekins. In a separate bowl, toss together the breadcrumbs with the remaining butter and sprinkle over the crab mixture.

3 Bake in the oven for 15–20 minutes until heated through and browned on top. Briefly place under a preheated grill, if necessary, to crisp up the crumbs.

4 In the meantime, prepare the salad. Cut the tomatoes into quarters or 1cm (½in) slices. Spread out in a single layer on a large flat plate and season to taste with salt, pepper and sugar. Add the lemon juice, drizzle over the olive oil and scatter with the basil leaves and toss gently together.

5 Serve the baked crab with the tomato salad and some fresh crusty bread on the side.

Sunday lunch

Roast chicken with stuffing, gravy and sauces

SERVES 4—6

Roast chicken is one of the most popular family recipes and can be stuffed simply with a few cloves of garlic and a lemon, a handful of herbs, a traditional stuffing like the one here, or with one of the delicious variations that follow. Of course, roast chicken is fantastic with a simple gravy, but why not experiment with a cream sauce, such as the tarragon cream sauce on page 97 — most definitely Zac's favourite! Always buy as good a chicken as you can afford, remembering not only that this is going to be great on the day you cook it, but that you can then use the leftovers in a soup, pie or pasta sauce, and even make a stock out of the carcass.

1 chicken (1.5–2.25kg/ 3lb 5oz–5lb)
15g (½oz) butter, softened
Sea salt and freshly ground black pepper

1 Preheat the oven to 180°C (350°F), Gas mark 4.

2 First make the stuffing (if using), choosing either the traditional herb stuffing or one of the variations (see page 96). Leave to cool.

3 Spoon the cooled stuffing into the chicken cavity and place the chicken in a roasting tin. Smear the butter over the skin and sprinkle with salt and pepper. Roast in the oven for 1½–1¾ hours (allowing about 20 minutes per 450g/1lb), basting occasionally, until cooked through. If the skin begins to look quite dark during cooking, cover the chicken with some foil or parchment paper.

4 While the chicken is cooking, prepare your choice of sauce (see pages 96–7) to accompany the chicken, unless you want to make the gravy or Tarragon Cream Sauce (see page 97), which use the juices of the chicken once it's cooked.

5 To check whether the chicken is fully cooked, stick a skewer into the thigh with a spoon placed underneath to catch the juices; the juices should run clear. Also, the legs should feel quite loose on the bird. When cooked, transfer the chicken to a serving plate and leave to rest, covered with foil and in the oven at the lowest temperature, if possible, while you make the gravy or sauce.

6 Spoon the stuffing out of the chicken into a serving bowl or onto a plate. Carve the chicken and serve with the stuffing, gravy or any other accompanying sauce, roast potatoes (see page 119) and your choice of vegetables — either your own favourite recipes or from those on pages 120–8.

(continued overleaf)

Traditional herb stuffing

MAKES 250G (9OZ)

This stuffing can be made in advance and kept in the fridge for a couple of days or frozen.

25g (1oz) butter
1 tbsp olive oil
1 onion, peeled and chopped
1 clove of garlic, peeled and finely chopped
3 tbsp chopped mixed herbs, such as parsley, thyme and sage
100g (3½oz) white breadcrumbs
Salt and freshly ground black pepper

Melt the butter in a saucepan with the olive oil, then add the onion and garlic, cover with a butter wrapper or a piece of greaseproof paper and then cover with a lid and cook on a low heat for 8–10 minutes or until the onions are soft but not browned. Take off the heat, then stir in the herbs and breadcrumbs. Season to taste with salt and pepper.

Variations

Lemony stuffing: (Makes about 300g/11oz.) Stir the finely grated zest of 1 lemon and the juice of ½ lemon into the stuffing mixture at the same time as the herbs and breadcrumbs (see above).

Chorizo stuffing: (Makes about 300g/11oz.) Cook 110g (4oz) very finely chopped chorizo sausage with the onions (see above). Basil, thyme and marjoram would go well with this as the mixed herbs.

Smoked bacon stuffing: (Makes about 350g/12oz.) Use a red onion in place of a yellow one and fry with 50g (2oz) chopped smoked bacon or pancetta. Use thyme and/or parsley as the herbs.

Ivan Whelan's chestnut stuffing: (Makes about 450g/1lb.) Stir 150g (5oz) finely chopped and toasted chestnuts (for toasting nuts, see Rachel's tip on page 50) into the stuffing mixture. Use sage and/or rosemary as the herbs. For Christmas stuffing, add 50g (2oz) dried cranberries as well.

Fruit and nut stuffing: (Makes about 450g/1lb.) This variation goes surprisingly well with the chicken. Stir 50g (2oz) chopped dried apricots, 50g (2oz) sultanas and 50g (2oz) chopped and toasted hazelnuts into the stuffing mixture.

Rachel's tip

If you don't have time to make a stuffing, pop a halved lemon or a halved head of garlic or a bunch of torn herbs inside the chicken cavity.

Bread sauce

SERVES 6–8 · VEGETARIAN

Bread sauce – you either love it or hate it!

600ml (1 pint) milk, plus extra if needed
110g (4oz) white breadcrumbs
2 onions, peeled and studded with 6 cloves each
50g (2oz) butter
Good pinch of ground cloves
75ml (3fl oz) double or regular cream
Salt and freshly ground black pepper

1 Place all the ingredients in a small saucepan, season with salt and pepper and bring to the boil. Cover with a lid, reduce the heat and simmer gently for 30 minutes. Alternatively, pour into an ovenproof dish and cook, covered with a lid or piece of foil, in a low–moderate oven (170°C/325°F/Gas mark 3) for the same length of time.

2 Remove the onions just before serving. Adjust the seasoning if necessary and add a little more milk if the sauce is too thick. Serve the bread sauce hot.

Chicken gravy

MAKES ABOUT 400ML (14FL OZ)

Gravy is, of course, the classic accompaniment to roast chicken. You can use the same method for making gravy for any roast meat.

600ml (1 pint) chicken stock (see page 326)
15–25g (½–1oz) roux (see page 327)
Salt and freshly ground black pepper

1 Once the chicken is cooked and removed from the roasting tin to rest and keep warm (see page 94), place the tin on a medium heat and deglaze with a little of the stock, stirring with a wooden spoon and scraping any sticky bits from the bottom of the tin.

2 Drain off the fat using a separating jug or, if you don't have one, pour the liquid into a bowl and add a handful of ice cubes. After a few minutes the fat will float to the surface. Remove and discard the fat, pour the remaining liquid into a saucepan with the remaining chicken stock on a medium heat.

3 Bring the stock to the boil, whisk in the roux a little at a time and continue to boil for 2–3 minutes to thicken very slightly. Season to taste with salt and pepper. Just before serving the chicken, strain the gravy through a fine sieve into a gravy boat or jug.

Tarragon cream sauce

MAKES ABOUT 250ML (9FL OZ)

This is particularly good with the smoked bacon stuffing (see page 96).

600ml (1 pint) chicken stock (see page 326)
100ml (3½fl oz) double or regular cream
2 tbsp chopped tarragon

Make the chicken gravy as above, less the roux, and add the cream and tarragon. Simmer for 3–4 minutes, uncovered, stirring regularly, until reduced and thickened, or add some roux (see page 327) to thicken it some more.

Francatelli sauce

MAKES ABOUT 250ML (9FL OZ)
VEGETARIAN

This autumnal sauce is based on one attributed to Charles Elme Francatelli, chief cook to Queen Victoria.

225g (8oz) cranberry sauce
2 tbsp port
1 cinnamon stick
4cm (1½in) strip of lemon rind

Place all the ingredients in a small saucepan on a gentle heat and simmer for 5 minutes, stirring occasionally. Leave to cool completely and refrigerate if not using straight away. Remove the cinnamon stick and lemon rind before serving and serve at room temperature rather than straight from the fridge.

Mushroom and watercress sauce

MAKES ABOUT 350ML (12FL OZ)
VEGETARIAN

This goes well with the chorizo stuffing (see page 96). Use any mushrooms you like, whether button, flat, chestnut or wild.

25g (1oz) butter
1 tbsp olive oil
1 onion, peeled and finely chopped
150g (5oz) mushrooms, sliced
Salt and freshly ground black pepper
200ml (7fl oz) single or regular cream
15g (½oz) watercress leaves, roughly chopped

Place the butter and olive oil in a saucepan on a medium heat and, when the butter has melted, tip in the onion and gently fry for 6–8 minutes or until soft but not browned. Add the mushrooms, season with salt and pepper and cook for a further 5–6 minutes or until softened and golden. Add the cream and the watercress and simmer for 2–3 minutes, uncovered, until slightly thickened.

Roast duck with gravy and sage and onion stuffing

SERVES 4

I love roast duck during the winter because I find it such a comforting meal. Sage and onion stuffing is a classic combination that really complements the flavour of the meat. It is also lovely with goose. You can use 600ml (1 pint) chicken stock (see page 326) if you'd rather not use this duck stock.

1 duck (about 1.8kg/4lb), plus the neck and giblets
Salt and freshly ground black pepper
15–25g (½–1oz) roux (see page 327)

For the stock (optional)
1 onion, peeled and quartered
1 carrot, peeled and sliced
1 stick of celery, trimmed
2 sprigs of parsley
1 sprig of thyme
3 peppercorns
OR
600ml (1 pint) ready-made stock

For the sage and onion stuffing
50g (2oz) butter
75g (3oz) (1 small) onion, peeled and finely chopped
100g (3½oz) fresh white breadcrumbs
1 tbsp chopped sage
Salt and freshly ground black pepper

1 Preheat the oven to 180°C (350°F), Gas mark 4.

2 First, make a stock for the gravy (if you are making your own). Place the duck neck and giblets in a large saucepan and add all the stock ingredients. Pour in enough cold water to just cover, bring slowly to the boil, reduce the heat and simmer, covered with a lid, for 2–3 hours. Strain through a fine sieve into a bowl, discarding the neck, giblets and vegetables. Then measure out 600ml (1 pint) of stock for making the gravy, adding water if you have to or refrigerating or freezing any that is left over to use another time.

3 Meanwhile, make the stuffing. Melt the butter in a frying pan on a gentle heat and sweat the onion for 8–10 minutes until soft but not browned. Add the breadcrumbs and sage and season to taste with salt and pepper. Remove the pan from the heat and set aside to cool.

4 Next, season the cavity of the duck with salt and pepper and spoon in the stuffing. Place the duck on a rack in a roasting tin and pierce the skin all over with the point of a sharp knife (this will help release the fat during cooking). Season the skin well, particularly with salt to help crisp it up during cooking.

5 Roast in the oven for 1½ hours (allowing about 20 minutes per 450g/1lb), basting occasionally and draining any excess fat from the tin (saving it for roast or sauté potatoes). When the duck is cooked, the legs should feel slightly loose and a metal skewer inserted into the thigh should be too hot to hold against the inside of your wrist. When cooked, transfer the duck to a serving plate and leave to rest, covered with foil and in the oven at the lowest temperature, if possible, while you make the gravy (see page 97).

6 Drain any fat from the roasting tin using a separating jug or, if you don't have one, pour the liquid from the tin into a bowl and add a handful of ice cubes. After a few minutes the fat will float to the surface. Remove and discard the fat (saving, if you wish, for roast potatoes on another day), then pour the remaining liquid into a saucepan.

7 Place the roasting tin on a medium heat and deglaze with a little of the cooking liquid or homemade or ready made stock, stirring with a wooden spoon and scraping any sticky bits from the bottom of the tin. Pour this into the saucepan with the cooking liquid, add the stock and bring to the boil. Whisk in the roux a little at a time and continue to boil for 2–3 minutes to thicken to the desired consistency. Season to taste with salt and pepper if necessary. Just before serving, strain the gravy through a fine sieve into a warm gravy boat or jug.

8 Finally, spoon the stuffing out of the duck into a serving bowl or onto a serving plate. Carve the duck breasts away from the carcass and cut each one in half. Remove the leg portions and divide them in half too. Serve a breast and leg portion per person, along with the stuffing and gravy.

Roast stuffed loin of pork with crackling and Bramley sauce

SERVES 10–12

Part of the pleasure of using pork is the crackling that comes with it, so make sure the skin is still on the joint when you buy it. You don't have to stuff the pork if you don't want to. If so, simply get your butcher to score the skin and roll and tie the pork. Any of the stuffings that accompany the roast chicken would be perfect to use here (see page 96).

1 long loin of pork (2.25kg/5lb), suitable for rolling, with the skin still on
Salt and freshly ground black pepper
About 300–450g (11oz–1lb) stuffing (see page 96), cooled

For the apple sauce
450g (1lb) Bramley apples
50g (2oz) caster or granulated sugar

For the gravy
600ml (1 pint) chicken stock (see page 326)
15– 25g (½–1oz) roux (see page 327)
Salt and freshly ground black pepper

1 Preheat the oven to 190°C (375°F), Gas mark 5.

2 First, prepare the pork. To achieve really good crackling (and to make it easier to carve later) use a sharp knife to score the skin at 5mm (¼in) intervals going in the direction from the eye (the fleshy part of the meat) to the streaky part. Put the pork skin side down on a clean surface running away from you and with the fleshy eye nearest you. Season all over with salt and pepper.

3 Spread the cooled stuffing down the centre of the pork, leaving the further end of the meat free of stuffing. Then, starting with the fleshy eye, roll the meat away from you into a long sausage shape. (That way, when you slice the pork for serving, each slice will have a piece of the streaky part of the meat and a piece of the eye as well as some stuffing.) Tie with string, at intervals, down the length of the meat to secure in place. Sit the pork, seam side down, on a rack in a large roasting tin and season generously with salt.

4 Roast the pork for 2–2¼ hours (allowing about 25 minutes per 450g/1lb), basting occasionally. About 10 minutes before the end of cooking time, increase the oven temperature to 230°C (450°F), Gas mark 8, and transfer the pork to a clean roasting tin before returning it to the oven (this is to avoid burning the sediment in the first tin). This high temperature will help give a really crisp and golden crackling. When the pork is cooked, the juices should run clear when the centre of the meat is pierced with a skewer. Remove from the oven and allow to rest in the tin.

5 While the pork is cooking, make the apple sauce. Peel, quarter and core the apples and cut each piece in half. Tip into a stainless-steel or cast-iron saucepan and add the sugar and 1 tablespoon of

(continued overleaf)

water. Cover with a lid and cook on a low heat for 6–8 minutes or until the apple has broken down. Stir and taste for sweetness, adding a little more sugar if you like. Keep warm in the pan.

6 Finally, make the gravy. Place the original roasting tin on a medium heat and deglaze with a little of the chicken stock, scraping any sticky bits from the bottom of the tin, then follow the instructions on page 97 for making gravy.

7 To carve the pork, use a very sharp knife to cut slices along the lines of the crackling and through the rolled up meat. Serve with the gravy and apple sauce. This, of course, is delicious with the roast potatoes (see page 119) and your choice of vegetable.

Rachel's tip
Apple sauce freezes perfectly, so make more than you need and freeze in small portions for ease of use.

Traditional roast rib of beef with Yorkshire puddings and horseradish sauce

SERVES 8–10

Roast beef is much tastier when cooked on the bone. Buy this from your butcher, asking him to remove the chine bone to make it easier to carve when cooked. In case you don't find beef on the bone, I have also included cooking times for beef off the bone. It's not right to serve roast beef without Yorkshire puddings, so I've included instructions for these too.

1 prime rib of beef (2.5–3.5kg/5½–7¾lb), on the bone, chine bone removed
Salt and freshly ground black pepper
Horseradish sauce (see page 328), to serve

For the Yorkshire puddings
110g (4oz) plain flour
2 eggs
300ml (½ pint) milk
15g (½oz) butter, melted
Salt and freshly ground black pepper
3 tbsp vegetable oil

For the gravy
600ml (1 pint) beef stock (see page 326)
15– 25g (½–1oz) roux (see page 327)
Salt and freshly ground black pepper

12-hole muffin tin

1 Preheat the oven to 240°C (475°F), Gas mark 9.

2 Weigh the joint and calculate the cooking time (see page 104). Score the fat and season generously with salt and pepper. Place the beef in a roasting tin fat side up so that as the fat melts during cooking it will baste the meat. The bones provide a natural rack to hold the meat clear of the fat in the roasting tray. (If you are cooking beef off the bone, then use a trivet or place a few metal spoons in the bottom of the tray.) Roast the beef in the oven for the calculated cooking time, turning the heat down to 180°C (350°F), Gas mark 4, after 15 minutes.

3 Meanwhile, make the Yorkshire pudding batter. Sift the flour into a large bowl, make a well in the centre and break in the eggs. Whisking continuously, gradually add the milk while drawing the flour in from the sides with the whisk to give a smooth batter. Whisk in the butter and season with salt and pepper. Allow to stand for about 1 hour if possible.

4 To check that the beef is cooked, insert a skewer into the thickest part of the joint, leave it there for about 30–45 seconds and then lay it against the back of your hand. If it still feels cool, the meat is rare, if it is warm it's medium rare, if it's hot it's medium and if you can't keep the skewer against your hand for more than a second, then you can bet it's well done! Also, if you check the colour of the juices that run out, you will find they are clear for well done and red or pink for rare or medium. If you own a meat thermometer, that will eliminate guesswork altogether, but make

(continued overleaf)

sure the thermometer is not touching a bone when you are testing. If the thermometer reads 60°C (140°F) then the beef is rare, 70°C (158°F) is medium and 75°C (167°F) is well done. Once cooked to your liking, remove the beef from the tin and leave to rest, covered with foil and in a warm place, if possible, for 15–30 minutes.

5 Meanwhile, cook the Yorkshire puddings. Increase the oven temperature to 230°C (450°F), Gas mark 8 and put in the muffin tin to heat up. When the tin is really hot, remove and, working quickly, grease each hole generously with the vegetable oil and half fill with the batter. Immediately return the tin to the oven and bake the Yorkshire puddings for about 20 minutes or until they are golden and well risen.

6 In the meantime, make the gravy. Place the roasting tin on a medium heat and deglaze with a little of the beef stock, stirring with a wooden spoon and scraping any sticky bits from the bottom, then follow the instructions on page 97 for making gravy.

7 Carve the now rested beef and serve with the gravy, Yorkshire puddings, horseradish sauce, lots of crispy roast potatoes (see page 119) and any of the vegetables included later in this chapter (see pages 120–8).

Calculating cooking times for beef

Beef on the bone

Rare	10–12 minutes per 450g (1lb)
Medium	12–15 minutes per 450g (1lb)
Well done	18–20 minutes per 450g (1lb)

Beef off the bone

Rare	8–10 minutes per 450g (1lb)
Medium	10–12 minutes per 450g (1lb)
Well done	15–18 minutes per 450g (1lb)

Roast leg of lamb with mint sauce and redcurrant jelly

SERVES 8–10

This is a classic Sunday lunch to savour (see the photography on page 108).
My favourite time to eat this dish is between spring and early summer when
mint and redcurrant are in season and the lamb has a mild, sweet flavour.
Serve both sauces with the lamb, if you wish, or just one or the other.

1 leg of lamb (2.5–3.5kg/
   5½–7¾lb)
1 large sprig of rosemary
4 cloves of garlic, peeled
   and sliced
Salt and freshly ground
   black pepper
Mint sauce or redcurrant
   jelly (see page 328),
   to serve

For the gravy
600ml (1 pint) chicken
   stock (see page 326)
15–25g (½–1oz) roux
   (see page 327)
Salt and freshly ground
   black pepper

1 Preheat the oven to 200°C (400°F), Gas mark 6.

2 Place the joint in a roasting tin and make several deep incisions
widthways across the top using a sharp knife. Pull the tufts of
rosemary from the stalk and push them into each incision with
a slice or two of garlic (it's fine if they are left poking out a bit).
Season generously with salt and pepper.

3 Roast the lamb for 20 minutes, then turn the heat down to
180°C (350°F), Gas mark 4, and cook for a further 1¼–1½
hours. Baste the lamb occasionally by spooning the hot melted
fat in the tin over the meat.

4 When the lamb is cooked, remove it from the tin, cover with
foil and allow it to rest for 15 minutes - somewhere warm if
possible (like on a plate/baking tray in a low oven). Meanwhile,
make the gravy.

5 Place the roasting tin on a medium heat and deglaze with
a little of the chicken stock, stirring with a wooden spoon
and scraping any sticky bits from the bottom, then follow
the instructions on page 97 for making gravy.

6 Carve the rested lamb into slices and serve with the gravy,
mint sauce or redcurrant jelly, roast potatoes (see page 119)
and your choice of vegetables. The sticky cumin and apricot
roast carrots and parsnips (see opposite) would go perfectly
with this.

Sticky cumin and apricot roast carrots and parsnips

SERVES 4–6 · VEGETARIAN

These are a real favourite of mine with a roast leg of lamb (see opposite). The natural sugars in the vegetables work beautifully with the apricot jam to give it the perfect sticky and flavourful finish (see the photograph on page 109).

500g (1lb 2oz) small carrots, peeled and tops trimmed
500g (1lb 2oz) small parsnips, peeled and halved (if larger than the carrots)
3 tbsp olive oil
1 tsp cumin seeds
Salt and freshly ground black pepper
2 tbsp apricot jam
2 tsp lemon juice
1 tbsp chopped coriander

1 Preheat the oven to 200°C (400°F), Gas mark 6.

2 Place the carrots and parsnips in a large roasting tin and drizzle with the olive oil. Scatter over the cumin seeds, season with salt and pepper and toss everything together to coat evenly. Roast in the oven for 40–45 minutes, tossing occasionally in the oil during cooking, until tender and golden.

3 In the meantime, heat the apricot jam and lemon juice for a few minutes in a small saucepan, stirring until you have a smooth, runny sauce. Pour this over the carrots and parsnips for the last 10 minutes of cooking, tossing the vegetables in the sauce to coat evenly. Scatter with the coriander just before serving.

Menu planning

Feeding a family is a great joy, but having to cook day in, day out can also seem like hard work. Some parents have more time to put thought and effort into the weekly family meals. Others may come home from work feeling tired and lacking inspiration. I find that planning meals for the week with a little foresight, and making use of the freezer and a well-stocked larder (see pages 170–1 and 334–5), can really help.

Shopping for the season

Don't underestimate the importance of shopping! It is the first part of menu planning. When I go to the farmers' market and my local shops, I think about what I'm getting for the week. Whether you shop for groceries online or locally, you can approach it in the same way. My weekly meals rely on what is locally and seasonally available. Locally grown and seasonal foods are generally better value than produce flown to us from the other side of the world. Eating food out of season is both expensive and makes the food in question seem less special if you can have it all year round.

When I think about a seasonal menu, I think about the time of year, what I feel like eating and its nutritional benefits. Nature really has it all worked out. We need the goodness of root vegetables in the winter, and at that time of year I crave hearty soups and stews. In the summer, my mind turns to fresh, palate-tingling flavours and vibrant colours – homemade tomato sauce, berry fools and crisp, tasty salads.

Being thrifty and thinking ahead

I like to think of economical and easy ways to stretch meals and use up all my leftover little bits. I know that on Sunday I'll make a roast and then for Monday supper I'll use the leftovers. So, I'll buy a chicken for lunch on Sunday (see page 94), then on Monday evening we'll have the leftover chicken with lasagne, tostadas (see pages 183 and 137) or in a pie or salad. Roast meats are easily re-used in stir-fries, fried rice, pasta sauces or sandwiches for school. Cooked vegetables can be used in an omelette or frittata (see pages 20 and 35) or whizzed into a soup. What you plan for a meal depends very much on how much time is available, of course. I might have time to make a fish pie one night (see page 168), while another night it will be a simple pasta dish or something pulled from the freezer.

Keeping things interesting

I keep the menu planning interesting for myself by following my changing tastes and cravings from day to day and depending on the weather. On one occasion I may want something spicy and warming like Chilli con Carne (see page 202). The next night it might be an Asian stir-fry, such as the Crispy Prawns with Chinese Noodle Stir-Fry on page 153. I like to experiment with new things as well as make the foods I know my family loves. It's also important to introduce your children to different cultures through food, opening them up to different flavours and textures as well as ways of eating. Our boys love using chopsticks, for instance, because it's a novelty and because we always have a bit of a laugh. Cheese fondue (see page 162) is another winner; you can't fail to have fun sitting around the table with everyone dipping pieces of bread into the melted cheese. Homemade pizza is a favourite finger food – and our children love to choose their own toppings (see pages 149–51) when making them with me.

I like to make a variety of foods for the family, but I don't offer our children a choice at mealtimes. I do take their tastes into consideration, of course, but I won't make different meals for everyone.

Planning for the week

When I'm planning the week's menu, I also think about what the children are eating over the course of a few days. So I won't give them several nights of pasta in a row or too much meat. As long as they are eating a variety of foods, I know they are getting what they need. One or two nights a week I like to make a special treat for the family. It might be a gorgeous comforting bread and butter pudding (see page 226) or some ice cream with homemade toffee or chocolate sauce (see pages 240 and 337).

If you are making two or three courses for a special meal or a dinner party, think about serving a variety of textures, flavours and colours. For a multi-course meal, you wouldn't want everything a bland-looking brown, beige and white. There needs to be balance, too, in the richness of the food you are serving: you might follow a creamy main course with a lighter pudding to counterbalance it, for instance. And try to avoid being repetitive with ingredients. For example, I wouldn't serve tomatoes or eggs for more than one course.

Sunday roast and pizza night

While variety is important, you may find it helpful to set aside a night or two for a particular type of meal, even make a tradition of it – the Friday pizza night, for instance, or the Sunday roast. Then you'll know that at least twice a week you'll never have to wonder what you are going to make that day. You don't have to be too rigid, of course, especially if you're not in the mood for a particular meal or simply too busy to shop on your regular day and have to rely on what's in the larder. Depending on what ingredients you have, you may decide to switch pasta night for fish night or have a casserole on Sunday instead of the usual roast.

Pecan and vegetable loaf

SERVES 4—6 · VEGETARIAN

Quite a few people have asked me for a good nutloaf recipe, so here is one that my brother-in-law makes. It's a classic dish for vegetarians and is so tasty and full of texture that meat lovers will enjoy it too. This dish goes beautifully with Sautéed Potatoes and Caramelised Onions (see opposite) and the Green Beans with Garlic (see page 124). Leftover slices can be easily frozen for later use. If pecan nuts are unavailable, walnuts can be used instead.

2–3 tbsp olive oil
25g (1oz) butter
350g (12oz) peeled and finely chopped onions
75g (3oz) mushrooms, finely chopped
25g (1oz) red pepper, finely chopped
Salt and freshly ground black pepper
350g (12oz) peeled and grated carrots
175g (6oz) finely chopped celery
175g (6oz) fresh white breadcrumbs
50g (2oz) chopped pecan nuts
25g (1oz) sunflower seeds
Leaves from 2 sprigs of thyme
Leaves from 1 large sprig of oregano or marjoram
Pinch of freshly grated nutmeg
5 eggs, beaten

900g (2lb) loaf tin
(12.5 x 23cm/5 x 9in)

1 Preheat the oven to 180°C (350°F), Gas mark 4. Grease the loaf tin with 1 tablespoon of the olive oil, line with parchment paper and grease again with a little more of the oil. Place the loaf tin on a baking sheet.

2 Add the remaining oil and the butter to a frying pan on a medium heat. When the butter has melted, sauté the onions, mushrooms and red pepper for 7–10 minutes, stirring occasionally, until soft and slightly golden. Season to taste with salt and pepper, remove from the heat and allow to cool a little.

3 Meanwhile, toss the carrots, celery, breadcrumbs, pecans, sunflower seeds and herbs together in a large bowl. Season with salt, pepper and the nutmeg. Add the cooled sautéed vegetables and the eggs and mix well together.

4 Spoon the mixture into the prepared loaf tin, pressing it down with the back of the spoon to expel any air trapped in the mixture. Bake in the oven for 1 hour, turning the loaf tin around once half-way through, until golden on top and firm to the touch. Remove from the oven and allow to rest for 10 minutes before turning out. Cut into 8–12 slices and serve.

Sautéed potatoes with caramelised onions

SERVES 4 · VEGETARIAN

This is delicious with any roast meat, a steak or even a burger. Use any leftover mixture in a frittata or omelette (see pages 35 and 20). You can omit the onions and just serve the sautéed potatoes if you like.

800g (1¾lb) floury potatoes, peeled and cut into 2cm (¾in) cubes
4 tbsp olive oil
Salt and freshly ground black pepper
25g (1oz) butter
1 large onion, peeled and finely sliced
2 cloves of garlic, peeled and finely chopped
2 tsp finely chopped thyme or rosemary leaves

1 Dry the potatoes well in a clean tea towel. Pour 3 tablespoons of the olive oil into a large, heavy-based frying pan on a high heat and add the potatoes. Turn the heat down to low–medium and sauté the potatoes for 30–35 minutes, tossing regularly, until softened, crisp and golden. Season well with salt and pepper.

2 In the meantime, add the butter and remaining oil to a separate frying pan, and when the butter has melted, add in the onion. Cook on a low–medium heat for roughly the same length of time, 30–35 minutes or until softened and caramelised to a golden colour. Add the garlic and thyme or rosemary to the onions for the last 5 minutes of cooking and season well with salt and pepper.

3 Tip the caramelised onions into the pan with the sautéed potatoes, toss together and serve immediately.

Smoked salmon, leek and potato pie

SERVES 4—6

Here is the perfect summer dish for a different Sunday lunch.
It's so quick and easy to put together you can then spend some time
with your friends or family while it bakes in the oven. Serve with
the Pea Purée or Minted Broad Beans (see pages 122 and 124).

850g (1lb 14oz) peeled
floury potatoes (weigh
when peeled), cut into
5mm (¼in) slices
175g (6oz) smoked
salmon, cut into 2cm
(¾in) slices
2 leeks (about 225g/8oz
when trimmed), cut into
3–5mm (⅛–¼in) slices
Salt and freshly ground
black pepper
2 large cloves of garlic,
peeled and chopped
15g (½oz) butter
375ml (13fl oz) double
or regular cream
40g (1½oz) Parmesan
cheese, finely grated

1.5 litre (2½ pint) pie dish

1 Preheat the oven to 180°C (350°F), Gas mark 4.

2 Divide the sliced potatoes into three piles and arrange one-third of the sliced potatoes on the base of the pie dish, followed by half the smoked salmon and half the leeks. Season with a pinch of salt, some pepper and half the garlic, then dot with the butter. Add another layer of potatoes, then the remaining smoked salmon and leeks, season again and add the remainder of the garlic, then add the final layer of potatoes.

3 Bring the cream to the boil in a saucepan and pour over the potatoes. Season with salt and pepper and sprinkle the Parmesan over the top. Season again, cover with some foil and cook in the oven for 1¼–1½ hours, removing the foil after 30 minutes. When cooked, the potatoes will be soft and the top golden, with the cream bubbling up the sides of the dish. Serve immediately or keep warm in the oven at the lowest temperature for 30 minutes or so, covering it again with foil to prevent it drying out.

Variation
Leek, chorizo and potato pie: In place of the smoked salmon, use 75g (3oz) chorizo, cut into about 5mm (¼in) thick slices.

Creamy mashed potato

SERVES 4 · MAKES ABOUT 1KG (2LB 3OZ) · VEGETARIAN

Good mashed potato is the best comfort food ever, eaten on its own with a great knob of butter melting in it. It is hugely popular in our family — we'd eat it for every meal! For the most nutritious version — and the fluffiest mash — boil the potatoes in their skins and peel afterwards. Floury potatoes are always best as new potatoes are too waxy for mashing.

1kg (2lb 3oz) floury potatoes
Salt and freshly ground black pepper
50g (2oz) butter
200ml (7fl oz) boiling milk, or 150ml (5fl oz) boiling milk and 50ml (2fl oz) single or regular cream

1 Clean the potatoes, but do not peel them. Place in a large saucepan, cover with cold water and add a good pinch of salt.

2 Bring the water to the boil and cook the potatoes for 10 minutes. Then pour out all but about 4cm (1½in) of the water and continue to cook the potatoes on a very low heat. Don't be tempted to stick a knife into them at any stage to see if they are cooked — the skins will split and the potatoes will just break up and become soggy if you do. About 20 minutes later, when you think the potatoes might be cooked, test them with a skewer; if they are soft, take them off the heat and drain them.

3 Peel the potatoes while they are still hot, holding them in a clean tea towel to avoid scalding your hands. Mash them immediately. Add the butter, but don't add any milk until the potatoes are free of lumps. When the potatoes are mashed, pour over the boiling milk (or milk and cream) — you may not need it all, or you may need more, depending on the texture of the potatoes. Season to taste with salt and pepper.

Rachel's tip

If you want to make the mash in advance, add a little extra milk, to keep the potatoes moist as they sit. The mash keeps well in a warm oven as long as it is covered with a lid, plate or foil.

Duchess potatoes

SERVES 4 · VEGETARIAN

Duchess potatoes are basically a rich mash made with egg yolk. It's fantastic for topping a pie as the egg yolk turns the mash a lovely golden brown.

1kg (2lb 3oz) floury
    potatoes
4 egg yolks
50g (2oz) butter, softened
100–200ml (3½–7fl oz)
    hot milk
Salt and freshly ground
    black pepper

1 Preheat the oven to 200°C (400°F), Gas mark 6.

2 Cook, peel and mash the potatoes as described in the mash recipe (see opposite). Place the warm mash in a large bowl and stir in the egg yolks and butter, mixing well. Add enough hot milk to soften the potatoes a little. Season to taste with salt and pepper.

3 Spoon into an ovenproof serving dish or place on top of a pie and bake in the oven for 8–10 minutes or until the top forms a crust and turns golden. Serve immediately.

Rachel's tip
Use the leftover egg whites to make meringues or Eton Mess (see pages 237 and 234).

Celeriac and sweet potato mash

SERVES 6–8 · VEGETARIAN

Celeriac is absolutely delicious roasted or mashed, especially with sweet potatoes. Make the most of it in winter when it's at its best.

Salt and freshly ground
    black pepper
1 celeriac, peeled
    and diced
1kg (2lb 3oz) sweet
    potatoes, peeled
    and diced
50g (2oz) butter
2 tbsp chopped parsley

1 Bring a large saucepan of water to the boil with 1 teaspoon of salt. Tip in the celeriac and sweet potatoes and cook for about 15 minutes or until tender when pierced with a sharp knife. Drain well and return to the pan to dry out for a minute or two on a low heat.

2 Remove from the heat and mash with the butter until smooth. Season to taste with salt and pepper and sprinkle with the parsley.

Baked sweet potato chips

SERVES 6—8 · VEGETARIAN

These healthy alternatives to potato chips are delicious dipped
into flavoured mayonnaises or other dips (see pages 330 and 72—3),
as well as accompanying your favourite roast.

1.5kg (3lb 5oz) sweet
  potatoes
3 tbsp olive oil
Salt and freshly ground
  black pepper

1 Preheat the oven to 220°C (425°F), Gas mark 7.

2 Wash the sweet potatoes and dry them well (or peel them, if you
prefer), then cut into chips 1cm (½in) wide. Toss them in the oil,
season with salt and pepper and scatter onto two large baking trays.

3 Bake in the oven for 35—40 minutes, tossing the chips halfway
through and swapping the trays around on the oven shelves at this
point too. The cooked chips will be soft but crisp in places and
just turning golden.

Variations
Flavoured oil: When tossing the chips in the oil before baking,
add 1 teaspoon of one of the following:
* crushed chilli flakes
* cayenne powder
* finely chopped rosemary leaves

Roast baby onions

SERVES 4 · VEGETARIAN

Roast onions really couldn't be easier; they are just thrown into the
oven in their skins. They caramelise slightly and have a sweet flavour,
making them delicious with roast chicken, lamb or beef.

12—16 onions (3–4 per
  person), unpeeled
  (any loose outer papery
  skins removed)

1 Preheat the oven to 200°C (400°F), Gas mark 6.

2 Place the onions in a roasting tin (either on their own or
with roasting meat) and roast in the oven for 30–40 minutes
or until they have softened and are a bit caramelised. The
onions will easily squeeze out of their skins for serving.

Garlic roast potatoes

SERVES 4–6 · VEGETARIAN

Garlic gives a lovely subtle flavour to the roast potatoes, although you can of course cook the potatoes without it or the herbs, for a plainer dish. Perfect to serve with roast meats of all types. The garlic, once roasted, becomes sweet and mild, a long way from its raw state.

1 tsp salt

8–10 large floury potatoes, peeled and halved if large

3–5 tbsp olive oil, duck or goose fat or beef dripping

Sea salt

1 head of garlic, broken into cloves but left unpeeled

1 tbsp chopped thyme leaves or 2 tsp chopped rosemary leaves

1 Preheat the oven to 220°C (425°F), Gas mark 7.

2 Bring a large saucepan of water to the boil with the salt. Drop in the potatoes and cook for 10 minutes. Drain off the water and shake the potatoes around in the dry saucepan with the lid on (this roughens the surface of the potatoes to help make them crispier when roasting in the oven).

3 Place a roasting tin on a high heat and drizzle in 3 tablespoons of the olive oil (or duck, goose or beef fat). Once really hot, add the potatoes and toss them in the oil or fat, making sure they are well coated (adding the remaining oil or fat if not). Sprinkle with sea salt and roast in the oven for 45–55 minutes.

4 Add the cloves of garlic after 15–20 minutes, tossing them in the oil or fat. At this stage, if you think the potatoes are dark enough, turn the oven down to 200°C (400°F), Gas mark 6. Baste the potatoes (spooning over the hot oil or fat) occasionally and turn them over halfway through cooking.

5 Finally, sprinkle the thyme or rosemary over the potatoes 10 minutes before the end of the cooking time. Serve immediately or keep warm in a low oven (without covering or they will go soggy). Push the soft, sweet garlic cloves out of their skins and eat with the crispy potatoes.

Crunchy-topped parsnip gratin

SERVES 4—6 · VEGETARIAN

If you fancy a change from roast parsnips, this creamy
gratin with its crunchy topping is ideal. It can be prepared
in advance and reheated.

25g (1oz) butter, diced,
    plus extra for greasing
250ml (9fl oz) double
    or regular cream
3 cloves of garlic, peeled
    and crushed
1 tsp thyme leaves
Good pinch of nutmeg
    (freshly grated,
    if possible)
Salt and freshly ground
    black pepper
800g (1¾lb) parsnips,
    peeled and very
    thinly sliced

For the topping
25g (1oz) white
    breadcrumbs
15g (½oz) finely grated
    Parmesan cheese
15g (½oz) butter, melted
Salt and freshly ground
    black pepper

*23 x 18cm (9 x 7in) oval gratin
dish with 5cm (2in) sides*

1 Preheat the oven to 180°C (350°F), Gas mark 4. Butter the
gratin dish and place on a baking sheet.

2 Pour the cream into a saucepan on a medium heat and add
the garlic, thyme and nutmeg. Season with salt and pepper
and bring just to the boil, then remove from the heat. Stir
in the parsnip slices and then pour everything into the gratin
dish, spreading the parsnips out evenly. Scatter the diced
butter over the top and bake in the oven for 35—40 minutes.

3 In the meantime, place the breadcrumbs with the Parmesan
cheese in a bowl, pour in the melted butter and season with salt
and pepper. Scatter the breadcrumb mixture over the top of the
gratin for the last 10 minutes of cooking to become crisp and
golden. The parsnips should be soft when pierced with a knife.

Cheese and garlic potato gratin

This is a lovely warming dish for a winter Sunday lunch.
A classic gratin that tastes just as delicious reheated the next
day, it is equally good with fish or a roast.

15g (½oz) butter
Salt and freshly ground
  black pepper
1kg (2lb 3oz) floury
  potatoes, peeled and cut
  into 5mm (¼in) slices
110g (4oz) Cheddar
  cheese, grated
4 cloves of garlic, peeled
  and crushed or grated
350ml (12fl oz) double
  or regular cream

*25 x 18cm (10 x 7in) gratin
dish with 5cm (2in) sides*

1 Preheat the oven to 180°C (350°F), Gas mark 4. Butter the gratin dish and place on a baking sheet.

2 Bring a large saucepan of water to the boil with 1 teaspoon of salt. Add the potato slices, bring back up to the boil and cook for 3–4 minutes. Drain well and leave for a few minutes until cool enough to handle.

3 Arrange a third of the potato slices in the bottom of the gratin dish, season well and scatter over a third of the cheese and a third of the garlic. Repeat with another layer, using another third of the ingredients. Finally, top with the remaining potatoes and scatter with the remaining garlic. Pour over the cream before scattering the remaining cheese on top.

4 Bake in the oven for 50–55 minutes or until golden on top and tender when pierced with a knife. Serve at once.

Creamy gratin of butternut squash

SERVES 4 · VEGETARIAN

This is lovely served as a side dish with roast chicken or lamb or even on its own as a vegetarian main course.

1 large butternut squash (500g/1lb 2oz needed when peeled and cut up)
Salt and freshly ground black pepper
1–2 cloves of garlic, peeled and crushed or finely grated
175ml (6fl oz) double or regular cream
75g (3oz) Parmesan or Gruyère cheese, finely grated

1 litre (1¾ pint) pie dish

1 Preheat the oven to 180°C (350°F), Gas mark 4.

2 Using a sharp knife, peel the skin off the butternut squash. Remove any seeds and cut into slices about 5mm (¼in) thick. Weigh out 500g (1lb 2oz), then place in the pie dish and season with salt and pepper.

3 Place the garlic and cream in a saucepan, bring to the boil then pour over the butternut squash in the dish. Sprinkle with the grated cheese. Cover the dish with foil and bake in the oven for ¾–1 hour, removing the foil after 30 minutes. When cooked, the butternut squash should be soft and the top golden and bubbly.

Pea purée

SERVES 4 · VEGETARIAN

Pea purée is naturally sweet and the green colour is wonderfully intense. Make sure the peas are only just cooked so they don't lose their bright colour and fresh flavour (see picture on page 115).

Salt and freshly ground black pepper
450g (1lb) fresh or frozen peas
75ml (3fl oz) olive oil
Good squeeze of lemon juice

Bring a saucepan of water to the boil with 1 teaspoon of salt. Tip in the peas and cook for 2–3 minutes (or a further minute for frozen peas) or until just soft, then drain well. Blend in a food processor or with a hand-held blender with the olive oil until smooth. Add lemon juice and salt and pepper to taste.

Green beans with garlic, chilli and mustard seeds

A great way to liven up green beans. Leave out the chilli if you like — the garlic and mustard seeds still combine wonderfully well with the beans. These are also delicious served as leftovers at room temperature as a salad dish.

Salt and freshly ground black pepper
450g (1lb) green beans, trimmed
25g (1oz) butter
2 cloves of garlic, peeled and thinly sliced
2 red chillies (deseeded – optional), finely chopped
2 tsp brown mustard seeds

1 Bring a large saucepan of water to a rolling boil with 1 teaspoon of salt. Add the beans and, keeping the heat turned up high, cook for about 5–6 minutes or until just tender but still with a little bite. Drain immediately.

2 Melt the butter in a wide frying pan or wok on a medium–high heat and add the garlic, chillies and mustard seeds. Quickly stir-fry for about 30 seconds or until the garlic turns golden and the mustard seeds begin to pop. Immediately tip in the cooked beans, tossing in the garlic mixture to coat. Season with salt and pepper and serve at once.

Minted broad beans

SERVES 2–4 · VEGETARIAN

Broad beans and mint are fantastic together and make the perfect light summer vegetable dish. Keep the leftovers and toss into a salad the next day.

Salt and freshly ground black pepper
500g (18oz) podded fresh or frozen broad beans
25g (1oz) butter
4 tbsp roughly chopped mint

1 Bring a large saucepan of water to the boil with 1 teaspoon of salt. Add the broad beans, bring back up to the boil and cook for 2–3 minutes if fresh or 5–6 minutes if frozen. Drain well and, once cool enough to handle, pop the beans out of their skins.

2 Melt the butter in a small saucepan on a medium heat and, once frothing, add the broad beans, tossing for 30 seconds to 1 minute to warm through. Add the mint, tossing it with the beans, and season well with salt and pepper. Spoon into a bowl and serve immediately.

Cabbage with bacon and cream

This dish turns cabbage into something truly luxurious. The saltiness of the bacon works really well with the cabbage. It is particularly good served with roast pork or chicken (see pages 100 and 94).

50g (2oz) butter
6 rashers of smoked
    streaky bacon,
    thinly sliced
1 large Savoy or green
    cabbage (about 600g/
    1lb 5oz), outer leaves
    removed
2 cloves of garlic, peeled
    and crushed
200 ml (7fl oz) single
    or regular cream
Salt and freshly ground
    black pepper

1 Melt the butter in a large frying pan or wok on a high heat, add the bacon and fry for 4—5 minutes or until crisp and golden. Remove with a slotted spoon and drain on kitchen paper.

2 Meanwhile, cut the cabbage into quarters, removing the core from each piece, and thinly shred across the grain. Add the cabbage to the pan or wok, along with the garlic and 1 tablespoon of water. Sauté for about 5 minutes on a medium—high heat, tossing frequently, until wilted and just tender.

3 Increase the heat a little and return the bacon to the pan. Pour in the cream and allow to bubble for a few minutes until thickened slightly. Season with salt and pepper to taste and serve immediately.

Buttered cabbage

SERVES 6—8 · VEGETARIAN

Cabbage so often gets a bad press as a dreary and over-boiled vegetable, but this method keeps all the flavour as the cooking water isn't thrown away and the cabbage is cooked for only a short time. So for anyone who doesn't like cabbage — give this one a try. Mix into mashed potato, too, to make colcannon.

1 large Savoy or green
    cabbage (about 600g/
    1lb 5oz), outer leaves
    removed
50g (2oz) butter
Salt and freshly ground
    black pepper

1 Cut the cabbage into quarters, remove the core from each piece and thinly shred across the grain.

2 Melt the butter in a large frying pan or wok and add the cabbage along with 1 tablespoon of water. Sauté for about 5 minutes, tossing frequently, until wilted and just tender. Season to taste with salt and pepper and serve immediately.

Carrots with nutty buttered crumbs

SERVES 4–6 · VEGETARIAN

Our children love carrots cooked in this way because the
nutty topping adds wonderful flavour and texture.

Salt and freshly ground
 black pepper
600g (1lb 5oz) carrots
 (about 4), peeled and
 cut into 1cm (½in) slices
75g (3oz) butter
15g (½oz) flaked almonds
15g (½oz) hazelnuts, finely
 chopped
110g (4oz) coarse fresh
 white breadcrumbs
25g (1oz) Gruyère cheese,
 finely grated
1 tbsp roughly chopped
 parsley

1 Bring a large saucepan of water to the boil with 1 teaspoon
of salt. Add the carrots and bring back up to the boil. Reduce
the heat a little and leave to simmer for 8–10 minutes or
until just tender when pierced with the point of a sharp knife.
Be careful not to overcook them as they will become soggy.

2 In the meantime, make the nutty crumb topping. Melt the
butter in a frying pan and, once frothing, pour a third of it
into a large bowl to reserve for the carrots. Add the almonds
and hazelnuts to the remaining butter in the pan and fry on
a low heat for 2–3 minutes or until turning golden. Tip in
the breadcrumbs, season with salt and pepper and continue
to cook for 2–3 minutes, stirring occasionally, until lightly
toasted and crisp. Remove from the heat and stir in the
Gruyère and parsley.

3 Drain the carrots really well and toss in the reserved melted
butter. Spoon them into a serving bowl or onto a plate and
scatter with the crumbs. Serve at once.

Variations

Cauliflower with nutty buttered crumbs: Replace the carrots
with 1 large cauliflower, broken into small florets and cooked
for about 10 minutes or until just tender.

Broccoli with nutty buttered crumbs: Replace the carrots with
1 large head of broccoli, broken into small florets and cooked
for about 6–8 minutes or until just tender.

Cauliflower cheese

This is particularly good with roast chicken or beef (see pages 94 and 103). Rather than using Cheddar, you can try using other local cheeses or Gruyère, Taleggio or even a blue cheese like Stilton.

Salt and freshly ground black pepper

1 cauliflower, broken into small—medium florets, leaves reserved

300ml (½ pint) white sauce (see page 327), made with 50g (2oz) of roux rather than 25g (1oz)

½ tsp English mustard

75g (3oz) Cheddar cheese, grated

Good pinch of nutmeg (freshly grated, if possible)

1 tbsp chopped parsley

Gratin dish large enough to hold the cauliflower florets in a single layer

1 Fill a large saucepan with water to a depth of about 2½cm (1in) and add a little salt. Arrange the cauliflower leaves in the bottom, sit the cauliflower florets on top, cover with a lid and bring to the boil. Cook for about 8—10 minutes or until the stalks are tender when pierced with a knife. Remove the cauliflower (discarding the leaves), drain well and arrange in the gratin dish.

2 In the meantime, make the cheese sauce. Start with the white sauce in a small saucepan on a low heat and add the mustard and most of the grated cheese, reserving a little to scatter over the top of the dish, and stir until melted. Season to taste with salt, pepper and nutmeg.

3 Preheat the grill to high. Pour the sauce over the cauliflower in the dish and then scatter with the reserved cheese. Place the dish under the grill for 2—3 minutes or until golden and bubbling on top. Scatter the chopped parsley over and serve.

Rachel's tip

Once the cauliflower cheese is assembled in the dish, but before grilling, it can be popped in the fridge for a few hours until you are ready to serve. Before grilling it, reheat the cauliflower cheese in the oven, preheated to 200°C (400°F) Gas mark 6, for about 20 minutes.

Supper

Homemade pasta and sauces

SERVES 3–4

Pasta is one of those fantastic family staples, great for children and adults alike. For cooking fresh or homemade pasta, see below. To cook dried pasta, place in boiling, salted water and cook for 10–12 minutes (or follow the instructions on the packet). I normally allow around 110g (4oz) of pasta per person, whether fresh or dried. Fresh pasta is surprisingly easy to make and delicious when served straight away. Simply tossed in butter or olive oil and a few herbs, it couldn't be nicer. It's well worth having a few sauce recipes up your sleeve to whip up quickly, or to make in advance and store in the freezer in convenient portions. There are so many sauces to try — see pages 132–6 for a few ideas.

For fresh pasta
200g (7oz) plain flour, strong white flour or '00' pasta flour, plus extra for dusting
Salt
2 eggs
Fine semolina, for tossing
Butter, melted, or extra-virgin olive oil, to serve

1 Sift the flour and ¾ teaspoon of salt into a bowl. Whisk the eggs together in a separate bowl, then make a well in the centre of the flour and add half of the egg. Mix into a dough using your hands, adding the remainder of the egg if you need it. The pasta should just come together but shouldn't stick to your hands – if it does, add a little more flour.

2 Knead in the bowl for a few minutes until smooth and then cover with cling film and place in the fridge for 30 minutes– 1 hour to relax. (It will keep for about two days in the fridge.) The dough can also be made in an electric food mixer or food processor, again being careful not to make it too wet.

3 Divide the dough into quarters and, using a rolling pin, roll out one piece at a time on a floured work surface into a very thin sheet, keeping the other pieces covered under the cling film or bowl. This can also be rolled really thinly using a pasta machine, working a piece of dough at a time through the machine, starting with the widest setting and ending with the narrowest. You should be able to read the headline print on a newspaper through the pasta.

4 From here, use the pasta to make ravioli (see pages 141–2) or cut into thin ribbons of tagliatelle, slightly wider fettucine or thick lengths of pappardelle. To shape by hand, roll each strip into a tube and, using a sharp knife, cut into slices 5mm (¼in) wide for tagliatelle, 3mm (⅛in) for fettucine or 1.5cm (⅝in)

for pappardelle. Again this can easily be done with a pasta machine, setting up the attachment to cut the pasta into strips of whatever width you like. Once made, unroll the strip and let it run through your fingers to separate the strands. Use immediately or allow to dry draped over a clean broom handle supported horizontally above the ground on two chair backs. The length of time that it takes to dry depends on the room temperature. For example, if drying near a radiator, it would take 30–45 minutes, but otherwise it could take up to a couple of hours. Once the pasta is semi-dry (dry to the touch), you can toss it in a fine polenta or semolina to prevent it sticking and then use your hands to wind it up into 3–4 coils or nests. If the pasta is completely dry (cracks when bent), store in an airtight box or plastic bag for up to 3 days.

5 When you are ready to cook the pasta, fill a large saucepan with water and bring to a fast, rolling boil. Add 1 teaspoon of salt and drop in the pasta, stirring well. Cover the saucepan with a lid until the water returns to the boil and cook for 1–2 minutes, depending on the thickness of the pasta. Drain well and toss immediately in some melted butter, olive oil or your chosen sauce (see pages 132–6) and serve immediately.

Variations
Tomato pasta: Add 2 tablespoons of tomato purée with the eggs when making the dough.
Green-speckled pasta: Add 3 tablespooons of finely chopped mixed herbs or spinach with the eggs when making the dough.

Rachel's tips
* Although pasta is best cooked and served immediately, it can be cooked a little in advance (up to 10–15 minutes): so instead of draining completely, reserve about 50ml (2fl oz) of the cooking water and stir this into the pasta with a glug of olive oil and then reheat when ready to serve.
* Once dried, the pasta can be stored in an airtight box or plastic bag and kept for a couple of days in a cool, dry place, or frozen.

Broad bean, mint and feta sauce

SERVES 4 · VEGETARIAN

For this healthy summer sauce, broad beans and mint are a great combination while feta adds a wonderful tanginess. Use fresh broad beans if possible, although frozen ones work just as well.

Salt and freshly ground black pepper
300g (11oz) podded fresh or frozen
    broad beans
Large handful of mint leaves,
    roughly chopped or torn
Zest of 1 large lemon
3–4 tbsp extra-virgin olive oil
150g (5oz) feta cheese

1 Bring a large saucepan of water to the boil with 1 teaspoon of salt and cook the broad beans for 2–3 minutes if fresh or 5–6 minutes if frozen. Drain well and, once cool enough to handle, pop the beans out of their skins.

2 Stir the broad beans into cooked pasta along with the mint leaves, lemon zest, olive oil and some salt and pepper to taste. Crumble over the feta cheese and serve immediately.

Tomato, garlic and basil sauce

SERVES 4 · VEGETARIAN

This is a super-fast, super-easy pasta sauce that has a zingy, fresh flavour. Ensure the tomatoes are perfectly ripe to achieve the best result. It is well worth keeping some of this classic sauce in the freezer as a standby.

375g (13oz) ripe tomatoes, roughly chopped
3 spring onions, trimmed and finely chopped
1 large clove of garlic, peeled and crushed
Large handful of basil leaves, several kept
    whole, the rest roughly torn
4 tbsp extra-virgin olive oil
Squeeze of lemon juice
Good pinch of caster sugar
Salt and freshly ground black pepper
110g (4oz) ricotta cheese (optional)

1 Place the tomatoes, spring onions, garlic and the torn basil leaves in a large bowl, add some freshly cooked pasta, pour over the olive oil and lemon juice and toss everything together.

2 Season with the sugar, salt and pepper, stir in spoonfuls of the ricotta cheese (if using), garnish with the whole basil leaves and serve.

Variation
Tomato and basil sauce: see the meatloaf recipe on page 191.

(sauces continued overleaf)

Spinach, garlic and walnut pesto

SERVES 4 · VEGETARIAN

Perfect with pasta, this pesto is also delicious on toast, with cheese and cold meats, or as a dip for crudités (see page 250). Kale can be used in place of the spinach. If not using all the pesto straight away, then pour into a clean sterilised jar (see tip on page 336), cover with a layer of olive oil, seal and store in the fridge for up to a month.

75g (3oz) spinach leaves, stalks removed
50g (2oz) roughly chopped walnuts (or pecans)
3 large cloves of garlic, peeled and roughly
    chopped
Salt and freshly ground black pepper
100ml (3½fl oz) extra-virgin olive oil
25g (1oz) Parmesan cheese, finely grated

1 Place the spinach leaves, walnuts or pecans and garlic in a food processor with a good pinch of salt and some pepper. Add the olive oil gradually by pouring it through the tube of the food processor while blending and blitz to a smooth paste.

2 Add the grated cheese and blend briefly again, then check the seasoning and adjust if necessary. Pour over cooked pasta and toss to coat, or stir into risotto (see page 146).

Creamy asparagus and Parmesan sauce

SERVES 4 · VEGETARIAN

A sinful and really delicious variation of a classic Italian *alfredo* sauce, this is truly divine. It is best made when asparagus is in season in late spring and early summer. Out of season, or if asparagus is not available, substitute with green beans or small broccoli florets

300ml (½ pint) double or regular cream
25g (1oz) butter, diced
75g (3oz) Parmesan cheese, roughly grated
Salt and freshly ground black pepper
150g (5oz) fine asparagus, each spear
    cut into three pieces

1 Place the cream, butter and Parmesan in a small saucepan, season with a little salt and pepper and simmer gently on a very low heat for about 20 minutes, stirring frequently, until reduced and thickened.

2 Once the sauce has been cooking for about 15 minutes, bring another small pan of water to the boil with ½ teaspoon of salt. Add the asparagus pieces and blanch for about 1 minute until just tender. Drain well.

3 Remove the sauce from the heat and stir in the asparagus. Check the seasoning and adjust if necessary. Serve the sauce immediately, stirred into cooked pasta along with a good grind of pepper.

Variation
Creamy asparagus with Parmesan sauce and pork: Serve the whole pasta dish sprinkled with chopped pieces of Parma ham, crisp pancetta or bacon.

Tomato and cream sauce

SERVES 4 · VEGETARIAN

As this takes a bit of time to cook, it is worth making a double batch of it. Cool and place in the fridge until ready to use or freeze in small portions.

75g (3oz) butter
½ onion, peeled and finely chopped
½ carrot, peeled and finely chopped
1 small stick of celery, trimmed
    and finely chopped
1 x 400g tin of tomatoes
Salt and freshly ground black pepper
Good pinch of caster sugar
75ml (3fl oz) double or regular cream
    or mascarpone

1 Melt the butter in a small saucepan on a medium heat, add the onion, carrot and celery and cook for about 5 minutes or until beginning to soften but without browning. Add the tomatoes, a pinch of salt and pepper and the sugar. Bring to the boil, reduce the heat and simmer very gently for 1 hour, uncovered and stirring occasionally, until reduced and thickened.

2 Pour the sauce into a blender, blitz until smooth and return to the saucepan. Alternatively, keep everything in the pan (removed from the heat) and use a hand-held blender to purée the sauce. Return the pan to the hob and bring the sauce to a simmer on a gentle heat, stirring regularly. Once it comes to a simmer, add the cream or mascarpone and cook for 1 minute more, still stirring. Check the seasoning and adjust if necessary. Pour the sauce over cooked pasta, toss everything together to coat evenly and serve immediately.

Carbonara sauce

SERVES 4

Another classic Italian sauce for pasta. The egg yolks give it a wonderful richness and complement the saltiness of the bacon.

2 tsp sunflower oil
6 rashers of smoked streaky bacon, diced
4 egg yolks
75ml (3fl oz) double or regular cream
Salt and freshly ground black pepper
3 tbsp finely grated Parmesan cheese
2 tsp finely chopped chives

1 Pour the oil into a small frying pan on a high heat, add the bacon and sauté for 1–2 minutes or until crisp and golden. Remove from the pan and drain on kitchen paper.

2 In a large bowl, beat the egg yolks and cream together and season lightly with salt and pepper. Tip in some freshly cooked pasta and quickly toss together – the egg will coat the pasta and cook a little in the heat. Add the Parmesan, chives and bacon and check the seasoning. Toss everything together and serve at once.

Rachel's tip
Use the leftover egg whites to make meringues or Eton Mess (see pages 237 and 234).

(sauces continued overleaf)

Bolognese sauce

SERVES 4

Bolognese reminds me of childhood; I was brought up on this recipe and always loved it. Served with spaghetti, it is the epitome of comforting family food. It's ideal for making in a large batch and freezing in small quantities to have on standby.

1 small onion, peeled and coarsely chopped
1 small carrot, peeled and coarsely chopped
1 stick of celery, trimmed and coarsely chopped
15g (½oz) butter
1 tbsp olive oil
2 cloves of garlic, peeled and crushed or grated
250g (9oz) minced beef or 125g (4½oz)
    minced beef and 125g (4½oz) minced pork
75ml (3fl oz) white wine
75ml (3fl oz) beef, chicken or vegetable stock
    (see page 326)
1 x 400g tin of chopped tomatoes
Salt and freshly ground black pepper
1–2 tbsp chopped basil, plus a few leaves
1 tbsp chopped parsley
Good pinch of caster sugar
Some grated Parmesan (optional), to serve
Handful of basil leaves, to serve

1 Place the onion, carrot and celery in a food processor and whiz until finely chopped, or finely chop by hand. Put the butter and olive oil in a saucepan on a medium heat. When the butter has melted, add the chopped vegetables and sauté for 3–4 minutes or until cooked and light golden.

2 Turn up the heat, add the garlic and minced meat, and fry, breaking up the lumps as it cooks, until evenly browned. Pour in the wine, stock and tomatoes (plus their juice) and season with the sugar, salt and pepper. Bring to the boil, reduce the heat to low and simmer uncovered for about 20 minutes or until the sauce is quite thick.

3 Add the chopped basil and parsley and adjust the seasoning to taste.

4 Pour the sauce over cooked spaghetti and toss together to coat. Divide between plates and sprinkle with the Parmesan (if using) and some torn basil leaves. Serve with garlic bread.

Creamy bacon and mushroom sauce

SERVES 4

Our children go through phases of not wanting to eat mushrooms, so Zac whizzes them up in this sauce to disguise them. Use wild mushrooms for a posher version.

1 tbsp olive oil
175g (6oz) back bacon (about 6 rashers),
    chopped
250g (9oz) button mushrooms
Salt and freshly ground black pepper
250ml (9fl oz) double or regular cream
75g (3oz) Gruyère cheese, grated
25g (1oz) Parmesan cheese, grated
1 tbsp finely chopped parsley
Squeeze of lemon juice

1 Pour the olive oil into a frying pan on a medium heat, add the bacon and fry for 3–4 minutes or until crisp and golden. Meanwhile, blend the mushrooms in a food processor for a few seconds until finely chopped (the processor saves time but you could of course chop the mushrooms by hand). Add the mushrooms to the bacon and sauté for a further 3–4 minutes or until softened. Season with a little salt and plenty of pepper.

2 Reduce the heat, add the cream to the pan and allow to simmer gently for 1–2 minutes. Remove from the heat and stir in the Gruyère and Parmesan, followed by the parsley and lemon juice, and check the seasoning. Pour the sauce over some cooked pasta, tossing together to coat evenly, and serve.

Chicken tostadas with refried beans, guacamole and tomato salsa

SERVES 6

The chicken and mayonnaise mixture is delicious as a snack when spread on crackers or crispbreads. Try adding fresh herbs and keep in the fridge for dipping into. This mixture can be made in advance, but it's best to make the tomato salsa and guacamole as close to serving as possible so they are really fresh.

2–3 tbsp olive oil
600g (1lb 5oz) skinless, boneless chicken breasts
110ml (4fl oz) mayonnaise (see page 330)
Juice of ½ lime
Salt and freshly ground black pepper

For the quick refried beans
50g (2oz) butter
1 large red onion, peeled and finely chopped
4 cloves of garlic, peeled and very finely chopped
1 x 400g tin of kidney beans, drained, or 125g (4½oz) dried beans, soaked and cooked (see page 329)
75ml (3fl oz) chicken or vegetable stock (see page 326)

For the tomato salsa
450g (1lb) ripe tomatoes (about 4), roughly chopped
1 spring onion, trimmed and finely chopped
1 clove of garlic, peeled and crushed

(continued overleaf)

1 First cook the chicken. Pour 1–2 tablespoons of the olive oil into a frying pan on a low heat, add the chicken breasts and gently fry for about 10 minutes on each side or until cooked through and golden. Remove from the pan and allow to cool a little on a chopping board. Use a rolling pin to flatten the chicken breasts. This also makes them quite stringy and easier to shred. Shred the chicken into small pieces, allow to cool completely and then place in a bowl. Add the mayonnaise, remaining olive oil and lime juice, season with and salt and pepper and mix well together, mashing a little as you go, to give a paste-like texture.

2 Next, make the quick refried beans. Melt the butter in a saucepan on a low heat, add the onion and garlic, cover with a lid and gently fry for 6–8 minutes or until soft and slightly golden. Add the kidney beans and cook in the pan, uncovered, for 3 minutes until heated through. Using a potato masher or fork, mash the bean mixture, keeping it chunky and not too smooth. Add the stock and continue to cook gently for 4–5 minutes, uncovered, until it is quite thick. Season to taste with salt and pepper and set aside. Either eat at room temperature or reheat when ready to serve.

3 Prepare the tomato salsa by simply mixing together all the ingredients (these are continued overleaf) and seasoning with salt and pepper. Put in the fridge until needed.

(continued overleaf)

1–2 red or green
   chillies, deseeded
   and finely chopped
1 heaped tbsp roughly
   chopped coriander
Juice of ½ lime
Pinch of caster sugar

For the guacamole
2 avocados
Juice of ½–1 lime
1 tbsp chopped coriander
   (optional)

For the tostadas
Sunflower oil, for
   deep-frying
12 x 18–20cm (7–8in)
   flour or corn tortillas,
   left whole, halved
   or cut into wedges

To serve
Finely shredded crisp
   lettuce
Soured cream or
   crème fraîche
Grated Cheddar cheese
Chopped coriander leaves
Lime wedges

4 For the guacamole, mash the avocado flesh with a fork in a small bowl, so that it stays fairly chunky. Mix in the lime juice and coriander (if using) and season to taste with salt and pepper. Place in the fridge until needed.

5 For the tostadas, heat a deep-fat fryer filled with sunflower oil to 180°C (350°F). Alternatively, pour the oil into a large saucepan to a depth of 2cm (¾in) and bring to the same temperature on the hob (checking with a sugar thermometer, or see tip on page 255). Deep-fry the tortillas for 1–2 minutes, one at a time if whole or halved, or in batches if cut into wedges, turning halfway through, to make them crisp and golden. Drain well on kitchen paper.

6 Serve everything on little plates or in bowls for people to share and make up themselves. To assemble, I like to spread a little refried bean mix on a crisp tostada, scatter some crunchy lettuce on top, add some of the shredded chicken mix, guacamole and tomato salsa and top with some soured cream or crème fraîche, a sprinkling of Cheddar, chopped coriander and finally a squeeze of lime juice!

Variation
Nachos: Cut the tortillas into wedges before deep-frying. Spread them out in the base of a large dish and sprinkle with plenty of Cheddar cheese (or Cheddar cheese mixed with mozzarella). Bake until the cheese has melted before serving with the rest of the ingredients.

Butternut squash ravioli with sage and pine nut butter

SERVES 4 · MAKES ABOUT 20 RAVIOLI · VEGETARIAN

This recipe is relatively time consuming, but the results are marvellous. The butternut squash is quite sweet and combines with the autumnal and wintry flavours of sage, butter and pine nuts. You could easily substitute the squash with pumpkin, if you prefer. The ravioli freezes well before cooking.

25g (1oz) butter
1 tbsp olive oil
500g (1lb 2oz) butternut
   squash, peeled and diced
Salt and freshly ground
   black pepper
½ tsp grated nutmeg
300g (11oz) homemade
   pasta dough (see
   page 130)
50g (2oz) plain flour,
   strong flour or '00'
   pasta flour, for dusting
1 egg, beaten

**For the warm sage
and pine nut butter**
110g (4oz) butter
Handful of sage leaves
25g (1oz) pine nuts

To serve
25g (1oz) Parmesan
   cheese, finely grated
Handful of rocket leaves

*6–8cm (2½–3in) ravioli
cutter or fluted scone cutter*

1 Add the butter and olive oil to a large frying pan on a low heat. When the butter has melted, tip in the squash. Season with salt and pepper and cook gently for 15–20 minutes until softened and becoming pulpy but not browned. Remove from the heat and blend to a fine purée in a blender or food processor. Alternatively, blitz using a hand-held blender.

2 Pour into a bowl, allow to cool and then cover with a plate or cling film and place in the fridge for about 30 minutes. Remove from the fridge, stir in the nutmeg and check the seasoning, adjusting if necessary. At this point you can cover and place in the fridge again until ready to use.

3 Divide the dough into four and put one piece through a pasta machine, starting at the widest setting and passing through until the final setting is reached and the pasta is almost paper thin and smooth. Alternatively, do this by hand using a rolling pin. Lay the strip of pasta out flat on a floured work surface, cover with a clean tea towel, set aside and repeat with a second piece of dough. (It is important that any pasta not being used is kept covered so that it doesn't dry out.)

4 Spoon about 10 tablespoons of the squash filling, spaced about 4cm (1½in) apart, down the length of the first strip. Brush a little of the beaten egg around each piece of filling. Lay the second strip of pasta loosely on top, squash the filling down a little and press the pasta down and around to completely enclose, squishing out any trapped air as you go. Using the ravioli cutter or scone cutter, stamp out the ravioli or simply cut out with a knife into squares.

(continued overleaf)

5 Toss them in a little flour to prevent sticking, arrange in a single layer on a well-floured baking tray and cover with a clean tea towel. Repeat with the remaining pasta and filling mixture and place in the fridge for at least 30 minutes (or up to 24 hours).

6 Prepare the sage and pine nut butter when ready to serve. Melt the butter in a small frying pan and, when frothing, add the sage leaves, pine nuts and a little salt and pepper. Gently cook for 4–5 minutes until the pine nuts turn golden and the butter becomes nutty brown in colour, being careful not to burn either.

7 Meanwhile, bring a large saucepan of water to a simmer with 1 teaspoon of salt and gently cook the ravioli for 2 minutes. Drain in a colander, return to the pan and pour over the sage and pine nut butter, tossing well to coat. Serve immediately with a scattering of grated Parmesan, the rocket leaves and a grind of pepper.

Rachel's tip

If using a special ravioli tin, simply lay strips of the pasta over the moulds in the tin, carefully pressing them into the holes. Spoon a little of the squash filling into each hole and then lay another sheet of pasta on top. Run a rolling pin over the top to seal and cut them into individual ravioli and pop them out of the tin. A ravioli tin will make many more ravioli as the individual holes are quite small.

Ham and cheese macaroni

SERVES 6

This is one of our children's favourite meals. The Emmental
and Gruyère cheeses add a wonderful flavour and texture to the
dish – making a change from the more traditional Cheddar.
Serve with a crisp green salad or peas.

50g (2oz) butter,
    plus extra for greasing
Salt and freshly ground
    black pepper
350g (12oz) macaroni
50g (2oz) plain flour
850ml (1½ pints)
    whole milk
150g (5oz) Cheddar
    cheese, grated
100g (3½oz) Emmental
    or Gruyère cheese, grated
1 tsp English mustard
250g (9oz) sliced ham

*1.8 litre (3 pint) gratin dish
(20 x 30cm/8 x 12in) with
5cm (2in) sides*

1 Preheat the oven to 200°C (400F), Gas mark 6. Butter
or grease the gratin dish and place on a baking sheet.

2 Bring a large saucepan of salted water to the boil and cook
the pasta for 10–12 minutes or follow the instructions on
the packet. Drain well.

3 Meanwhile, prepare a speedy version of white sauce. Melt the
butter in a large saucepan on a medium heat and add the flour,
stirring for a few seconds. Take off the heat and gradually add
the milk, stirring continuously until it is fully incorporated and
the sauce is lump free. Return the pan to a gentle heat and cook
the sauce for 6–8 minutes, stirring constantly, until thickened
and smooth.

4 Mix the Cheddar with the Emmental or Gruyère, reserving
a third of it to use as a topping. Remove the white sauce from
the heat and add the other two-thirds of the cheese, the mustard
and some salt and pepper, stirring until the cheese has melted
and is fully incorporated into the sauce.

5 Add the cooked macaroni to the sauce and stir to combine
evenly. Spoon a third of the mixture into the gratin dish and
spread evenly. Lay half of the ham slices in a single layer on top
and spread over another third of the macaroni mixture. Repeat
with the remaining ham and pasta. Scatter with the reserved
cheese and bake in the oven for 15 minutes or until heated
through and bubbling and golden on top.

Spaghetti with herby pork meatballs

SERVES 4 · MAKES 16–20 LITTLE MEATBALLS

These pork meatballs are equally delicious served as canapés with a dip, such as sweet chilli sauce, raita or a flavoured mayonnaise (see pages 73 and 330). You can also use beef or lamb mince instead of pork mince.

450g (1lb) minced pork
1 tsp finely chopped
    parsley
1 tsp thyme leaves
3 cloves of garlic,
    peeled and crushed
    or finely grated
1 egg, beaten
Salt and freshly ground
    black pepper
1–2 tbsp olive oil
300g (11oz) spaghetti
Grated mozzarella or
    Parmesan cheese,
    to serve

**For the tomato
and herb sauce**
3 tbsp olive oil
1 onion, peeled and sliced
1 clove of garlic, peeled
    and crushed
2 x 410g tins chopped
    tomatoes or 900g (2lb)
    fresh, ripe tomatoes,
    skinned (see tip below
    right) and chopped
1 tsp caster sugar
3 tsp finely chopped
    marjoram or 2 tsp
    finely chopped sage

1 Place the minced pork, parsley, thyme, garlic and egg in a large bowl, season with salt and pepper and mix well together. (To check the seasoning at this stage, see tip on page 70.)

2 Using wet hands, form the mixture into 16–20 tiny little meatballs, each about 2cm (¾in) in diameter, and then place in the fridge (for up to 24 hours) or store in the freezer (defrosting well before use) until you are ready to cook them.

3 Next, prepare the sauce. Heat the oil in a large saucepan and cook the onion and garlic on a gentle heat for about 6 minutes until they are soft and slightly golden. Add the tomatoes, sugar and 2 teaspoons of the marjoram or sage and season well with salt and pepper. Simmer the sauce gently, uncovered, for about 30 minutes until reduced and thickened.

4 When you are ready to cook the meatballs, pour the olive oil into a large frying pan on a medium heat, add the meatballs and fry for 12–15 minutes, turning regularly, until evenly browned and cooked through. Alternatively, fry them for a minute all over until well browned, then transfer to the oven, preheated to 230°C (450°F), Gas mark 8, for 10 minutes until cooked through.

5 Meanwhile, bring a large saucepan of water to the boil with 1 teaspoon of salt and cook the spaghetti for 8–10 minutes or following the instructions on the packet until al dente, stirring every now and again. Drain well and return to the saucepan.

6 To serve, pour the sauce over the cooked spaghetti and add the meatballs. Toss everything together and serve with a scattering of mozzarella or Parmesan and the remaining marjoram or sage.

Rachel's tip
To skin tomatoes, score a cross through the skin of each tomato with a sharp knife, then place in a bowl and cover with boiling water. Leave in the water for 15–20 seconds, then drain, rinse in cold water and peel the skin from each tomato — it should come away very easily.

Basic risotto with variations

SERVES 6

Risotto is an Italian dish using a short-grain rice such as Arborio or Carnaroli. Depending on where it is made in Italy, the consistency of the dish varies from runny to quite thick. It can be prepared simply, with just cheese added to the basic dish, or cooked with a whole range of ingredients from vegetables to meat and seafood. See the variations overleaf for some ideas.

1 tbsp olive oil
25g (1oz) butter
1 onion, peeled and
    finely chopped
350g (12oz) risotto rice
150ml (5fl oz) white wine
1 litre (1¾ pints) chicken
    stock (see page 326)
75g (3oz) Parmesan,
    Manchego or Desmond
    cheese, finely grated
Salt and freshly ground
    black pepper

Basic risotto

1 Heat the olive oil and butter in a large saucepan. When the butter has melted, add the onion, cover with a lid and sweat on a gentle heat for about 10 minutes, stirring halfway through cooking, until soft but not browned. Add the rice and stir around in the saucepan for a minute or so before adding the wine. Bring the mixture to the boil, reduce the heat and simmer for 2–3 minutes or until the wine has been absorbed (at this point the alcohol has been burnt off).

2 Meanwhile, pour the stock into another saucepan and bring to the boil. Reduce the heat and simmer gently to keep warm.

3 Continuing to cook the risotto on a gentle heat, add a ladleful of stock at a time, stirring continuously and not adding another until the previous one has been absorbed. Repeat this process until all the stock has been used up and the rice has cooked to a runny and creamy consistency. This should take about 20–25 minutes.

4 Stir in the cheese, reserving a little for serving and check the seasoning. At this stage serve as it is or add your choice of flavourings from overleaf. Spoon the risotto into warm bowls or onto plates and scatter the remaining grated cheese over the top. Serve with a crisp green salad.

(variations given overleaf)

Spring vegetable risotto with baby carrots, mangetout and spring onions

Prepare the risotto as described on page 146. Melt 25g (1oz) butter in a large frying pan on a gentle heat and sauté 150g (5oz) sliced carrots (or halved lengthways if using baby carrots) for 4–5 minutes. Add a thinly sliced courgette, 110g (4oz) sliced mangetout and 2 finely sliced spring onions and sauté for a further 3–4 minutes or until just tender. Stir into the cooked risotto with 1 tablespoon of roughly chopped marjoram.

Red wine risotto with chorizo and peas

When making the risotto (see page 146), substitute white wine with red. In a separate pan, gently fry 200g (7oz) sliced or diced chorizo for 1–2 minutes or until the oils are released. Drain on kitchen paper, reserving the chorizo oil for serving. Stir the chorizo into the cooked risotto with 125g (4½oz) fresh or frozen and defrosted peas and 2 tablespoons of roughly chopped parsley. Drizzle the reserved oil over the finished risotto and serve.

Risotto with potatoes and spinach garlic and walnut pesto

Prepare the risotto as described on page 146. Boil 450g (1lb) peeled and diced potatoes (use a waxy variety such as Desirée) in salted water for 15–20 minutes until just tender but not falling apart, and drain well. Stir into the cooked risotto along with 75ml (3fl oz) of the Spinach, Garlic and Walnut Pesto (see page 134).

Butternut squash risotto with blue cheese and toasted pumpkin seeds

Peel and dice a butternut squash (about 750g/1lb 10oz peeled weight) and place in a large saucepan with 25g (1oz) butter and 250ml (9fl oz) water together with a pinch of salt. Cover with a lid and simmer gently for 5 minutes. Remove the lid, increase the heat and simmer for a further 5–10 minutes or until all of the water has evaporated. Reduce the heat slightly, add 2 teaspoons of finely chopped sage and sauté for 4–5 minutes or until tender and just turning golden. Stir the squash mixture into the cooked risotto with 50g (2oz) lightly toasted pumpkin seeds (see tip on page 50), reserving a few for sprinkling over the dish. Scatter over 110g (4oz) crumbled blue cheese with the reserved pumpkin seeds when serving.

Homemade pizzas

Making pizzas with children is great fun and a favourite pastime of our young ones, keeping them occupied for ages. Put the ingredients out in small bowls so everyone can help themselves to their favourite combinations. If you have any tomato sauce leftover, it is delicious as a pasta sauce the next day.

350g (12oz) strong white flour
1 tsp salt
2 tsp caster sugar
50g (2oz) butter
1 x 7g sachet fast-acting yeast
2 tbsp olive oil, plus extra for brushing
175–200ml (6–7fl oz) lukewarm water
Plain flour, semolina or fine polenta, for dusting
450g (1lb) mozzarella, grated, or 225g (8oz) mozzarella and 225g (8oz) Gruyère cheese, grated

For the tomato sauce
450g (1lb) ripe tomatoes, halved
3 cloves of garlic, peeled and kept whole
5 tbsp olive oil
3 tbsp balsamic vinegar
Good pinch of caster sugar
Salt and freshly ground black pepper

Baking tray and at least 2 baking sheets

1 First make the pizza dough. Place the flour, salt and sugar in a large bowl. Rub in the butter until the mixture resembles fine breadcrumbs, add the yeast and mix together. Make a well in the centre of the dry ingredients, add the oil and most of the water and mix to a loose dough. Add more water or flour, if needed.

2 Transfer the dough from the bowl to a lightly floured work surface, cover with a clean tea towel and allow to rest for 5 minutes. Uncover and knead the dough for 10 minutes or until it feels smooth and slightly springy. You can also do this in an electric food mixer with the dough hook attachment for half the time. Let the dough relax again for a few minutes, covered with the tea towel.

3 Shape the dough into six equally sized balls, each weighing about 110g (4oz). Lightly brush the dough balls with olive oil. Cover the oiled dough with cling film and place in the fridge for 30 minutes while you make the tomato sauce. The dough will be easier to handle when cold but it can also be used immediately.

4 Preheat the oven to 230°C (450°F), Gas mark 8.

5 To make the sauce, first lay the tomatoes on a baking tray, cut side up. Add the garlic, drizzle with the olive oil and balsamic vinegar, and season with the sugar and some salt and pepper. Cook in the oven for 20–30 minutes or until the tomatoes are completely soft and blistered.

6 Remove from the oven, blitz until smooth in a blender or using a hand-held blender and then strain through a fine sieve into a bowl. Check the seasoning and the consistency of the sauce. It should be thick enough to coat the back of a spoon.

(continued overleaf)

If it needs thickening, pour it into a saucepan, bring to the boil and reduce to thicken, which could take up to 10 minutes.

7 Place 1–2 baking sheets in the oven to heat up (I find it best to cook just one or two pizzas at a time). Then, on a floured work surface, roll each dough ball out to a disc about 25cm (10in) in diameter. Place each pizza base on a cold baking sheet (with no edges, so that the pizza can slide off) or upturned baking tray that has been dusted with flour, fine polenta or semolina to prevent it from sticking. Spread the tomato sauce all over each base, leaving a 2.5cm (1in) border around the edge. Scatter the grated cheese over the sauce, followed by your choice of additional toppings (if using – see below).

8 Slide each pizza off the cool baking sheet onto a hot sheet in the oven and cook for 5–10 minutes, depending on the thickness of the pizza and heat of the oven, until the pizza is golden underneath and bubbling on top. Serve immediately.

Toppings
Try adding some of the following to the tomato and cheese base:
* A sprinkling of diced cooked ham
* Thinly sliced chorizo, arranged on top, plus a scattering of thinly sliced red onion
* A little goat's cheese, crumbled over, and some slivers of roasted red or yellow pepper
* A few strips of Parma ham, arranged on top, followed by a drizzle of pesto
* A sprinkling of basil and some dried chilli flakes

Crispy prawns with Chinese noodle stir-fry

SERVES 4—6

Salt and freshly ground
    black pepper
400g (14oz) medium
    Chinese egg noodles
2 tsp sesame oil
3 tbsp groundnut oil
375g (13oz) raw, peeled
    large tiger prawns (about
    500g/1lb 2oz in weight
    with the shells on) or
    about 24 shrimps or
    small prawns, split in
    half lengthways if large
3 tbsp plain flour
2 cloves of garlic, peeled
    and finely chopped
2 tsp finely chopped root
    ginger
1 red chilli, deseeded
    and finely chopped
1 carrot, peeled and cut
    into fine strips
110g (4oz) green beans,
    topped and tailed and
    halved
2 tsp dark soy sauce
1 tsp caster sugar
Bunch of spring onions,
    trimmed and cut into
    strips
110g (4oz) beansprouts
2 tbsp roughly chopped
    peanuts, toasted
    (see tip on page 50)

1 Bring a large saucepan of water to the boil with 1 teaspoon of salt and cook the noodles for 3—4 minutes or following the instructions on the packet until tender. Drain well and return to the pan. Drizzle the sesame oil over and toss to coat. Cover the noodles and set aside in the pan to keep warm.

2 Pour 2 tablespoons of the groundnut oil into a wok or large frying pan on a medium—high heat. Season the prawns with salt and pepper and toss in the flour to coat lightly, shaking off any excess. Fry the prawns for 2—3 minutes until golden and cooked through. Set aside to keep warm, but do not cover.

3 Add the remaining groundnut oil to the wok or frying pan. When hot, add the garlic and ginger and sauté for about 30 seconds until just golden. Tip in the chilli, carrot and beans and sauté for a further 3—4 minutes. Season with the soy sauce and sugar. Add the noodles and all but a handful of each of the spring onions and beansprouts and stir-fry for 1 minute more.

4 To serve, divide the noodle stir-fry between warm plates or bowls. Arrange the prawns on top and sprinkle over the remaining spring onions and beansprouts. Scatter with the toasted peanuts and serve immediately.

Rachel's tips
* Using a mandolin to slice or julienne the carrot into fine strips will make the job much easier.
* Serve the prawns from this recipe as party nibbles with a dip (such as the mayonnaise dips on page 330).

Sweet and sticky pork noodle stir-fry

SERVES 4—6

400g (14oz) lean pork,
  cut into thin strips
1 tsp salt
400g (14oz) medium
  Chinese egg noodles
400g (14oz) button
  mushrooms, quartered
1 tbsp soy sauce
150g (5oz) finely shredded
  Savoy cabbage
4 large spring onions,
  trimmed and cut into
  2.5 cm (1in) pieces

For the marinade
2 cloves of garlic, peeled
  and finely chopped
2 tsp finely grated root
  ginger
3 tbsp groundnut oil
1 tsp soy sauce
3 tbsp fish sauce (nam pla)
3 tbsp caster sugar

1 Place the pork in a bowl or resealable food bag and add all the ingredients for the marinade. Toss the pork to coat evenly and cover the bowl with cling film or seal the bag and leave to marinate in the fridge for at least 4 hours or overnight if possible.

2 Bring a large saucepan of water to the boil with the salt. Add the noodles and cook for 3—4 minutes or follow the instructions on the packet until tender. Drain well and return to the pan, then cover and set aside to keep warm.

3 Once ready to cook, place a wok or large frying pan on a very high heat and, once hot, add the pork and the marinade. Stirring constantly, fry for 4—5 minutes until the pork is cooked through. Remove the pork with a slotted spoon and set aside. Reduce the heat so that the marinade is simmering, add the mushrooms and soy sauce and continue to cook for 2—3 minutes. Add the cabbage and spring onions and stir-fry for a further 2 minutes.

4 Finally, tip in the cooked noodles along with the pork. Cook for 1 minute more, tossing everything together. Divide between warm bowls and eat with chopsticks if you wish.

Stir-fried noodles with chicken dumplings

SERVES 4—6

1.2 litres (2 pints) chicken
    stock (see page 326)
400g (14oz) medium
    Chinese egg noodles
1 tbsp vegetable oil
4 cloves of garlic, crushed
2 small red chillies,
    deseeded (optional)
    and finely chopped
6 spring onions, trimmed
    and sliced diagonally
3 tbsp soft dark brown sugar
225g (8oz) beansprouts
4 tbsp fish sauce (nam pla)
4 tbsp finely chopped
    salted peanuts
Juice of 2 limes
Bunch of coriander
    (15g/½oz), leaves
    picked and chopped
Lemon wedges, to serve

**For the dumplings (makes
about 500g/1lb 2oz)**
300g (11oz) minced
    chicken
100g (3½oz) minced
    pork belly
50g (2oz) finely chopped
    salted peanuts (optional)
1 tsp finely chopped root
    ginger
1 tsp finely chopped garlic
1 tsp finely chopped,
    deseeded red chilli
    (optional)
2 large spring onions,
    trimmed and chopped
2 tsp finely chopped
    coriander
1 small egg
50g (2oz) breadcrumbs
2 tbsp vegetable oil
Salt and black pepper

1 First, prepare the chicken dumplings. Mix all of the ingredients except the oil together in a large bowl until well blended and season with a little salt and pepper. Divide the mixture into 48 walnut-sized pieces and roll them into small balls. Pour the oil into a large frying pan on a medium heat and, working in batches, gently fry the dumplings for 6—8 minutes, turning frequently, until cooked through and golden all over.

2 In the meantime, bring the stock to the boil in a large saucepan and add the noodles. Cook for 3—4 minutes or following the instructions on the packet until tender, then drain well into a bowl (reserving the stock to make soup at another time, if you wish).

3 While the noodles are cooking, pour the oil into a wok or large frying pan on a high heat and, once hot, add the garlic, chillies, spring onions and sugar. Fry for 1—2 minutes, stirring continuously until everything has softened and the sugar dissolved. Add the cooked noodles with the beansprouts and fish sauce, toss everything together and continue to cook for a few more minutes to warm through. Remove from the heat and stir in the peanuts, lime juice and coriander.

4 Pile the noodles into serving bowls and arrange the dumplings on top (allowing six per person). Serve immediately with lemon wedges to squeeze over.

Rachel's tips
* Chicken dumplings are also great served as a snack, starter or canapé with a dipping sauce. To make a quick Thai dipping sauce, mix 50ml (2fl oz) fish sauce (nam pla) with 50ml (2fl oz) lime or lemon juice in a small bowl. Stir in 2 tablespoons of caster sugar until dissolved and then add 1 peeled and crushed clove of garlic and 3 finely sliced red or green chillies (with seeds left in). Add 25ml (1fl oz) water to dilute the sauce if you find that it is a little too strongly flavoured.
* You can freeze the raw dumplings, if you wish, so consider making extra so that you have some easily to hand the next time you want to make this dish.

Beef, oyster mushroom and Savoy cabbage stir-fry with noodles

SERVES 4—6

1.2 litres (2 pints) chicken stock (see page 326)
350g (12oz) fine Chinese egg noodles
2 tbsp sesame oil
3 tbsp tasteless oil such as groundnut or sunflower
3 tsp finely chopped root ginger
2 large cloves of garlic, peeled and finely chopped
1 large red onion, peeled and cut into 1cm (½in) slices
400g (14oz) chump steak, thinly sliced
1 large carrot, peeled and thinly sliced on the diagonal
150g (5oz) oyster mushrooms, torn in half
2 tbsp soy sauce
Bunch of spring onions, trimmed and sliced on the diagonal into 1cm (½in) pieces
175g (6oz) Savoy cabbage leaves, thick veins removed, thinly shredded
75g (3oz) salted peanuts, roughly chopped

1 Pour the chicken stock into a large saucepan, bring to the boil and cook the noodles for 4—5 minutes or following the instructions on the packet until just tender. Drain the noodles well and place back in the pan, off the heat and with the lid on to keep warm.

2 Place a wok or large frying pan on a very high heat and when the pan is very hot, add the sesame and peanut or sunflower oils. Add the ginger, garlic, red onion and beef and sauté for 2 minutes until the meat is well browned all over.

3 Add the carrot and sauté for a further minute before adding the mushrooms and soy sauce. Cook for 2—3 minutes until the mushrooms have softened. Next, add the spring onions, cabbage and two-thirds of the peanuts. Cook for 1—2 minutes, stirring continuously, until the cabbage has wilted.

4 Finally, tip in the cooked noodles and toss everything together until well combined. Serve in warm bowls with the remaining peanuts sprinkled over. Eat using chopsticks, if you wish.

Rachel's tip
If you can't get hold of oyster mushrooms, just use sliced button or flat mushrooms instead.

Thai peanut, vegetable and coconut noodles

SERVES 4–6 · VEGETARIAN (IF MADE USING SOY SAUCE)

I love this quick delicious noodle dish. It's warming
and filling, yet not too heavy.

1 x 400ml tin of
  coconut milk
1 tbsp sunflower or
  groundnut oil
2 tbsp red curry paste
3 tbsp crunchy peanut
  butter
300ml (½ pint) vegetable
  stock (see page 326)
3–4 tbsp fish sauce (nam
  pla) or soy sauce for
  a vegetarian version
1 tbsp light brown sugar
350g (12oz) medium
  rice noodles
150g (5oz) baby corn,
  cut into slices on
  the diagonal
150g (5oz) broccoli,
  cut into small florets
150g (5oz) mangetout, cut
  in half on the diagonal
50g (2oz) spring onion,
  trimmed, sliced into
  strips and dropped into
  a bowl of iced water to
  make them curly
100g (3½oz) peanuts,
  toasted (see tip on
  page 50) and roughly
  chopped
2 tbsp torn basil leaves
  or roughly chopped
  coriander

1 If the coconut milk has divided into two parts (watery and
thick), separate the two and set both aside. Place a wok or
a large frying pan on a high heat and, when the pan is hot,
add the sunflower or groundnut oil, then the thick part of
the coconut milk (if it has not separated into two, add all
the coconut milk at this stage). Stir until the coconut milk
starts to separate and thicken.

2 Add the curry paste and the peanut butter and mix together,
then add the stock, fish sauce or soy sauce, watery part of the
coconut milk, if remaining, and sugar, and bring to the boil.

3 Meanwhile, place the noodles in a bowl and cover with boiling
water. Leave for 5 minutes to soften before draining and
rinsing with water to prevent them sticking.

4 Add the corn and broccoli to the wok or frying pan and
cook, uncovered, for a minute then add the mangetout and
spring onion and cook for a further 1–2 minutes. Stir in
half the chopped peanuts and half the herbs and check the
seasoning, adding more fish sauce or soy sauce if you want
it to be saltier.

5 Add the drained noodles and toss to mix. Place in a large
warm serving bowl, or individual bowls, then scatter with the
remaining peanuts and herbs before serving.

Gnocchi with Gorgonzola cream, walnuts and rocket

SERVES 4—6 · VEGETARIAN

The word *gnoccho* literally means 'little lump' and gnocchi — soft little dumplings or noodles (see the photographs on pages 160—1) — have been eaten in Italy since Roman times. If you prefer, you can substitute the Gorgonzola with any other blue cheese or even with Cheddar.

750g (1lb 10oz) floury potatoes
1 egg yolk, beaten
125g (4½oz) plain flour, plus extra for dusting
Salt and freshly ground black pepper
50g (2oz) Parmesan cheese, finely grated
50g (2oz) chopped walnuts, toasted (see tip on page 50), to serve
Rocket leaves, to serve

For the Gorgonzola cream
250ml (9fl oz) single or regular cream
125g (4½oz) Gorgonzola cheese, crumbled into pieces
Freshly grated nutmeg

1 Following the instructions on page 116, cook, peel and mash the potatoes until really smooth (but without adding butter and milk).

2 Add the egg, flour and salt and pepper, stirring together to give a soft dough. Turn out onto a lightly floured work surface and knead gently. Divide the dough into four and roll each piece into a long sausage shape about 2cm (¾in) in diameter and cut each one into 3cm (1¼in) sections. Roll each section into a ball and press it with the tines of a fork to mark the surface. Place in a single layer on a floured baking sheet (the gnocchi can be made in advance up to this point and stored in the fridge for up to 24 hours or frozen).

3 To make the sauce, place the cream and Gorgonzola in a small saucepan on a low—medium heat. Once the cheese has melted, allow the sauce to simmer gently for about 5 minutes. Season to taste with pepper and nutmeg.

4 Bring a large saucepan of water with 1 teaspoon of salt to the boil and then reduce the heat to a simmer and cook the gnocchi in batches for 2—3 minutes. They will rise to the surface when they are cooked. Remove each batch of gnocchi from the water with a slotted spoon, drain well and place in a large warm bowl.

5 Preheat the grill to high. Pour the Gorgonzola sauce over the gnocchi and toss. Spoon into heatproof serving bowls and scatter with the Parmesan. Arrange the bowls on a baking sheet and grill the gnocchi for 2—3 minutes or until the sauce is bubbling and turning golden. Serve immediately, each bowl topped with a grind of pepper and some toasted walnuts and rocket leaves.

Variation
Gnocchi in sage and pine nut butter: For a lighter dish, toss the cooked gnocchi in sage and pine nut butter (see Butternut Squash Ravioli, pages 141—2).

Quick Swiss cheese fondue

SERVES 4 · VEGETARIAN

Children and adults alike love cheese fondue because it's a bit of
a novelty. Definitely something to enjoy as a family — especially when
a piece of bread disappears into the cheese sauce and everyone
hunts around for it with their skewer!

75ml (3fl oz) dry
white wine
2 large cloves of garlic,
peeled and crushed
2 tbsp chopped parsley
(optional)
300g (11oz) Gruyère
cheese, grated
400g (14oz) Emmental
cheese, grated
200g (7oz) crusty white
bread, cut into 2cm
(¾in) chunks

1 Place the wine, garlic and parsley (if using) in a fondue
pot or small saucepan, stir together and then add the grated
cheeses. The fondue can be prepared ahead up to this point.

2 Preheat the oven to 200°C (400°F), Gas mark 6.

3 Tip the chunks of bread onto a non-stick baking tray and
bake in the oven for 8–10 minutes, tossing halfway through,
until they are crisp and golden.

4 Place the fondue pot or saucepan on the hob at a low heat
and cook until the cheese melts and begins to bubble, stirring
occasionally. Serve the fondue immediately with the toasted
bread. To eat, place a piece of bread on a fork or fondue
skewer, dip in the fondue and enjoy!

Baked potatoes

SERVES 1 · VEGETARIAN

Baked potatoes are the ultimate economical and convenient meal,
and require no effort to pop in the oven. There are so many different
fillings and toppings that you can enjoy. Try one of the suggestions
below or use whatever you have to hand.

1 large baking potato
(such as Maris Piper,
King Edward or
Desirée), scrubbed
clean and dried
15g (½oz) butter, to serve

1 Preheat the oven to 230°C (450°F), Gas mark 8.

2 Pierce the potato all over with a fork, metal skewer or the
point of a sharp knife. If you stick the skewer right through the
potato once before cooking, it will help speed up the cooking
time slightly. Place on a baking sheet and bake for 45–50
minutes or until the skin is crispy and the potato feels soft
when you pinch it with your fingers or insert a knife.

3 Once baked, remove the potato from the oven and slice
the top with a cross. Open it out and serve with butter and/
or your choice of topping from below.

Toppings

Leek and cheese: Gently fry 75g (3oz) finely sliced leek in
25g (1oz) of butter for 12–15 minutes or until soft but not
browned. Remove from the heat and stir in 25g (1oz) crumbled
blue cheese. Season to taste with salt and pepper and spoon
onto the baked potato. Serve with a tomato relish, cranberry
sauce or redcurrant jelly (see page 328).

Steak and onion: Fry 1 finely sliced small onion in 25g
(1oz) butter on a very gentle heat for 15–20 minutes until
caramelised. Remove the onion with a slotted spoon and set
aside. Increase the heat and add 100g (3½oz) thinly sliced
beef steak and fry for 2 minutes or until browned and cooked
through to taste. Remove from the heat and return the onions
to the pan with 1 tablespoon of finely chopped parsley. Season
to taste with salt and pepper. Serve with a dollop of horseradish
sauce or a flavoured mayonnaise (see pages 328 and 330).

Mexican-style: Serve topped with guacamole and tomato
salsa (see pages 137–8), 1–2 tablespoons of soured cream
and 25g (1oz) grated Cheddar cheese. Make even more of
a meal of it by using up Chilli con carne (see page 202).

Wild mushroom and goat's cheese: Sauté 100g (3½oz) sliced or halved wild mushrooms and 1 peeled and crushed clove of garlic in 25g (1oz) butter on a high heat for 3–4 minutes until softened. Stir in 2 teaspoons of finely chopped parsley and season to taste with salt and pepper. Spoon onto the baked potato and scatter 2 tablespoons of grated Parmesan over the top. Grill to melt the cheese, if you wish.

Baked trout with herb butter

SERVES 4

This works equally well with mackerel or sea bass. Cooking it wrapped in foil or parchment paper – known as cooking *en papillote* (literally, 'in parchment') – allows the fish to steam, ensuring it is kept moist. Like any baked fish, it should be eaten immediately or it will quickly go mushy.

4 trout, gutted and
   heads removed
1 large handful of herbs,
   such as chervil,
   marjoram, tarragon
   or corriander
50g (2oz) butter, diced
Salt and freshly ground
   black pepper
Herb butter (see page 327)
   using the same herbs
   as above, to serve
Lemon wedges, to serve

1 Preheat the oven to 180°C (350°C), Gas mark 4.

2 Stuff the cavity of each trout with herbs and use a sharp knife to make an incision down the spine to split the skin (to make it easier to peel off once cooked). Tear off four generous sheets of parchment paper or foil (they need to be large enough to wrap up each fish), place a fish in the centre of each sheet, dot with the butter and season with salt and pepper. Fold up the paper or foil around each fish so that it forms a loose parcel, scrunching the open ends together to seal, and place on a baking sheet.

3 Bake in the oven for 20–25 minutes or until cooked through. Make the herb butter while the fish is cooking. Once the fish is cooked, carefully peel off the skin and either serve on or off the bone (you should be able peel the flesh off the bones easily once cooked) with the juices from the parcel, the herb butter and lemon wedges.

Sole à la meunière

SERVES 2

It's very important to try to eat fish as often as you can as it's excellent brain food! This is an especially delicious and simple way to eat it. You can substitute the sole with another flat fish, such as plaice.

2 tbsp plain flour
Salt and freshly ground
    black pepper
2 skinned fillets of sole
50g (2oz) butter, softened
1 tbsp finely chopped
    parsley
Good squeeze of
    lemon juice

1 Sift the flour onto a large plate and season with salt and pepper. Pat the fish fillets dry with kitchen paper and lay in the flour, dusting each side with a light coating. Spread half of the butter over the top of the fish.

2 Place a large frying pan on a medium heat and place the fish, buttered side down, into the pan and gently fry for 2–3 minutes until a nutty golden brown in colour. Carefully turn over and cook for a further 2–3 minutes on the other side.

3 Lift the fish out and place on warm serving plates. Add the remaining butter to the pan and, once melted and frothing, add the parsley and lemon juice and stir everything together. Cook for 10–15 seconds on a high heat and then spoon the sauce over the fish. Serve immediately with some boiled potatoes and a simple green salad.

Rachel's tip
You can leave the skin on the fish, if you wish, to help keep the fish intact while frying.

Fish pie

SERVES 4—6

This is the fish pie that Zac makes and it's a wonderful family supper. Use whatever fish is in season so you know it is ultra-fresh. Prepared fish can be frozen for up to six weeks.

1 large onion, peeled and chopped
800g (1¾lb) skinless fillets of fish, either one type or a mixture, such as salmon, cod, whiting, hake or haddock
150ml (5fl oz) white wine
Juice of ½ lemon
125g (4½oz) butter, diced
Salt and freshly ground black pepper
150g (5oz) mushrooms, sliced
225ml (8fl oz) double or regular cream
1 heaped tbsp Dijon mustard
4 tbsp finely chopped mixed herbs, such as chives, parsley, tarragon, thyme or dill
1kg (2lb 3oz) mashed potato (see page 116)

22cm (8½in) square ovenproof dish or 4—6 smaller individual dishes

1 Preheat the oven to 180°C (350°F), Gas mark 4.

2 Place the onion in the bottom of a large saucepan and lay the fish on top in an even layer (cutting to fit, if necessary). Pour in the wine, add the lemon juice (the liquid is unlikely to cover the fish, but that's fine), scatter with 100g (3½oz) of the butter and season with salt and pepper. Cover with a lid and simmer on a low heat for 15—20 minutes or until the fish is cooked.

3 In the meantime, melt the remaining butter in a small frying pan and sauté the mushrooms on a gentle heat for 5—6 minutes or until softened. Season well with salt and pepper.

4 Once cooked and using a slotted spoon, carefully transfer the fish from the saucepan (leaving the onions and cooking liquid in the pan) to the ovenproof dish or divide between individual dishes. While there is no need to flake the fish, you needn't worry if the fish breaks up as you move it. Add the cream to the onions and cooking liquid in the pan and continue to simmer, with the lid off, for 10—15 minutes or until the sauce is reduced and thick enough to coat the back of a spoon. Stir in the mustard, herbs and sautéed mushrooms and check the seasoning.

5 Pour the sauce over the fish in the dish (or dishes) and then spoon over the mashed potato, spreading with the back of a spoon or fork. Alternatively, pipe the mash over the fish with a piping bag and nozzle for a more professional-looking finish. The fish pie can be prepared to this stage, left to cool and then placed in the fridge overnight until ready to bake, if wished.

6 Bake in the oven for about 30 minutes or until bubbling and golden on top. If cooking from chilled then bake for about 40 minutes instead. Serve immediately.

Home freezing

Freezing food is a great way for home cooks to be more economical in the kitchen, saving both time and money. Generations before us were a lot more frugal and there was never any waste. Today, almost one-third of the food we buy gets thrown out, yet with a little foresight much of this waste can be avoided simply by making better use of our freezers. Foods such as bread, muffins and cookies go stale quite quickly, and you can avoid that by popping some in the freezer for another time. Freezing food is also an excellent way of using up leftovers and I regularly look through my fridge for things I can cook and then freeze. If there are some leftover vegetables, I'll make them into a soup and then pop it into the freezer. It's also a great time saver. Whenever I make family dishes — such as a lasagne or Shepherd's pie (see pages 183 and 193) — I make more than is needed for one meal and put the remainder in the freezer. It takes only a bit more preparation to increase the quantities in a recipe, but then you save so much time another day by having a ready-cooked meal to hand.

First in, first out

Sometimes food goes into the freezer and never comes out. It's worth every couple of months looking in the freezer and then using up things or rotating items by placing the most recent ones at the back or at the bottom. It's also helpful to allocate different drawers or sections in your freezer for different foods — raw meat, poultry and fish in one, for instance, or soups, stocks and sauces in another. However you organise it, the rule with freezing food is first in, first out. Also, make sure to freeze things when they are as fresh as possible. Fish freezes beautifully, whether raw or cooked in a fish pie. But don't forget: if the fish wasn't fresh when it went in, it's not going to taste good when it comes out. Freezing food straight away preserves the freshness. Don't let food sit around in the fridge for 2–3 days and then put it in the freezer.

What can be frozen and for how long

While almost any food can be frozen safely, some foods take better to freezing than others. Emulsified sauces such as mayonnaise or hollandaise don't freeze well as the sauces don't retain their consistency during the freezing process. Whole eggs and tinned food can't be frozen. But most other foodstuffs freeze perfectly: tomato-based sauces, stews, soups, casseroles, pies, lasagne, raw meat and fish, bread and baked goods. I always have some fruit in the freezer, such as berries and rhubarb for smoothies, crumbles and pies. If you have a glut of over-ripe bananas, freeze them for making banana bread or muffins another time.

Freezing food stops the growth of microbes such as bacteria, yeast and mould that cause spoiling. So frozen food remains safe to eat pretty much indefinitely, as long as it stays frozen. However, the longer food remains frozen, the more the colour, flavour and texture quality will be affected. So while food left in the freezer for a long time may be safe to eat, you may not be happy with the quality and consistency of it once it's defrosted. For this reason, most cooked foods should be eaten within 2–3 months. Raw meat, poultry and fish should be used up within 4–6 months. Bear in mind, too, that uncooked food that has been defrosted mustn't be refrozen, or not without cooking it first, as freezing and refreezing can allow bacteria to grow.

Containers and labelling

Always having an indelible black pen and some labels to hand will make your life easier. You may think you'll remember what's in that little white tub in the freezer, but a month later you won't and you'll end up throwing it out. I always hang on to different-sized airtight containers: water bottles, cleaned-out milk containers, ice-cube trays and yoghurt tubs with lids are all perfect for freezing different quantities of foods. I find that when I freeze, say, soup in small containers, then I can reheat it from frozen in 10–15 minutes and lunch is ready. You'll also want some clear plastic bags. Foil, however, should be avoided once it's frozen as it sticks to food and breaks.

'Tray freezing' certain items — placing them in the freezer on a baking sheet or foil tray — is quite useful for maintaining the shape of foodstuffs such as fish cakes, strawberries or chicken and stops them sticking together. Once they are frozen solid, you can take them off the tray and put them into a container.

For homemade stock (see page 326), I label different-sized containers with a 'C' for chicken, 'B' for beef , 'V' for vegetable or 'F' for fish. You can also make your own stock cubes by boiling stock, uncovered, and reducing it until it is quite concentrated, then freezing it in ice-cube trays. This works quite well with chicken and beef stock, though not fish stock as it gets bitter in flavour if over-boiled. Freezing foods can intensify the salt content due to some moisture loss, so do bear this in mind if you are cooking specifically for the freezer.

Forward planning

Many foods can be used straight from the freezer: peas, nuts, breadcrumbs and berries or chopped pieces of fruit can be taken out and used immediately for cooking. But home-cooked frozen meals and raw meats and fish are best thawed in the fridge overnight. This may take a bit of forward planning, but once you get the hang of using the freezer properly, you won't be able to do without it!

Steamed mussels with cream and herbs

SERVES 4

A great big bowl of steaming mussels in the centre of the table is a tempting treat for everyone. The novelty of removing each mussel from its shell can be very enticing for young and old alike. In this recipe you can use a mixture of your favourite fresh herbs or whatever you have to hand. Tarragon, chervil, dill and marjoram would all work perfectly, in addition to the ones suggested below. There is no need to season this dish as the juices from the mussels will probably be salty enough.

2.5kg (5½lb) mussels
150ml (5fl oz) double
   or regular cream
1 tbsp chopped parsley
1 tbsp chopped chives
2 tsp chopped thyme leaves
2 tsp chopped fennel (the
   herb, not the bulb)

1 Scrub the mussels very well, discarding any that are open and don't close when tapped against a hard surface. Remove the beard – the little fibrous tuft – from each mussel.

2 Pour the cream into a large saucepan and bring slowly to the boil. Stir in the herbs and add the mussels. Reduce the heat to a simmer, cover with a lid and continue to cook on a medium heat for about 5–8 minutes or until all the mussels are completely open. (Discard any that remain closed.)

3 Scoop the mussels out into one large or four individual serving bowls and ladle the creamy juices over. Place another bowl on the table for the empty shells, some finger bowls and lots of napkins. Serve with plenty of crusty bread.

Fried squid with tomato aioli

SERVES 4

Aioli is one of the best accompaniments for fried squid and this one is flavoured with tomato as well as lots of garlic. It can be made in advance and kept in the fridge for 3–4 days. Cook the squid very quickly to prevent it from becoming rubbery. If you wish to include the tentacles, add them to the total weight and coat and fry in the same way.

Sunflower oil, for
    deep-frying
100ml (3½fl oz) milk
110g (4oz) plain flour
Salt and freshly ground
    black pepper
400g (14oz) small–
    medium cleaned/
    prepared squid, cut into
    rings 1cm (½in) wide
Lemon wedges, to serve

For the tomato aioli
150g (5oz) tinned
    chopped tomatoes
3 cloves of garlic, peeled
    and crushed
Salt and freshly ground
    black pepper
300ml (½ pint)
    mayonnaise
    (see page 330)
1½ tbsp finely chopped
    basil or coriander

1 First, make the aioli. Tip the tomatoes and garlic into a saucepan and simmer on a medium heat for 15–20 minutes or until reduced by almost half to a thick paste. Season with salt and pepper, remove from the heat and leave to cool completely. Once cool, stir the tomato paste into the mayonnaise and add the basil or coriander. Check the seasoning and adjust if necessary. Spoon into a serving bowl and place in the fridge until needed.

2 Next, heat the oil in a deep-fat fryer to 180°C (350°F). Alternatively, pour the oil into a large saucepan to a depth of 2cm (¾in) and bring to the same temperature on the hob (checking with a sugar thermometer, or see tip on page 255).

3 Pour the milk into a bowl and place the flour on a plate, seasoning both with salt and pepper. Working in batches, dip the squid first in the milk and then in the flour, to coat. Deep-fry for 1–2 minutes until crisp and golden, turning the squid halfway through cooking. Drain well on kitchen paper and keep warm in a low oven while cooking the remaining squid in the same way.

4 Serve immediately with the lemon wedges for squeezing over the squid and the aioli for dipping.

Fish and chips with tartare sauce

SERVES 4

I like a thin and crisp batter on my fish. You can use a fillet of any
flat fish — my favourites are plaice and lemon sole. Although a little bit
more expensive, try brill, black sole or John Dory for a special occasion.
Either serve with chunky chips or with the frites on page 200–1.
It's also great with Pea Purée (see page 122).

250g (9oz) plain flour
500ml (18fl oz) milk
　or water
Salt and freshly ground
　black pepper
Sunflower oil, for deep-
　frying
900g (2lb) potatoes
4 x 150g (5oz) fillets of flat
　fish, such as plaice or
　lemon sole, or 8 fillets
　if half this size

To serve
Sea salt
Vinegar of your choice
Tartare sauce (see page 328)

1 Sift the flour into a large bowl and gradually whisk in the
milk or water to give a smooth, thin batter. Season with salt
and pepper. (The batter can be made up to 8 hours in advance
and kept in the fridge until needed.)

2 Heat the oil in a deep-fat fryer to 140°C (275°F). Alternatively,
pour the oil into a large saucepan to a depth of 2cm (¾in) and
bring to the same temperature on the hob (checking with a sugar
thermometer, or see tip on page 255).

3 To make the chips, peel the potatoes (or leave unpeeled) and
cut into square-sided chips each about 2cm (¾in) thick. Wash
and dry really well and then place in the fryer or saucepan, a few
handfuls at a time, and cook for 8–10 minutes or until soft but
not browned. Remove, drain well and set aside. The chips can
be cooled and placed in the fridge at this point, for up to
24 hours, until needed.

4 Increase the temperature of the oil in the deep-fat fryer or
saucepan to 180°C (350°F) (or see tip on page 255) and remove
the basket from the fryer (I find the fish tends to stick to it). Dip
a fillet of fish in the batter to coat evenly and carefully lower into
the hot oil to deep-fry for 3–4 minutes until crisp, golden and
cooked through, turning halfway through cooking. Drain well
on kitchen paper and deep-fry the remaining pieces of fish in
the same way. Keep the cooked fish warm (uncovered, so the
batter doesn't become soggy) in a preheated low oven.

5 To finish the chips, deep-fry them for 6–8 minutes, again working
in batches, until crisp and golden. Drain again and season lightly
with salt and pepper. Keep the cooked chips warm in the oven
with the fish, but don't cover them or they will go soggy.

6 Place the crisp battered fish on warm plates and sprinkle with
sea salt and pepper. Serve with the golden chunky chips, vinegar
and a small bowl of tartare sauce for sharing.

Family chicken burgers with roast tomato and lime mayonnaise

MAKES 8

These burgers are delicious on their own, but it is definitely worth making the roast tomato and lime mayonnaise to go with them. If you don't have a mincing machine, ask your butcher to mince the chicken and pork for you.

For the white sauce
100ml (3½fl oz) milk
A couple of slices of carrot
A couple of slices of onion
1 sprig of thyme
1 sprig of parsley
2 peppercorns
Roux (see page 327), made with 1 tbsp butter and 1 tbsp plain flour
Salt and freshly ground black pepper

For the burgers
600g (1lb 5oz) minced chicken
400g (14oz) minced pork belly or shoulder
100g (3½oz) fresh breadcrumbs
1 egg, beaten
1 tsp finely grated nutmeg
2 tbsp chopped tarragon
Salt and freshly ground black pepper
2 tbsp vegetable or olive oil

To serve
8 burger buns, halved and toasted
Sliced tomatoes and shredded lettuce
Roast Tomato and Lime Mayonnaise (see page 330) and/or Rachel's Ketchup (see page 329)

1 To make the white sauce, follow the instructions on page 327 and allow to cool. Once cooled, transfer the sauce into a large bowl and mix in the minced chicken and pork, breadcrumbs, egg, nutmeg, tarragon and some salt and pepper. (To check the seasoning at this point, see tip on page 70.) Shape the mixture into eight even-sized burgers. These can be made to this stage in advance and kept in the fridge for up to 24 hours or in the freezer until ready to use.

2 To cook the burgers, pour the oil into a large frying pan on a medium heat and fry the burgers (in batches if necessary) for 8–10 minutes on each side or until well browned and cooked through. Alternatively, fry the burgers in an ovenproof pan for 3–4 minutes on each side until deep golden, then pop in the oven, preheated to 200°C (400°F), Gas mark 6, for 10 minutes or until cooked.

3 Place each burger in a toasted bun and add some tomato slices and shredded lettuce. Serve with the tomato and lime mayonnaise and/or the ketchup.

Rachel's tip
If you'd prefer not to make your own mayonnaise, just add the roast tomatoes, lime juice and basil (see the variation on page 330) to some shop-bought mayonnaise.

Egg-fried rice

This is one of the best ways to use up cooked rice, not to mention leftover chicken or seafood. For a vegetarian version, simply omit the chicken, pork or seafood. Either way, throw in some sliced and sautéed mushrooms too if you wish, adding them at the end of cooking. When cooking this with shrimps or prawns, I sometimes use oyster sauce instead of the soy sauce. Feel free to add in grated root ginger too, before the rice goes in.

2 eggs
Salt and freshly ground
    black pepper
4 tbsp tasteless oil, such as
    sunflower or rapeseed
1 large clove of garlic,
    peeled and crushed
500g (1lb 2oz) cold,
    cooked basmati or long-
    grain rice (see tips below
    right)
100g (3½oz) shelled fresh
    or frozen (and
    defrosted) peas
150g (5oz) cooked shrimps
    or small prawns, or
    sliced cooked chicken
    or pork
3 spring onions, trimmed
    and sliced
1—2 tbsp soy sauce

1 Break the eggs into a bowl, season with a good pinch of salt and pepper and gently mix with a fork. Place half the oil into a wok or large frying pan on a low—medium heat and pour the eggs in. Stirring all the time, cook the eggs for 1—2 minutes until they are lightly scrambled but not dry. Transfer them to a plate, cover and keep warm. Wipe the wok or pan with a piece of kitchen paper to remove any traces of egg.

2 Place the wok or frying pan back on the heat, allow it to heat up and then add the remaining oil. Fry the garlic for 30 seconds on a high heat. Tip in the cooked rice and stir-fry for 2—3 minutes. (It's best to use a metal spoon for this as it will be less likely to mash the rice than a wooden one.) Add the peas and the shrimps/small prawns or chicken/pork and stir-fry for a further 3—4 minutes.

3 Finally, stir in the spring onions and soy sauce and carefully mix in the cooked egg. Warm through for 1 minute, then check the seasoning, adding more soy sauce if necessary, and serve immediately.

Rachel's tips
* Leftover rice should be cooled down as quickly as possible to prevent bacteria spores from forming. Once cool, cover and place in the fridge immediately, and use within two days.
* If you are starting with uncooked rice, you will need about 200g (7oz) dry rice to give the amount of cooked rice required. Boil in a large saucepan of salted water for 10—12 minutes or follow the instructions on the packet.

Chicken casserole with cheesy herb dumplings

SERVES 6—8

You can serve this casserole without the dumpling topping and cook it on its own or topped with peeled whole potatoes.

1 chicken (1.8kg/4lb)
Salt and freshly ground
    black pepper
2 tbsp olive oil
350g (12oz) unsliced
    rindless streaky bacon,
    cut into 1—2cm
    (½—¾in) chunks
1 large onion, peeled and
    roughly chopped
2 large carrots, peeled
    and cut into 2cm (¾in)
    slices on the diagonal
700ml (1¼ pints) chicken
    or vegetable stock
    (see page 326)
Few sprigs of thyme

For the cheesy herb
dumplings
350g (12oz) plain flour,
    plus extra for dusting
¾ tsp bicarbonate of soda
1 tsp salt
300ml (½ pint)
    buttermilk or soured
    milk (see tip on
    page 24)
2 tbsp finely chopped
    mixed herbs, such
    as parsley, thyme,
    rosemary, tarragon
    or chives
25g (1oz) Cheddar
    cheese, finely grated

5cm (2in) scone cutter (optional)

1 Preheat the oven to 180°C (350°F), Gas mark 4. Remove the breasts from the chicken and cut them in half. Remove the leg portions and divide them into thighs and drumsticks. This will give eight chicken pieces in total. Season them well with salt and pepper.

2 Pour the olive oil into a large casserole dish on a high heat, add the bacon and fry quickly for 1—2 minutes or until crisp. Remove with a slotted spoon and drain on kitchen paper. Add the chicken in batches and sear on each side until golden, then remove. Add the onion and carrots and fry for 2—3 minutes or until golden.

3 Return the bacon and chicken to the dish, pour on the stock, add the thyme and season with salt and pepper. Bring slowly to the boil, cover with a tight-fitting lid and bake in the oven for 20 minutes.

4 In the meantime, prepare the dumplings. Sift the flour, bicarbonate of soda and salt into a large bowl, add the herbs, mix, then make a well in the centre. Pour in most of the buttermilk or soured milk (leaving about 50ml/2fl oz in the measuring jug). Using one hand with your fingers outstretched like a claw, bring the flour and liquid together, adding a little more buttermilk if necessary. Don't knead the mixture or it will become too heavy. The dough should be soft but not too wet and sticky.

5 Tip the dough onto a floured work surface and bring together, forming it into a round. Using a rolling pin, roll the dough out to about 2cm (¾in) thick. With the scone cutter stamp out 10—12 dumplings, or divide the dough into 10—12 pieces and roll each one between your hands into a small ball.

6 Remove the casserole dish from the oven and turn the heat up to 230°C (450°F), Gas mark 8. Arrange the dumplings on top, leaving a slight gap between them to allow for spreading. Scatter with the cheese. Return to the oven, uncovered, for 10 minutes, then reduce the heat to 200°C (400°F), Gas mark 6, and cook for a further 20 minutes until the dumplings are crisp and golden and the chicken is cooked through.

Chicken and coconut Indian curry

This is a really easy curry, which is quick to prepare. It is a great dish for teenagers to try out their cooking skills. Substitute the chicken with pork, beef or lamb. Use fresh or frozen peas instead of the green beans, if you wish.

1 tbsp vegetable or sunflower oil

1 large onion, peeled and roughly chopped

2 cloves of garlic, peeled and crushed

2.5cm (1in) piece of root ginger, peeled and finely grated

2 large green chillies, deseeded (optional) and finely chopped

15g (½oz) coriander, leaves picked and stalks roughly chopped

1 tbsp garam masala

1 tbsp curry powder (mild, medium or hot, to taste)

1 x 400g tin of coconut milk

150ml (5fl oz) chicken stock (see page 326)

450g (1lb) skinless, boneless chicken thighs, cut into 2.5cm (1in) cubes

Salt and freshly ground black pepper

75g (3oz) green beans, trimmed and halved

Lime wedges, to serve

1 Pour the oil into a large saucepan, add the onion and garlic and fry on a gentle heat for 6–8 minutes until soft but not browned. Add the ginger, chillies, coriander stalks, garam masala and curry powder and fry for a further 1–2 minutes. Pour in the coconut milk and stock and bring slowly to the boil. Add the chicken and season with a little salt and pepper.

2 Reduce the heat and simmer, covered with a lid, for 30 minutes. Remove the lid and simmer for a further 15 minutes, adding the green beans for the last 5 minutes of cooking, by which time the chicken should be completely cooked and the sauce thickened.

3 Remove from the heat and stir in the coriander leaves. Serve at once with the lime wedges and some boiled rice and naan breads.

Variation

Prawn and coconut curry: Substitute the chicken with raw, peeled prawns instead (and use fish stock instead of chicken stock, if you wish). Add these to the sauce at the same time as the beans for the last 5 minutes of cooking.

Mum's chicken and ham lasagne

SERVES 4–6

I love my Mum's lasagne. It really reminds me of when I was little.
This is a great way of using up any leftover cooked chicken and ham.
You can also make this just with chicken.

75g (3oz) butter
1 onion, peeled and
  finely chopped
1 clove of garlic, peeled
  and crushed
50g (2oz) plain flour
700ml (1¼ pints) milk
300ml (½ pint) chicken
  stock (see page 326),
  heated
¼ tsp freshly grated
  nutmeg
Salt and freshly ground
  black pepper
400g (14oz) cooked
  chicken, diced
200g (7oz) cooked ham,
  cut into 1–2cm
  (½–¾in) cubes
8 sheets of dried lasagne
110g (4oz) Cheddar
  cheese, grated

*20 x 30cm (8 x 12in) ovenproof
dish with 6cm (2½in) sides*

1 Preheat the oven to 180°C (350°F), Gas mark 4.

2 Melt a third of the butter in a large saucepan on a low heat.
Add the onion and gently fry for 3 minutes, then add the garlic
and sauté for a further 2 minutes. Remove the onion and
garlic from the pan with a slotted spoon and set aside.

3 Melt the remaining butter in the saucepan, still on a low heat.
Add the flour and beat with the melted butter to make a smooth
paste. Remove from the heat and gradually add the milk, bit by
bit and whisking all the time, until it is fully incorporated and
you have a smooth sauce.

4 Return the pan to the heat and simmer for 3–4 minutes,
stirring constantly, until the sauce thickens enough to coat the
back of the spoon. Whisk in the hot chicken stock and return
the onion and garlic to the pan. Add the nutmeg, season to
taste with salt and pepper, stir everything together and remove
from the heat.

5 Toss the diced chicken and ham together and sprinkle half
of it into the ovenproof dish. Pour over a third of the sauce
and arrange four lasagne sheets on top to cover. Scatter the
remaining meat mixture over, pour over another third of sauce
and top with the remaining lasagne sheets. Pour over the
remaining sauce, spreading evenly to cover the lasagne sheets,
and then scatter with the cheese to finish.

6 Place the dish on a baking sheet and bake for 55 minutes or
until it is enticingly golden and bubbly on top. Leave to stand
for a few minutes before serving.

Roast chicken legs with new potatoes and summer herb dressing

SERVES 6

Equally good for lunch or supper, this is a lovely light and summery dish with delicious fresh flavours from the herbs and lemon.

6 chicken legs (each with a thigh and drumstick)
1kg (2lb 3oz) small new potatoes
Cloves from 1 head of garlic, left unpeeled
Zest and juice of 1 lemon
2 tbsp olive oil
Salt and freshly ground black pepper

For the summer herb dressing
25g (1oz) bunch of mixed herbs, such as tarragon, mint, parsley, chives or basil, leaves picked
1 slice of white bread, crusts removed
2 tbsp red wine vinegar
1 tsp caster sugar
8 tbsp extra-virgin olive oil

1 Preheat the oven to 190°C (375°F), Gas mark 5.

2 Arrange the chicken legs in a large roasting tin or ovenproof dish and nestle the potatoes and garlic cloves in between the pieces of chicken. Whisk together the lemon zest and juice with the olive oil and plenty of salt and pepper and pour over the chicken and potatoes. Toss everything together to coat evenly and roast in the oven for 40–50 minutes or until the chicken is cooked and the potatoes are tender, basting occasionally with the juices.

3 Meanwhile, make the dressing. Put the herbs and bread in a food processor and blend until finely chopped. Alternatively, finely chop the herbs, grate the bread into crumbs and mix together before stirring in the remaining ingredients. Add the remaining ingredients, season with salt and pepper and blend again to give a thick dressing.

4 Place a roasted chicken leg on each plate, along with some potatoes and a few softened garlic cloves. Drizzle over some of the juices from the roasting tin, spoon over some of the dressing and serve with a crisp green salad.

Crumbed bacon chops with sweet whiskey sauce

SERVES 4—6

This is a dish often made at Ballymaloe. I adore the crispy coating around the bacon chops and the way the sweetness of the sauce combines perfectly with the saltiness of the bacon. If you're feeding children, leave the whiskey out of the sauce as the alcohol isn't burnt off. Substitute it with orange or pineapple juice.

900g (2lb) loin of bacon (boneless and without the streaky end)
110g (4oz) plain flour
1 egg
110g (4oz) fresh white breadcrumbs
Salt and freshly ground black pepper
25g (1oz) butter
1 tbsp olive oil

For the whiskey sauce
225g (8oz) caster sugar
50ml (2fl oz) hot water
3—4 tbsp Irish whiskey

1 Follow the instructions on page 190 for cooking the bacon loin, boiling it for about 40 minutes or until fully cooked (a skewer stuck into the centre of the meat should come out easily).

2 Meanwhile, prepare the sauce. Put the sugar in a saucepan with 75ml (3fl oz) cold water and bring slowly to the boil on a gentle heat, stirring until the sugar dissolves. Boil without stirring for about 10 minutes until it turns a chestnut-brown colour, swirling the pan to caramelise evenly. Remove from the heat and immediately add the hot water. Stir to give a smooth sauce and then add the whiskey. Keep warm in the pan.

3 Once the loin of bacon is cooked, lift out of the water, drain well and allow to cool a little. Sift the flour into a wide shallow bowl, beat the egg in a small bowl, place the breadcrumbs in a third dish and season all three with salt and pepper. Remove the bacon rind, trimming away excess fat (so that it is about half its original thickness), and slice into chops 1—2 cm (½—¾in) thick. Dip each chop first in the flour, then in the egg and finally the breadcrumbs to coat.

4 Add the butter and oil to a large frying pan on a medium heat and, when the butter starts to froth, fry the chops for 3—4 minutes on each side or until crisp and golden. Serve the crumbed bacon chops with the sweet whiskey sauce and some vegetables (see pages 120—8) and boiled new or mashed potatoes (see page 116).

Kinoith pork casserole

SERVES 6–8

My father-in-law created this recipe and we eat it regularly. The ginger flavour is quite subtle, so feel free to increase the amount if you wish. If you use loin chops, there is probably no need to remove any fat after cooking.

1.5kg (3lb 5oz) shoulder of pork chops, cut about 1.5cm (⅝in) thick and on the bone
3 tbsp olive oil
Salt and freshly ground black pepper
12 baby onions, peeled (see tip below right), or 3–4 standard onions, peeled and cut into quarters lengthways through the root
3 carrots, peeled and thickly sliced, or 12 baby carrots, scrubbed and left whole
8cm (3in) piece of root ginger, peeled and finely grated
1 litre (1¾ pints) chicken stock (see page 326)
1.3kg (3lb) potatoes (about 12 small), peeled and halved if large
3 tbsp chopped coriander

1 Preheat the oven to 170°C (325°F), Gas mark 3.

2 Cut the pork chops in half, without removing the bones as they will greatly add to the flavour. Pour the olive oil into a casserole dish or large ovenproof pan with a tight-fitting lid and set on a high heat. When the oil is really hot, add the meat in batches, searing the chops for about 1 minute on each side or until golden brown, seasoning with salt and pepper as it cooks. Remove from the pan and set aside.

3 Sauté the onions and carrots in the hot oil for 3–4 minutes and season with salt and pepper. Return the chops to the casserole or pan, add the ginger, pour in the stock and bring to the boil. Place the potatoes on top, cover with a lid and cook in the oven for 1½–1¾ hours or until the meat is very tender and the sauce has thickened slightly.

4 Once cooked, strain the stew through a colander over a large bowl to catch the cooking liquid. Return the meat and vegetables to the casserole dish or pan with the lid on to keep warm and leave the liquid to stand for a minute or so to allow the fat to float to the top (adding some ice cubes will help speed up the cooling process). Remove the fat with a spoon and return the liquid to the casserole. Warm through on a gentle heat, stir in the coriander and serve.

Rachel's tips

* You can substitute the olive oil with 3 tablespoons of fat rendered from pork fat. Heat any pork fat trimmings from the meat in a small saucepan until melted to an oil.
* If the potatoes are quite small, add them to the dish 20–30 minutes after the stew starts cooking to prevent them breaking up too much.
* To quickly peel the baby onions, place them in a bowl, cover with boiling water and allow to stand for a few minutes before draining. The skins should then peel off very easily.

Homemade sausages

These sausages are completely unlike any that you might buy. They are a lot coarser and don't have a casing, which makes them more straightforward to prepare. Make them to eat straight away or place in the fridge and cook within 24 hours. You can also freeze them. It is important to use a fatty pork mince for this recipe. If it is too lean, the sausages will be too dry. If necessary, ask your butcher to mince the pork for you. You can also try blending it with a little beef mince.

450g (1lb) fatty minced pork
50g (2oz) fresh white breadcrumbs
1 egg, beaten
Salt and freshly ground black pepper
2 tbsp olive oil

1 Mix the minced pork in a large bowl with the breadcrumbs and beaten egg. Season with salt and pepper, then add your choice of flavouring from below, stirring to mix all the ingredients.

2 Using dampened hands, shape the mixture into 12 evenly sized sausages. These can be placed in the fridge or frozen until ready to cook (defrosting before use).

3 To cook the sausages, pour the olive oil into a large frying pan on a low heat, add the sausages and gently fry for 12–15 minutes, turning regularly, until evenly golden and cooked through.

4 Serve with Celeriac and Sweet Potato Mash, Pea Purée or Cauliflower Cheese (see pages 117, 122 and 128) and with apple sauce (see pages 100–2) or mustard.

Variations
Stir one of the following flavourings into the sausage mixture:
Tarragon, wholegrain mustard and honey: 1 tablespoon of chopped tarragon, 2 teaspoons of wholegrain mustard and 1 teaspoon of honey.
Sage and onion: 1 crushed clove of garlic, 1 very finely chopped onion and 4 finely chopped sage leaves.
Grated apple and Dijon mustard: 1 eating apple (e.g. Granny Smith, Gala or Braeburn), peeled, cored, grated and squeezed dry, 2 teaspoons of Dijon mustard and 1 teaspoon of finely chopped parsley.
Fennel seeds and thyme: 1 crushed clove of garlic, 1 teaspoon of fennel seeds, lighted toasted (see tip on page 50) and crushed, and 1 teaspoon of thyme leaves.
Cumin and coriander: 1 teaspoon each of ground cumin and ground coriander, 2 trimmed and very finely chopped spring onions and 2 teaspoons of finely chopped coriander.

Turkey and ham potato pie

SERVES 6—8

This makes a good sustaining family meal, not only at Christmas
to use up all the leftover turkey and ham, but at any time of year.
You could easily use leftover chicken in place of turkey.

50g (2oz) butter
1 onion, peeled and
  finely chopped
450g (1lb) mushrooms,
  sliced
350ml (12fl oz) double
  or regular cream
100ml (3½fl oz) turkey
  or chicken stock
  (see page 326)
675g (1½lb) mixture of
  leftover cooked turkey
  and ham, cut into 2cm
  (¾in) chunks
1 tbsp chopped tarragon
  or marjoram
Salt and freshly ground
  black pepper
1kg (2lb 3oz) mashed
  potato (see page 116)

3 litre (5 pint) shallow gratin dish

1 Preheat the oven to 180°C (350°F), Gas mark 4.

2 To prepare the filling, melt half the butter in a large saucepan
on a low heat, add the onion and fry gently for 8—10 minutes
or until completely soft but not browned. Remove from the
pan and set aside, then increase the heat and add the remaining
butter to the pan. Tip the mushrooms into the pan and sauté
them for 4—5 minutes or until they are soft and golden brown
(you may need to do this in two batches).

3 Return the onion to the pan and pour in the cream and stock.
Bring to the boil, then reduce the heat and simmer for 3—4
minutes or until the sauce has thickened a little. Add the turkey,
ham and tarragon or marjoram and season to taste with salt
and pepper. Pour into the gratin dish, set on a baking sheet
and spread evenly. (If you are popping the sauce in the freezer
to use another time, allow it to cool before adding the meat.)
Top with the mashed potato, spooning it on in dollops and
spreading with a fork.

4 Bake in the oven for 25—30 minutes or until golden brown on
top and bubbling hot. Serve with buttered carrots and/or peas.

Rachel's tip
Rather than making one large pie, divide the ingredients
between 6—8 individual pie dishes. This is also particularly
handy if you choose to freeze them (fully made with the mashed
potato on top) as you can take them out as you need them.

Bacon and cabbage with parsley sauce

SERVES 6

This is a traditional Irish dish in which the cabbage is boiled in the water used for cooking the bacon. Many people recall it with affection, while others chiefly remember it for the overcooked cabbage. Providing the cabbage is cooked for only 3–5 minutes, you won't be disappointed.

900g (2lb) loin or
    collar of bacon
1 small Savoy cabbage,
    outer leaves removed
25g (1oz) butter
Salt and freshly ground
    black pepper

For the parsley sauce
300ml (½ pint) white
    sauce (see page 327)
1 tsp Dijon mustard
25g (1oz) finely
    chopped parsley
Salt and freshly ground
    black pepper

1 Place the piece of bacon in a large saucepan, cover with water and bring slowly to the boil. Drain, refill the pan with fresh water and repeat. This is to get rid of the salt (which appears as white froth on top of the water), so may need to be done again, depending how salty the bacon is. Taste the water to check for saltiness and keep checking and boiling again in fresh water until you are happy with the flavour.

2 Cover with fresh hot water and bring to the boil for the final time. Reduce the heat, cover with a lid and simmer for about 40 minutes (allowing 45 minutes per kg/20 minutes per lb), occasionally skimming any sediment that rises to the surface. Once the bacon is cooked (a skewer inserted in the middle should come out easily), remove from the pan (reserving the cooking liquid) and leave to rest, covered with foil, a clean tea towel or upturned bowl.

3 In the meantime, prepare the parsley sauce. Make the white sauce following the instructions on page 327 and then stir in the mustard and parsley. Check the seasoning and adjust if necessary. Set aside, cover and keep warm in the pan.

4 Cut the cabbage into quarters, remove the core pieces and finely shred across the grain. Bring the cooking liquid for the bacon to a fast boil. Cook the cabbage in the water for about 3 minutes or until just tender (it's easy to overcook). Drain well, squeezing out any excess water, and return to the saucepan. Add the butter to the cabbage, tossing to melt, and season to taste with salt and pepper .

5 Remove the rind from the bacon and slice into thick pieces. Serve with the buttered cabbage and parsley sauce. This dish is also delicious served with mashed potato (see page 116), or boiled or baked potatoes, and some hot mustard.

Meatloaf with tomato and basil sauce

SERVES 4—6

My sister makes this mealoaf, which is great served hot for a weekday
supper or cold for picnics or in lunchboxes, with relish and mustard.
Leftover slices of meatloaf can be easily frozen. The sauce is also
excellent served with pasta (see page 130).

900g (2lb) minced beef
2 eggs, beaten
75g (3oz) fresh white
  breadcrumbs
3 tbsp finely chopped
  parsley
50g (2oz) Parmesan
  cheese, finely grated
Salt and freshly ground
  black pepper

**For the tomato
and basil sauce**
2 tbsp olive oil
1 onion, peeled and
  finely chopped.
2 cloves of garlic,
  peeled and crushed
  or finely grated
1 x 400g tin of whole
  tomatoes
1 tsp caster or granulated
  sugar
2 tbsp chopped basil

1 Preheat the oven to 180°C (350°F), Gas mark 4.

2 To make the meatloaf, mix together the minced beef, eggs,
breadcrumbs, parsley and Parmesan in a large bowl and season
with salt and pepper. (To check the seasoning, see tip on
page 70.)

3 Tip the mixture out onto a clean work surface and use your
hands to gather it together into a slightly flattened loaf shape
(about 15cm x 23cm/6in x 9in). Grease a roasting tin slightly
larger than this and carefully transfer the meat loaf onto it,
adjusting the shape of the loaf to fit, if necessary. Bake in the
oven for 1½ hours, covering with foil for the last 30 minutes,
until set and firm. Remove from the oven and allow to rest
for 10 minutes before serving.

4 Meanwhile, make the sauce. Pour olive oil into a saucepan on
a gentle heat, add the onion and cook for 4—5 minutes without
browning. Add the garlic, tomatoes, sugar and some salt and
pepper and mix together using a wooden spoon to gently break
up the tomatoes. Cook, partially covered with a lid, for 10—12
minutes or until reduced a little. Remove from the heat and add
the basil. Check the seasoning, adjusting if necessary, and then
leave to cool. Blend the sauce to a smooth purée in a blender
or using a hand-held blender.

5 Slice the meatloaf and serve with the sauce on the side. This
is delicious served with the Cheese and Garlic Potato Gratin
(see page 121) and green beans.

Shepherd's pie

I couldn't write a book on home cooking without including shepherd's pie. This classic was originally made using leftover roast lamb, which was then minced. Every family has its favourite dishes, and this is definitely one of ours.

50g (2oz) butter
1 large onion, peeled and chopped
1 large carrot, peeled and finely chopped
2 sticks of celery, trimmed and finely chopped
Salt and freshly ground black pepper
1kg (2lb 3oz) minced lamb (not too lean)
250ml (9fl oz) chicken stock (see page 326)
1 tbsp Worcestershire sauce
2 tbsp tomato purée
2 tbsp roux (see page 327)
1–2 tbsp tomato chutney (optional)
1kg (2lb 3oz) mashed potato (see page 116)

Large pie dish or four individual dishes

1 Melt the butter in a large saucepan (or lidded, ovenproof pan, if cooking in the oven – see below) on a low heat, add the onion, carrot and celery and season with salt and pepper. Cover with a butter wrapper, or a disc of greaseproof paper, and a lid and cook for 8–10 minutes until soft but not browned.

2 Remove the lid and paper, add the minced lamb, increase the heat and cook, stirring regularly, for a few minutes until the meat changes colour. Pour in the stock and stir in the Worcestershire sauce and tomato purée. Bring to the boil, then reduce the heat, cover the pan with the lid and continue to cook for about 20 minutes or until the meat is fully cooked, taking care not to let it burn on the bottom.

3 Strain the cooked mince and vegetables through a sieve placed over another large saucepan to catch the cooking liquid. Return the mince to the original pan, cover with a lid to keep warm, then bring the liquid back up to the boil. Add 1 tablespoon of the roux, a little at a time, and whisk into the liquid until it has thickened, adding the rest of the roux if you would like the sauce a little thicker. Tip the mince mixture back into the sauce, stir in the tomato chutney (if using) and check the seasoning, adjusting if necessary.

4 Preheat the grill to high and (if eating straight away) the oven to 180°C (350°F), Gas mark 4.

5 Pour the mixture into the pie dish or individual dishes. Spoon the mashed potato over the top, spread with a fork and grill for a few minutes to brown the potato slightly. (The pie can easily be prepared in advance and, once assembled, left to cool before placing in the fridge for up to 48 hours or freezer until needed.) Bake the shepherd's pie in the oven for 20–25 minutes or longer if from the fridge or freezer, until hot and bubbling. Serve at once with your favourite green vegetable.

Individual steak and mushroom pies

SERVES 6

Very quick and easy to make, hot water crust pastry is an excellent topping for any meat pie. You can also use 250g (9oz) puff pastry if you prefer. If you don't want to top with pastry, simply serve as a casserole with mash (see page 116). The alcohol from the stout evaporates during cooking, so it's fine for children.

For the hot water crust pastry
75g (3oz) butter, cubed
225g (8oz) plain flour, plus extra for dusting
Pinch of salt
1 egg (plus another for glazing), beaten

For the filling
4 tbsp olive oil
600g (1lb 5oz) stewing beef, trimmed and cut into 2cm (¾in) chunks
Salt and freshly ground black pepper
400g (14oz) baby button mushrooms
350g (12oz) carrots, peeled and thickly sliced
12 baby onions, peeled (see tip on page 187)
4 large cloves of garlic, peeled and chopped
500ml (18fl oz) beef or chicken stock (see page 326)
1 x 250ml bottle of stout, such as Guinness, Beamish or Murphy's
1 tbsp thyme
1 egg, beaten, for glazing

Six 10cm (4in) diameter individual pie dishes with 5cm (2in) sides

1 First, prepare the pastry. Place the butter and 100ml (3½fl oz) water in a saucepan and heat gently, stirring occasionally, until the butter melts, then allow the mixture to come to a rolling boil.

2 Meanwhile, sift the flour and salt into a large bowl. Make a well in the centre and add the egg. Pour the hot liquid into the flour and quickly stir with a wooden spoon to mix to a dough. Use the wooden spoon to spread the dough out on a large plate and allow to cool for about 15 minutes. Knead the dough into a ball, flatten slightly, wrap in cling film and place in the fridge for about 30 minutes to firm up.

3 While the dough is chilling, prepare the pie filling. Pour 2 tablespoons of the olive oil into a casserole dish or large ovenproof frying pan on a medium heat. Season the beef with salt and pepper and, cooking it in batches, sear all over for a few minutes until brown. Remove from the casserole dish or pan with a slotted spoon and set aside.

4 Heat another tablespoon of the oil in the casserole dish and add the mushrooms and carrots. Season with salt and pepper and sauté for 3–4 minutes until golden. Remove and set aside. Finally, heat the remaining oil in the casserole and fry the onions for 4–5 minutes, adding the garlic for the last minute of cooking.

5 Return the beef, mushrooms and carrots to the casserole dish, pour in the stock and stout and sprinkle with the thyme. Cover with a lid, bring to the boil, then reduce the heat and simmer gently on the hob for 1¼–1½ hours or until the meat is lovely and tender. Alternatively, cook for the same length of time in the oven, preheated to 150°C (300°F), Gas mark 2. Remove from the hob or oven, check the seasoning, adjusting if necessary, and allow to cool a little.

(continued overleaf)

6 Preheat the oven to 230°C (450°F), Gas mark 8.

7 Arrange the six pie dishes on a baking sheet. Divide the pastry into six equal-sized pieces and roll each one out between two large pieces of cling film or on a lightly floured surface, to give a circle about 3mm (⅛in) thick and slightly larger, by about 1cm (½in) all round than the top of the pie dish, plus a bit extra to make a strip to go round the dish. Turn the pie dish over on top of the pastry to check it has been rolled out to the correct size, cut around the dish with a knife to make a circle and cut the remaining pastry to make the strip. Repeat with each piece of pastry.

8 Divide the pie filling between the dishes and brush the rim or top edge of each pie dish with the beaten egg. Lay the pastry strip around the edge of the dish, pressing it in place, and then brush with more egg. Drape the pastry circle over the filling and press the pastry edges together to seal. Trim off any excess pastry and then, working round the top of the pie dish, use a knife to fluff up the very edges of the pastry with horizontal cuts for an attractive flaky finish. Give the pastry a scalloped effect by repeatedly pressing the index finger and thumb of one hand into the top edge of the pastry, gently pressing outwards. At the same time, press the point of a small blunt knife into the gap between your fingers, pushing inwards. Repeat all the way around. Use any leftover pastry to decorate the top of the pie and then brush all over with the beaten egg.

9 Cook in the oven for 10 minutes, then reduce the temperature to 200°C (400°F), Gas mark 6 and cook for a further 20–25 minutes or until the filling is bubbling and the pastry is golden. Allow to cool a little before serving.

Variations
Steak and kidney pie: Substitute the mushrooms with 400g (14oz) diced beef kidney. Soak the chopped kidney in a bowl of water with a good pinch of salt for about 1 hour. Fry the kidney separately, after the beef, for 2–3 minutes and add with the beef and carrots to the casserole before pouring in the stock and stout.
For one large pie: Use an oval pie dish measuring 18 x 23cm (7 x 9in) and about 4cm (1½in) deep. Cook at 220°C (425°F), Gas mark 7 for 10 minutes, reduce to 200°C (400°F), Gas mark 6 and cook for a further 25–30 minutes or until golden brown and bubbling.

Lamb cutlets with chickpea, caramelised onion and smoked paprika mash

SERVES 4

This is a lovely dish for a cold, wintry evening – the fragrant, smoky chickpea mash makes a nice change from potatoes. The lamb cutlets are also great served as a snack with the homemade garlic and herb mayonnaise (see the variations on page 330).

25g (1oz) butter
7 tbsp olive oil
1 large onion, peeled and finely sliced
2 cloves of garlic, peeled and finely chopped
2 tsp thyme leaves
½ tsp smoked paprika
2 x 400g tins of chickpeas, drained, or 250g (9oz) dried chickpeas, soaked and cooked (see page 329)
Salt and freshly ground black pepper
Juice of ½ lemon
8–12 lamb cutlets (2–3 per person)
50ml (2fl oz) red wine
100ml (3½fl oz) chicken stock (see page 326)
1 tbsp balsamic vinegar

1 Place the butter and 2 tablespoons of the olive oil in a large frying pan on a very low heat, add the onion and sauté for about 20 minutes until really soft and golden. Stir in the garlic, half the thyme and the paprika 5 minutes before the end.

2 Heat the chickpeas for 2–3 minutes in a saucepan of boiling, salted water, then drain them well. Place in a food processor with three-quarters of the caramelised onions, the lemon juice and 4 tablespoons of the olive oil, seasoning well with salt and pepper. Blend to a smooth purée, then return to the saucepan to keep warm. Alternatively, blitz all the ingredients in the pan using a hand-held blender.

3 Meanwhile, place another large frying pan on a high heat. Season the lamb cutlets and drizzle over the remaining tablespoon of oil. Adding the cutlets in batches, place them in the hot pan and quickly sear on both sides, then reduce the heat to medium and fry for 2 minutes on each side for rare, 2–3 minutes on each side for medium and 4–5 minutes on each side for well done. Remove from the pan and leave to rest, covered in foil to keep warm for a few minutes.

4 Drain the fat from the pan and then deglaze with the wine, stirring with a wooden spoon and scraping any sediment from the bottom. Allow the liquid to bubble for a few minutes and then add the stock, vinegar and remaining thyme and simmer for 3–4 minutes until reduced and slightly thickened.

5 Spoon the chickpea mash onto each plate, arrange the lamb cutlets on top, drizzle over the sauce, scatter with the remaining caramelised onions and serve.

Beefburgers with gherkin relish

The gherkin relish that accompanies these burgers is refreshing and packs a bit of punch. It is fresh and crunchy and is equally good with lamb or chicken burgers (see page 178). These burgers are made using beef, but you could, of course, make them with minced lamb instead.

4 tbsp olive oil
1 medium–large onion, peeled and chopped
Salt and freshly ground black pepper
800g (1¾lb) minced beef
4 tbsp chopped mixed herbs, such as tarragon, chives, thyme and parsley
4 cloves of garlic, peeled and crushed or grated
1 large egg, beaten
50g (2oz) fresh white breadcrumbs
8 toasted burger buns, ciabatta rolls or yeast rolls (see page 331), to serve

For the gherkin relish
75g (3oz) gherkins, very finely chopped
1 tomato, very finely chopped
1 spring onion, trimmed and finely chopped
1 clove of garlic, peeled and finely chopped
1 tbsp olive oil

1 To make the burgers, pour half the olive oil into a saucepan on a low heat, add the onion, season with salt and pepper, cover and sweat on a low heat for 10 minutes or until completely cooked and very soft but not browned. Remove from the pan and allow to cool.

2 Put the cooled onion in a bowl and mix with the remaining ingredients. Season with salt and pepper. (To check the seasoning, see tip on page 70.) Shape the mixture into eight evenly sized burgers. The burgers can be made to this stage in advance and kept in the fridge for up to 24 hours or frozen (and then defrosted) until ready to use.

3 Pour the remaining olive oil into a large frying pan on a medium heat and fry the burgers (in batches if necessary) for 8–10 minutes on each side or until well browned and cooked through. Alternatively, fry the burgers in an ovenproof pan for 3–4 minutes on each side until deep golden, then pop in the oven, preheated to 200°C (400°F), Gas mark 6, for 10 minutes or until cooked.

4 Meanwhile, prepare the gherkin relish by tossing all the ingredients together and seasoning with salt and pepper to taste.

5 Serve the burgers on a bun or your choice of toasted bread along with the gherkin relish and one of the toppings below, if you wish.

Toppings
Roast portabello mushrooms with lime cream cheese:
Remove the stalks from 8 portabello mushrooms, arrange on
a baking tray, drizzle with 2 tablespoons of olive oil and scatter
over 25g (1oz) finely grated Parmesan cheese, 2 finely chopped
cloves of garlic, 1 teaspoon of chopped thyme leaves and some
salt and pepper. Roast in the oven, preheated to 200°C
(400°F), Gas mark 6, for 10–15 minutes or until softened.
Meanwhile, stir together 150g (5oz) softened cream cheese
with 1 heaped tablespoon of chopped mint, the zest and juice
of 1 lime, the juice of ½ lemon and some salt and pepper to
taste. Sit a cooked mushroom on top of a cooked burger and
spoon some lime cream cheese on top to serve.
Buffalo mozzarella and crisp pancetta: Slice a ball of buffalo
mozzarella into eight and arrange a slice on top of each burger
to melt for the last 1–2 minutes of cooking time. Arrange
1–2 pieces of grilled crisp pancetta or streaky bacon on top
of each burger and serve.

Variation
Blue cheese burgers with rocket and onion jam: Add 50g
(2oz) crumbled blue cheese (such as Stilton, Roquefort or
Cashel Blue) to the burger mixture, being careful not to blend
it in too much so it stays in chunks. Cook as opposite and serve
with rocket or watercress leaves and onion jam (see page 336).

Steak and frites with garlic and herb butter and onion rings

SERVES 2

This is a classic combination, perfect for Father's Day. Steaks suitable for pan-frying include fillet, sirloin, T-bone and rib-eye. Remove the steaks from the fridge about 30 minutes before cooking to bring them to room temperature. The Creamy Mushroom and Bacon Sauce and Black Olive Tapenade (see pages 136 and 252) are also wonderful served with steak.

Sunflower oil, for deep-frying
450g (1lb) potatoes, peeled or unpeeled and cut into very thin chips about 5mm (¼in) thick
2 x 175–225g (6–8oz) fillet or sirloin steaks, at room temperature
2 tbsp olive oil
Salt and freshly ground black pepper
25ml (1fl oz) milk
2 tbsp plain flour
1 small–medium onion, peeled and cut into 0.5–1cm (¼–½in) slices, separated into rings
2 slices or 1 tsp Garlic and Herb Butter (see page 327)

1 Heat a deep-fat fryer filled with the sunflower oil to 140°C (275°F). Alternatively, pour the oil into a large saucepan to a depth of 2cm (¾in) and bring to the same temperature on the hob (checking with a sugar thermometer or see tip on page 255). To cook the frites, first wash and dry the chips really well and then fry a few handfuls at a time for 4–5 minutes or until beginning to soften but not turn brown. Remove and drain well on kitchen paper. The frites can be placed in the fridge at this point for up to 24 hours until needed.

2 Heat a heavy-based frying pan until really hot. To prepare the steaks, brush the olive oil all over, grind over plenty of pepper and sprinkle with salt on both sides. If using sirloin steaks, score the fat at 2.5cm (1in) intervals. Add the steaks to the pan and cook on each side (without touching the meat when cooking on the first side) for the recommended times opposite. To check whether the meat is cooked, press the steak with your finger. It will feel soft and supple for rare, firm for well done and somewhere in between for medium. Once the steaks are cooked to your liking, remove from the pan and leave to rest on a warm plate or plates, covered with foil, for 5–10 minutes.

3 Meanwhile, prepare the onion rings. Heat the deep-fat fryer or oil in a large frying pan again to 180°C (350°F) (check with the sugar thermometer or see tip on page 255). Pour the milk into a small wide bowl, sift the flour onto a plate and season both with salt and pepper. Dip the onion rings first in the milk and then in the flour to coat lightly, dusting off any excess. Deep-fry the onion rings in batches, trying to keep them as separate as possible, for 1–2 minutes until crisp and golden. Drain well on kitchen paper.

4 To finish the frites, deep-fry in batches for 3–5 minutes or until crisp and golden. Drain again on kitchen paper and season lightly with salt and pepper.

5 To serve, spoon or place slices of the garlic and herb butter on top of each steak. Divide the frites and onion rings between the plates and serve immediately.

Variation
Steak and frites with a cream sauce: Once the steaks have been removed from the frying pan, deglaze the pan with a splash of brandy (being careful as it may flame) or with a little stock, stirring with a wooden spoon and scraping up any sediment from the bottom of the pan. Pour in 100ml (3½fl oz) beef or chicken stock (see page 326), increase the heat and simmer rapidly for 4–5 minutes. Reduce the heat, pour in the cream, stir in either 1 tablespoon of Dijon mustard, 1 teaspoon of roughly crushed black peppercorns or 2 teaspoons of wholegrain mustard and simmer gently for 3–4 minutes until thickened. Check the seasoning, adding some salt and pepper if necessary, remove from the heat and serve either spooned over the steak or on the side in a separate small bowl or jug.

Rachel's tip
If keeping the frites or onion rings warm in the oven for any length of time, do not cover them as they will go soggy.

Frying times for steak (each side)

For steaks about 2.5cm (1in) thick
2 minutes for rare
3 minutes for medium rare
4 minutes for medium
5 minutes for well done

For steaks about 4cm (1½in) thick
5 minutes for rare
6 minutes for medium rare
7 minutes for medium
8–9 minutes for well done

Chilli con carne

This is a terrific dish for feeding a large number of people – just multiply the quantities as necessary. It can be made in advance and reheated or even popped in the freezer for another time. Chilli con carne is fabulous served with guacamole and tomato salsa (see Chicken Tostadas, page 137) as well as all the additions listed below in the ingredients.

2 tbsp olive oil
700g (1½lb) minced beef
1 large onion, peeled and roughly chopped
5 cloves of garlic, peeled and crushed
2 red or yellow peppers, deseeded and roughly chopped
3 red or green chillies, deseeded (optional) and finely chopped
2 x 400g tins of chopped tomatoes
1 tbsp tomato purée
Salt and freshly ground black pepper
1 x 400g tin of kidney beans, drained, or 125g (4½oz) dried beans, soaked and cooked (see page 329)
2 tsp ground cumin
2 tsp ground coriander
1 tsp brown sugar

To serve
Boiled rice, such as long-grain or basmati (see page 330)
Coriander leaves
Soured cream
Grated Cheddar cheese
Lime wedges

1 Pour the olive oil into a large casserole dish or saucepan (ovenproof and with a lid, if cooking in the oven – see below) on a high heat. Working in batches, sear the meat quickly until well browned. Remove each batch with a slotted spoon and set aside. Reduce the heat to medium, add the onion and garlic, cover with a lid and gently fry for 6–8 minutes, stirring occasionally, until soft.

2 Return the meat to the casserole dish or pan and add the peppers, chillies, tomatoes, tomato purée and some salt and pepper. Bring to the boil, cover with the lid, reduce the heat and simmer for about 1 hour or until the meat is nice and tender and the sauce has thickened a little. Alternatively, cook in the oven, preheated to 150°C (300°F), Gas mark 2, for an hour.

3 When the meat is cooked, add the remaining ingredients and leave to simmer, uncovered, on a low–medium heat for a further 10 minutes. Check the seasoning and adjust if necessary.

4 Serve the chilli con carne with boiled basmati or long-grain rice and with coriander leaves scattered over the top. Place small bowls of soured cream, Cheddar cheese and lime wedges on the table for people to help themselves.

Lassis

A lassi is a cooling Indian yoghurt drink, made with sweet or savoury ingredients (see picture on page 207). Lassis are very refreshing, particularly on a hot day. Try one for breakfast, or drink it ice cold to help you cool down. They are also an ideal antidote to a spicy curry — much better than water.

Basic recipe

Blitz all the ingredients together in a blender or using a hand-held blender until smooth. Push any fruit pulp through a fine sieve to get rid of the bits and pour into glasses to serve.

Spiced tumeric

Blend together 150ml (5fl oz) natural yoghurt, 150ml (5fl oz) milk, 2 teaspoons of lemon juice, ½ teaspoon each of cayenne pepper and ground turmeric and ¼ teaspoon of salt.

Mango and cardamon

Blend together 200ml (7fl oz) natural yoghurt, 100ml (3½fl oz) milk, 1 large ripe mango, peeled and roughly chopped, 2–3 teaspoons of caster sugar or honey and the seeds of 2 cardamom pods.

Banana and cumin

Blend together 200ml (7fl oz) natural yoghurt, 100ml (3½fl oz) milk, 1 large banana, peeled and broken into pieces, the juice of ½ lime, 1 teaspoon of ground cumin and ¼ teaspoon of salt.

Pineapple and lime

Blend together 150ml (5fl oz) natural yoghurt, 50ml (2fl oz) ice-cold water, 275g (10oz) roughly chopped pineapple, a good squeeze of lemon or lime juice and 2 teaspoons of caster sugar or honey.

Mild lamb curry with coriander rice and accompaniments

SERVES 6

My children adore the gentle flavour of this creamy mild curry. If you prefer a slightly hotter kick, then add the chilli as suggested in the recipe.

2 tsp coriander seeds
2 tsp cumin seeds
¼ tsp seeds from about 8 cardamom pods
4 cloves
3 tbsp sunflower oil
4 onions, peeled and sliced
1kg (2lb 3oz) lamb shoulder, cut into 2cm (¾in) dice and fat removed
2 tsp ground turmeric
4 cloves of garlic, peeled and finely chopped
1 tbsp finely chopped root ginger
1 red chilli, deseeded (if wished) and finely chopped (optional)
Salt and freshly ground black pepper
450ml (16fl oz) double or regular cream
150ml (5fl oz) beef or chicken stock (see page 326)
Juice of 1 lime or ½ lemon
Coriander leaves, to garnish

For the rice
500g (1lb 2oz) basmati rice
25g (1oz) butter
8 tbsp roughly chopped coriander

1 Toast the seeds and cloves (see tip on page 50), then crush using a pestle and mortar or spice grinder or, when cool, put them in a plastic bag and crush with a rolling pin.

2 Pour 2 tablespoons of the sunflower oil into a large lidded casserole dish or heavy-based saucepan on a high heat, add the onions and sauté for 5 minutes until softened and nicely golden. Transfer to a bowl and add the remaining oil. Place the lamb in the pan and sear until well browned all over, preferably working in batches so as not to overcrowd the pan and stew the meat.

3 Return the onions and all the seared meat to the pan and add the crushed spices along with the turmeric, garlic, ginger and chilli (if using). Season with salt and pepper, then toss everything together to combine and stir in the cream and stock, scraping any sediment from the bottom of the pan.

4 Bring slowly to the boil, then immediately reduce the heat and cover with a lid. Leave to gently simmer for about 1 hour, removing the lid for the last 15 minutes. Alternatively, make in an ovenproof dish or pan and cook in the oven, preheated to 150°C (300°F), Gas mark 2, for an hour, leaving the lid on for the whole cooking time. Check that the lamb is tender, cooking for a little longer if necessary. Add the lime or lemon juice and check the seasoning.

5 In the meantime, place the rice in double its volume of salted water, bring to the boil, cover with a lid and cook for 10–12 minutes (or following the instructions on the packet) until the rice is cooked and all the moisture has been absorbed. Remove the saucepan from the heat and allow to stand for a few minutes, with the lid on, then stir in the butter and coriander, using a fork in order not to mash the rice.

(continued on page 208)

6 While the rice is cooking (or a few minutes before this, depending on how many dishes you plan to serve), prepare your choice of accompaniments from below to serve with the curry, spooning them into lots of little serving bowls. Divide the cooked rice between each plate, spoon over the curry, decorate with coriander leaves and serve with the accompaniments (see below).

Accompaniments
Make a selection from the following:
Chutney: Use either mango or tomato chutney.
Raita: See Middle Eastern Spiced Lamb Koftas (page 73).
Tomato salsa: Mix 200g (7oz) diced ripe tomatoes with 1 chopped spring onion (or 1 tablespoon of finely chopped red onion), 1 tablespoon of chopped coriander and 2 teaspoons of lime juice, and season to taste with salt, pepper and a pinch of caster sugar.
Sliced bananas: Peel and slice 2 bananas, squeeze over the juice of 1 lime and scatter with 1 tablespoon of desiccated coconut.
Poppadoms: Either buy a pack of ready-made poppadoms from the supermarket, reheating them as per the instructions on the packet, or buy papads (uncooked poppadom discs) from an Asian grocery shop and either deep-fry, grill or microwave.

Variations
Coconut lamb curry: Substitute the cream with coconut milk for a different flavour.
Lamb and tomato curry: Use passata (or blended tinned tomatoes) in place of the stock for a more tomatoey taste.

Dessert

Fruit tarts

A fruit tart is tasty whatever the time of year and can be filled with fruits that are in season (or whatever you have in the freezer). The pastry can be difficult to handle so it is important to refrigerate the dough for at least an hour.

175g (6oz) butter,
    softened, plus extra
    for greasing
50g (2oz) caster sugar,
    plus extra for sprinkling
2 eggs
250g (9oz) plain flour,
    plus extra for dusting

*23cm (9in) diameter ovenproof
shallow pie dish or tart tin*

1 To make the pastry use an electric beater or an electric food mixer fitted with a dough hook. Cream the butter and sugar together until pale and creamy. Add one egg, beating continuously, then beat the second egg in a separate bowl. Pour half of it into the mixture (reserving the remainder for later) and beat again. Sift over the flour and stir in gently to give a smooth, soft dough. Tip the dough onto a clean work surface and knead a little before dividing in two. Shape each piece into a flat round, cover with cling film and leave in the fridge for at least 1 hour.

2 Preheat the oven to 180°C (350°F), Gas mark 4. Lightly butter the plate or tin. Place each pastry half on a floured work surface and roll out to about 3mm (⅛in) thick. Use one piece to line the dish or tin, trimming off the excess pastry with the back of a knife. Brush a little of the reserved beaten egg around the edge of the pastry.

3 Add your chosen fruit filling (see below) to the pastry case in the tin or dish and top with the second rolled-out piece, trimming the excess pastry once again and pressing the edges together to seal. Use any leftover pastry to decorate the top by rolling out and cutting into shapes. Brush all over with the remaining beaten egg.

4 Bake in the oven for 45–50 minutes or until the fruit is tender when tested with a skewer and the pastry golden. Remove from the oven, sprinkle with a light dusting of sugar and leave to cool slightly. Cut into wedges and serve with whipped cream or custard.

Fruit fillings

Apple: Peel, core and dice 700g (1½lb) Bramley cooking apples and toss with 150g (5oz) caster sugar and 2–3 cloves.

Plum, nectarine or peach: Halve, stone and quarter 900g (2lb) plums, nectarines or peeled peaches with a peeler (or see tip on page 144) and toss with 75g (3oz) caster sugar and 2 tablespoons of cornflour (adding an extra teaspoonful if the fruit is very ripe).

Strawberry: Toss 700g (1½lb) hulled strawberries (halved if large) with 1 tablespoon of cornflour and 50g (2oz) caster sugar.

Poached fruits

SERVES 4–6 (DEPENDING ON USE) · VEGETARIAN

All these are delicious served with ice cream, softly whipped cream
or custard. Pears poached in plain sugar syrup are particularly good with
chocolate sauce (see page 337). Alternatively, for a breakfast option, serve
the poached fruits with Greek yoghurt (or homemade yoghurt – see page 10)
and a scattering of nuts, such as the peaches and strawberries with toasted
flaked almonds or the apricots with chopped pistachios. Poached fruits
are also delicious served with meringues (see page 237).

For the sugar syrup
200g (7oz) caster sugar

**Flavouring choices for
the syrup (optional)**
1 vanilla pod, split
2 star anise
1 cinnamon stick
½ tsp ground cardamom
Splash of brandy

Fruit choices
450g (1lb) whole plums OR
450g (1lb) halved apricots,
    nectarines or peaches OR
450g (1lb) rhubarb, cut
    into 2.5cm (1in) pieces
300g (11oz) sliced
    strawberries, for
    adding to the apricots,
    nectarines, peaches,
    or rhubarb, once
    poached and cooled

1 Make a sugar syrup (see page 338) using the caster sugar and
200ml (7fl oz) cold water, plus your choice of flavouring (if
using). After boiling the syrup for 2 minutes, reduce the heat
and add your choice of fruit.

2 Poach one type of fruit gently for 10–15 minutes (except for
rhubarb, which will take only 1–2 minutes) until it is completely
softened. Transfer to a bowl, add the sliced strawberries if
using, and serve warm or cool.

Rachel's tip
Once the poached fruits have been used up, save any leftover
fruit syrup as a base for a refreshing fruit drink by diluting it
with water and lemon juice and then serving with lots of ice
(see soft drinks, page 296).

Chocolate and raspberry Swiss roll

SERVES 8 · VEGETARIAN

Despite appearances, Swiss roll is in fact very simple to make. The cake has no butter in it, so you can feel justified in spreading it with plenty of whipped cream.

Knob of butter, melted, for greasing
100g (3½oz) plain flour, plus extra for dusting
4 eggs
125g (4½oz) caster sugar, plus 3 tbsp for sprinkling
2 tbsp warm water
1 tsp vanilla extract
50g (2oz) best-quality cocoa powder
Icing sugar, for dusting

For the filling
225ml (8fl oz) raspberry coulis (see page 337) or 6 tbsp raspberry or strawberry jam
225ml (8fl oz) double or regular cream, whipped

Swiss roll tin measuring either 25 x 38cm (10 x 15in) or 10 x 35cm (4 x 14in)

1 Preheat the oven to 190°C (375°F), Gas mark 5. Line the base of the Swiss roll tin with greaseproof or parchment paper, brush all over with the melted butter (including the sides) and dust with flour, shaking off any excess.

2 Whisk the eggs and caster sugar together in a large bowl or in an electric food mixer until light and fluffy, then add the water and vanilla extract and whisk for a further few seconds. Sift the flour and cocoa powder together, then fold into the egg mixture, about a third at a time.

3 Pour the mixture into the prepared Swiss roll tin and spread out evenly, filling every corner. Bake in the oven for 12–15 minutes or until the centre of the cake is springy to the touch and the edges have shrunk slightly from the sides of the tin.

4 In the meantime, lay a large piece of greaseproof paper, slightly larger than the size of the tin, on a work surface and sprinkle evenly with 3 tablespoons of caster sugar. Turn the cooked Swiss roll from the tin onto the sugared greaseproof paper and carefully remove the tin and greaseproof paper from the bottom of the cake. Allow to cool, placing a slightly damp, clean tea towel over the cake while it cools to help prevent it from drying out and cracking when you are rolling it up.

5 Meanwhile, simmer the raspberry coulis (if using) in a small saucepan on a medium heat until reduced by about half and thickened slightly. Remove and allow to cool.

6 Spread the jam or raspberry coulis all over, followed by the cream. With the long side facing you, roll up the Swiss roll away from you, using the greaseproof paper underneath to guide it along. Transfer to a long plate and dust with icing sugar to serve.

Variation
Sweet liqueur cream: Omit the raspberry coulis and flavour the cream with coffee or orange liqueur and 1–2 tablespoons of sifted icing sugar. Perfect if serving for a dinner party (grown-ups only).

Fruit crumbles

SERVES 6 · VEGETARIAN

A fruit crumble is one of the most comforting puddings, especially when served with flavoured homemade custard (see page 338). It is very versatile; you can use whatever fruit you have to hand. This dessert takes no time to put together.

75g (3oz) butter, diced, plus extra for greasing
150g (5oz) plain flour
75g (3oz) soft light brown sugar
Icing sugar, for dusting

1 litre (1¾ pint) pie dish (15 x 20cm/6 x 8in) with 5cm (2in) sides, or six individual large ramekins

1 Preheat the oven to 180°C (350°F), Gas mark 4. Lightly butter the pie dish or ramekins and set on a baking sheet.

2 Prepare your choice of fruit filling from the following list and spread evenly in the bottom of the dish or ramekins.

3 For the crumble topping, rub the flour and butter together in a large bowl until it resembles very coarse breadcrumbs (don't rub it in too much or the crumble won't be crunchy once cooked). Stir in the sugar and then scatter the topping over the fruit. At this point you can place the crumble in the fridge for up to 48 hours or freezer until you need to cook it.

4 Bake the crumble in the oven for 35–40 minutes (or 15–20 minutes for the ramekins) until golden and bubbly. Serve dusted with icing sugar and with a dollop of lightly whipped cream, ice cream or custard.

Fruit fillings

Apple and raspberry: Cook 600g (1lb 5oz) (about 2) peeled, cored and roughly chopped cooking apples (such as Bramley) with 50g (2oz) caster sugar and 1 tablespoon of water for 6–8 minutes or until soft. Spoon into the prepared pie dish and scatter over 200g (7oz) fresh or frozen raspberries.

Apple and sweet mincemeat: Cook 800g (1¾lb) (or 3–4) peeled, cored and roughly chopped cooking apples (such as Bramley) with 75g (3oz) caster sugar and 2 tablespoons of water for 6–8 minutes or until just softened. Toss with 110g (4oz) sweet mincemeat (mince pie filling) and arrange in the prepared pie dish before adding the crumble.

Strawberry and rhubarb: Cook 450g (1lb) roughly chopped rhubarb with 75g (3oz) of sugar and 1 tablespoon of water for about 5 minutes until beginning to soften. Spoon into the prepared pie dish and scatter over 225g (8oz) hulled and quartered strawberries before topping with the crumble.

Plum and vanilla: Dissolve 75g (3oz) caster sugar in 100ml (3½fl oz) red wine (or water) in a saucepan on a gentle heat. Stone and quarter 600g (1lb 5oz) plums, add to the pan with 1 split vanilla pod and cook for 5 minutes or until beginning to soften. Remove the plums and place in the prepared pie dish. Simmer the liquid further until it has reduced by half to a thick syrup. Remove the vanilla pod and drizzle the syrup over the plums before topping with the crumble.

Variations

Sugars: In place of the soft light brown sugar use demerara, caster or granulated sugar in the crumble topping.

Topping texture: When adding the sugar, stir in any of these: 25g (1oz) rolled oats; 75g (3oz) chopped pecans or hazelnuts or flaked almonds; 2 teaspoons of ground spices, such as cinnamon, nutmeg or mixed spice.

Rachel's tip

Keep a large batch of the crumble mixture in a food bag in the freezer. Even when frozen, it will easily crumble so you can take handfuls of the mixture to use straight away as you need it.

Banana split

A banana split is something children love to make as they can play around with the food as much as they like, having fun at the same time. Let your children be as imaginative as they like, scattering all sorts of things (providing they're edible!) over their creations. Quantities in this recipe are for one, but just multiply them as needed.

1 banana, peeled and halved lengthways

2–3 scoops of ice cream

50ml (2fl oz) double or regular cream

15g (½oz) chopped nuts, toasted (see Rachel's tip on page 50), such as pecans, almonds or hazelnuts

15g (½oz) dark or white chocolate shavings

15g (½oz) honeycomb (see page 310) or chocolate-coated honeycomb, crumbled

½ tsp hundreds and thousands or other sweets for sprinkling

1 tbsp dark chocolate sauce (see page 337)

1 tbsp toffee sauce (see page 337)

1 Arrange the banana on a plate (or a long dish, if you have one) and spoon the ice cream down the centre of the two halves. Pipe the cream using a piping bag fitted with a star nozzle (or dollop it over with a spoon, shaping the cream with the back of the spoon).

2 To decorate, scatter over the nuts, chocolate shavings, crumbled honeycomb and hundreds and thousands. Then drizzle with the chocolate and toffee sauces and serve immediately.

Variation

Baked banana split: Preheat the oven to 200°C (400°F), Gas mark 6. Place a peeled banana in the centre of a large rectangle of foil, scrunch up the sides and drizzle over 1 tablespoon of maple syrup and 1 tablespoon of orange juice. Seal the parcel to enclose and bake in the oven for 20 minutes before carefully turning out onto a plate and assembling the banana split from this point.

Peaches and raspberries with lime and honey

SERVES 4 · VEGETARIAN

This is a perfect zesty and light dessert but is also
wonderful for breakfast served with Greek yoghurt
or your own homemade yoghurt (see page 10).

Finely grated zest and juice
of 1 lime
1 tbsp runny honey
3–4 peaches or nectarines,
stoned and cut into
slices 5mm (¼in) thick
125g (4½oz) fresh or
frozen (and defrosted)
raspberries

1 Mix the lime zest and juice with the honey in a large bowl.
Gently stir in the peaches or nectarines and raspberries.

2 Leave the fruit to sit for a few minutes to allow the flavours
to mingle before serving with some vanilla ice cream.

Rachel's tip
Don't leave the fruit for any longer than a few minutes
or it will become soggy.

Raspberry fool with shortbread biscuits

SERVES 4–6 · VEGETARIAN

A fool should be quite light and airy. A simple pudding, it's lovely made with raspberries and goes so well with these little shortbread biscuits.

350g (12oz) fresh or frozen (defrosted) raspberries
2–3 tbsp icing sugar
200ml (7fl oz) double or regular cream
200ml (7fl oz) natural yoghurt

For the shortbread biscuits
75g (3oz) plain flour, plus extra for dusting
50g (2oz) butter, diced
25g (1oz) caster sugar

1 Preheat the oven to 180°C (350°F), Gas mark 4.

2 To make the shortbread biscuits, rub the flour and butter together in a large bowl until the mixture resembles fine breadcrumbs. Add the sugar and bring the whole mixture together to form a stiff dough. Alternatively, briefly mix the ingredients in a food processor until they come together.

3 Roll out the dough on a floured work surface to a thickness of 5mm (¼in) and cut into 12–18 fingers, rounds or any shape you like. Carefully lift from the work surface with a palette knife and place on a baking sheet spaced evenly apart. Bake in the oven for 8–10 minutes until pale golden. Remove and immediately pierce with a fork in several places to decorate, if you wish. Allow to cool on the sheet for just a minute before carefully lifting onto a wire rack to cool.

4 Meanwhile, prepare the fool. Place the raspberries in a small bowl with the icing sugar and crush with a fork or potato masher or hand-held blender. Whip the cream to soft peaks and then gently fold in the yoghurt. Fold in the crushed raspberries but without stirring them in completely so that they create a marbled effect.

5 Cover and place in the fridge for about 20 minutes or until ready to serve. (The fool can be made up to a day in advance.) Spoon into glasses, small bowls or simply onto plates and serve with the shortbread biscuits on the side.

Variation
Blackberry and apple fool: Peel, core and dice 1 cooking apple – about 250g (9oz) prepared fruit – and place in a saucepan with 3 tablespoons of caster sugar and 2 tablespoons of water. Cover and cook on a low heat for 7–8 minutes, stirring every so often, until softened. Pour into a bowl and leave to cool. Add 125g (4½oz) fresh or frozen (and defrosted) blackberries and mash to a purée, then fold into the cream and yoghurt mixture as above, in place of the crushed raspberries.

Blueberry and buttermilk sherbet

Adapted from an American recipe, this is like a cross between a sorbet and an ice cream. The palate-pleasing sherbet 'fizz' comes from the tart buttermilk.

300g (11oz) fresh or frozen (and defrosted) blueberries

225g (8oz) caster sugar

500ml (18fl oz) buttermilk or soured milk (see tip on page 24)

1 tsp vanilla extract

1 egg white (unless freezing in an ice-cream machine)

1 Whiz the blueberries in a food processor or blender (or using a hand-held blender) until as smooth as possible. Press the purée through a sieve into a large bowl, discarding what's leftover in the sieve.

2 Stir the sugar, buttermilk or soured milk and vanilla extract into the blueberry purée and whisk really well, ensuring the sugar dissolves.

3 Pour the blueberry mixture into an ice-cream machine, and freeze according to the manufacturer's instructions. Alternatively, pour the mixture into a shallow dish and place in the freezer for about an hour. Take out of the freezer, whisk the mixture well and return to the freezer for another few hours until semi-frozen. Then beat the egg white until it forms soft peaks and immediately remove the sherbet from the freezer. Whisk it and fold the egg whites into the freezing mixture. Return the sherbet to the freezer and leave overnight or until completely frozen.

4 Place the sherbet in the fridge to soften a little — about 10 minutes — before you want to serve it. Scoop out and serve in chilled cups, glasses or bowls or in cones on a hot day.

Date and orange syrup pudding

SERVES 6—8 · VEGETARIAN

This is a terrific, gooey steamed pudding, full of rich autumnal flavours.
It's not something that you would eat every day of the week, but it is
perfect cold-weather fare. The dates and oranges combine beautifully
and have a lovely citrusy, toffee-like flavour.

125g (4½oz) butter,
   softened, plus extra
   for greasing
50g (2oz) pitted dates,
   sliced into 4—5 strips
25g (1oz) raisins (small
   ones are best)
Finely grated zest of
   1 small orange
75ml (3fl oz) golden syrup
Juice of 1 orange
100g (3½oz) caster sugar
2 eggs, lightly beaten
140g (5oz) self-raising
   flour, sifted
2 tbsp milk

1.25 litre (2 pint) pudding basin

1 Place the dates, raisins and orange zest in a small bowl and
mix together. Lightly butter the pudding basin. Mix together
the golden syrup and half the orange juice and pour it into
the bottom of the basin.

2 Cream the butter in a large bowl or in an electric food mixer
until soft. Add the sugar and beat until the mixture is light and
fluffy. Gradually add the eggs, beating well between each addition
and adding a little of the flour if the mixture appears to be
curdling. Stir in the flour, then the milk and the remaining
orange juice, mixing them thoroughly.

3 Fold in the dried fruits and spoon the cake mixture into the
pudding basin, taking care not to mix it in with the syrup at the
bottom of the basin. The mixture should come about two-thirds
of the way up. Flatten the mixture with the back of the spoon.

4 Butter a piece of greaseproof paper and fold a pleat across the
centre. Cover the basin with the paper, butter side down, and
secure with string under the lip of the basin (see picture on page
224). Cook in a steamer or large saucepan, following the
instructions for Steamed Ginger Treacle Pudding (see opposite).

5 Remove from the steamer or pan and slide a palette knife gently
around the pudding to loosen it, then invert onto a warm serving
plate (one that is wider than the top of the basin). Spoon over any
remaining sauce and eat while hot, served with cream or custard.

Rachel's tips
* Remove the pudding from the basin within 10 minutes
otherwise it will stick.
* This pudding is also great eaten cold as a cake.

Steamed ginger treacle pudding

SERVES 6 · VEGETARIAN

This pudding is a real winter treat (see picture on page 225). The treacle flavour is not too strong but almost toffee-ish. You can buy stem ginger in syrup in most supermarkets or any good deli or speciality food store. Alternatively, you can use crystallised ginger in the cake mix and then golden syrup in place of the ginger syrup in the treacle mix.

125g (4½oz) butter, diced and softened plus extra for greasing
50ml (2fl oz) treacle
50ml (2fl oz) ginger syrup (from the stem ginger jar – see below)
110g (4oz) soft light brown sugar
2 eggs
150g (5oz) self-raising flour, sifted
1–2 tbsp milk
75g (3oz) stem ginger, very finely chopped

1.2 litre (2 pint) pudding basin

1 Butter the pudding basin. Mix the treacle and the stem ginger syrup together and pour into the bottom of the basin.

2 Cream the butter and sugar together in a bowl or in an electric food mixer until light and fluffy. Beat in the eggs a little at a time, fold in the flour and add enough milk to give a dropping consistency. Stir in the stem ginger and spoon the mixture into the pudding basin to come two-thirds of the way up, smoothing the top with the back of the spoon. (The treacle will come up the inside of the basin, so be careful not to mix it into the cake mixture.)

3 Butter a piece of greaseproof paper and fold a pleat across the centre. Cover the basin with the paper, butter side down, and secure with string under the lip of the basin (see picture on page 224). Place in a steamer with a tight-fitting lid and simmer on a low heat for 1¼–1½ hours or until the top of the pudding is firm to the touch and a skewer inserted into the middle comes out clean. Remember to top up the water if necessary.

4 Alternatively, if you don't have a steamer, sit the pudding basin on an upturned saucer in the bottom of a large saucepan. Pour enough boiling water to come halfway up the sides of the basin and cover with a tight-fitting lid, then cook for the same length of time. Again, remember to keep the water topped up all the time.

5 Remove from the steamer or pan, carefully loosen the pudding by running a spatula around the inside of the basin and invert onto a warm serving plate (one that is wider than the top of the basin). The treacle sauce will ooze down the sides of the pudding. Spoon over any sauce remaining in the basin and serve with ice cream, softly whipped cream or custard.

Rhubarb and ginger bread and butter pudding

SERVES 4–6 · VEGETARIAN

This variation on the classic bread and butter pudding uses rhubarb and ginger, which go together so well. You can use fresh or frozen rhubarb and enjoy the pudding year round.

450g (1lb) rhubarb, cut into 1cm (½in) slices
2 tsp finely grated root ginger
150g (5oz) caster sugar
50g (2oz) butter, softened
12 slices of white bread, crusts removed
350ml (12fl oz) single or regular cream
350ml (12fl oz) milk
2 tsp finely grated root ginger
4 eggs
Pinch of salt
2 tbsp granulated sugar
Icing sugar, for dusting

25cm (10in) square ovenproof dish or similar-sized dish

1 Scatter the rhubarb in a baking dish and sprinkle with the grated ginger and half the caster sugar. Toss together and then leave to sit for about 30 minutes to soften a little.

2 Preheat the oven to 180°C (350°F), Gas mark 4. Butter the bread and arrange four slices, buttered side down, in the ovenproof dish. Scatter over half of the prepared rhubarb and top with four more slices of bread, again buttered side down. Repeat with the remaining rhubarb mixture and bread.

3 Place the cream, milk and grated ginger in a saucepan and bring just to the boil. While this is coming to the boil, whisk the eggs, salt and remaining caster sugar in a bowl. Continuing to whisk, pour the hot liquid into the egg mixture until well mixed. Slowly pour this custard over the bread and leave to soak for 10 minutes. Sprinkle the granulated sugar over the top.

4 Place the dish into a deep-sided baking tray and pour in enough boiling water to come halfway up the sides (known as a bain-marie). Carefully place in the oven to bake for 45–50 minutes or until it feels just set in the centre. Remove from the oven and serve warm with a light dusting of icing sugar and some softly whipped cream.

Variations

Bread and butter pudding with dried fruits and mixed spice: Use 200g (7oz) mixed dried fruits, such as sultanas, raisins and/or chopped apricots, prunes, figs or dates instead of the rhubarb. As dried fruit doesn't need to soften with sugar, unlike the rhubarb, reduce the caster sugar to 100g (3½oz) for the custard mixture. Substitute the ginger with the same quantity of mixed spice.

Raspberry jam bread and butter pudding: Spread 75g (3oz) raspberry jam over the buttered bread slices. Omit the rhubarb and ginger and therefore reduce the overall caster sugar in the recipe to 100g (3½oz).

Rice pudding

SERVES 4–6 · VEGETARIAN

Rice pudding is delicious served with poached fresh or dried fruit
(see pages 212 and 44), stewed fruit like apple, pear or rhubarb,
a scattering of toasted nuts or seeds or just a spoonful of jam.

110g (4oz) pearl or short-
grain pudding rice
75g (3oz) caster sugar
850ml (1½ pints) whole
milk (or half milk
and half single or
regular cream)

1 Place the rice, sugar, milk and any flavouring (if using –
see the variations below) in a saucepan (non-stick if possible)
and bring slowly to the boil.

2 Reduce the heat to low and cook gently for 45–50 minutes,
stirring frequently to prevent the mixture burning on the
bottom of the pan, particularly towards the end of cooking.
The cooked rice will be swollen, tender and creamy. Ladle
into bowls and serve immediately.

Variations
Add your choice of flavouring from the list below with
the other ingredients at the start of cooking:
Nutmeg: Good pinch of freshly grated nutmeg
Orange: Finely grated zest of 1 large orange
Vanilla: The seeds from 1 vanilla pod or 1 teaspoon of
vanilla extract
Dried fruits and cinnamon: 100g (3½oz) mixed dried
fruits (chopped if large), such as sultanas, raisins, apricots,
figs and dates, and ¼ teaspoon of ground cinnamon

Gooseberry sponge tart

SERVES 8 · VEGETARIAN

This is lovely served with some cream and a sprinkling of brown sugar as a dessert or as a treat with a cup of tea or coffee. If you can't get hold of fresh gooseberries, then frozen ones work equally well.

110g (4oz) butter, melted and cooled, plus extra for greasing
350g (12oz) shortcrust pastry (see page 333)
500g (1lb 2oz) green or red gooseberries, topped and tailed
100g (3½oz) brown sugar, plus extra for sprinkling
225g (8oz) self-raising flour
110g (4oz) caster sugar
2 eggs
2 tbsp milk
25g (1oz) flaked almonds
Icing sugar, for dusting
Brown sugar, for sprinkling

23cm (9in) diameter, straight-sided, loose-bottomed tart tin with 4cm (1½in) sides

1 Preheat the oven to 180°C (350°F), Gas mark 4. Lightly grease the tart tin.

2 Prepare the pastry, line the tart tin with it and bake 'blind' following the instructions on page 333.

3 Place the gooseberries in a saucepan with the brown sugar and 1 tablespoon of water, cover with a lid and cook on a low heat for 8–10 minutes until just beginning to soften. Remove and strain through a colander over another saucepan. Reduce the liquid in the pan on a high heat for a few minutes until thickened and syrupy. Stir in the gooseberries and allow to cool.

4 Meanwhile, make the sponge topping. Sift the flour into a bowl, stir in the caster sugar and make a well in the centre. Mix the egg, melted butter and milk in another bowl or jug and pour the mixture into the dry ingredients, stirring as you go. Beat well to give a smooth, thick cake mixture with a loose dropping consistency that will slide off the spoon fairly easily when held above the bowl.

5 Spoon the cooled gooseberry filling into the cooked pastry case, spreading it out evenly. Dot spoonfuls of the cake mixture over the gooseberries and spread it out with the back of a spoon. Scatter with the flaked almonds and place the tart tin on a baking sheet. Bake in the oven for 30–35 minutes or until risen and golden and a skewer, inserted into the middle of the cake mixture, comes out clean.

6 Remove from the oven and leave to cool in the tin before removing. Dust with icing sugar and serve with a sprinkling of brown sugar and whipped cream or custard.

Dark and white chocolate fudge puddings with zesty orange

SERVES 6 · VEGETARIAN

This recipe has to be one of my favourite ever; it is adapted from a pudding we make at the Ballymaloe Cookery School. Adults and children alike love it, and it is so simple to make. As it cooks the mixture separates divinely into a soft chocolate sponge on top and a very delicious chocolate fudgy sauce underneath.

150g (5oz) butter, plus extra for greasing
175g (6oz) good dark chocolate, broken into pieces
110g (4oz) caster sugar
Finely grated zest of 1 large orange
150ml (5fl oz) warm water
4 eggs, separated
25g (1oz) self-raising flour, sifted
Pinch of cream of tartar
100g (3½oz) roughly chopped white chocolate or white chocolate chips
Icing sugar, for dusting

1.2 litre (2 pint) oval pie dish (17 x 23cm/6½ x 9in) with 4cm (1½in) sides

1 Preheat the oven to 200°C (400°F), Gas mark 6. Lightly butter the pie dish and place in a deep-sided roasting tin.

2 Place the dark chocolate, butter, sugar, orange zest and water in a saucepan on a low heat to very gently melt. Remove from the heat, pour into a large bowl, stir until the mixture is smooth and allow to cool a little. Whisk in the egg yolks and then fold in the flour.

3 In a separate bowl, whisk the egg whites with the cream of tartar, until they form stiff peaks. Gently fold the stiff whites into the chocolate mixture until well incorporated and then pour into the prepared dish. Scatter the white chocolate chips evenly over the top (they will begin to sink a little).

4 Pour boiling water into the roasting tin to come about 2cm (¾in) up the sides of the dish (known as a bain-marie, this protects the pudding from the heat of the oven and prevents it drying out).

5 Carefully transfer to the oven to bake for 10 minutes, then reduce the heat to 170°C (325°F), Gas mark 3 for a further 10 minutes. The pudding should be firm on top but with a fudgy chocolate sauce underneath. Leave to sit for 3–4 minutes before serving with softly whipped cream or vanilla ice cream and dredged with icing sugar.

Variations
Individual puddings: use six ramekins or dariole moulds instead of the pie dish. Bake for 8–10 minutes at 200°C (400°F), Gas mark 6.
Plain chocolate fudge pudding: Omit the orange zest and white chocolate chips.
Chocolate and raspberry fudge pudding: Substitute the white chocolate chips with 75g (3oz) fresh or frozen (and defrosted) raspberries, scattering them over the top before cooking.

Baked raspberry and ricotta cheesecake

SERVES 8–10 · VEGETARIAN

In this variation on the classic American dessert, ricotta is used rather than cream cheese for a lighter texture, while the raspberries add a tangy, refreshing touch.

50g (2oz) butter, melted, plus extra for greasing
150g (5oz) (about 12) digestive biscuits
1 x 500g tub of ricotta cheese
200g (7oz) crème fraîche
3 eggs
175g (6oz) caster sugar
1 tbsp runny honey
Grated zest of 1 lemon
2 tsp vanilla extract
275g (10oz) fresh raspberries
Icing sugar, for dusting

20cm (8in) diameter spring-form/loose-bottomed cake tin

1 Preheat the oven to 180°C (350°F), Gas mark 4. Grease the sides and base of the cake tin.

2 Place the biscuits in a food processor and blend until quite fine. Alternatively, place them in a plastic bag and bash with a rolling pin. Mix the crushed biscuits with the melted butter and tip into the prepared tin. Press down into the base of the tin to form an even layer.

3 Wash the processor bowl and blade, reset and add the ricotta, crème fraîche, eggs, sugar, honey, lemon zest and vanilla extract. Blend for a few seconds until smooth and well combined. Alternatively, place all the ingredients in a large bowl and blend using a hand-held electric beater. Crush 100g (3½oz) of the raspberries with a fork and stir them into the mixture.

4 Pour the mixture onto the biscuit base in the tin and gently shake and tilt the tin so that the ricotta mixture forms a level layer (minding the loose bottom of the tin!). Bake in the oven for 40–45 minutes or until the cheesecake is pale golden and wobbles slightly in the middle when you shake the tin. Remove, cover with foil and leave in a warm place to completely cool before storing in the fridge overnight. Don't worry if the top has cracked when you take it out again as the remaining raspberries will cover this.

5 Run a knife around the edge to loosen the cheesecake and remove it from the tin. Transfer to a serving plate and scatter the remaining raspberries on top. Dust with icing sugar and serve.

Apricot and cardamom upside-down cake with pistachios

SERVES 8 · VEGETARIAN

I love the combination of apricots and cardamom with its Middle Eastern overtones. This moist dessert keeps really well for a few days. It is also delicious made with other fruits such as bananas or pears. You can also substitute the cardamom with other spices such as cinnamon, mixed spice or ground ginger. If apricots aren't in season, just use tinned ones instead.

50g (2oz) butter
150g (5oz) soft light brown or demerara sugar
550g (1lb 3oz) (about 10) fresh apricots, halved and stoned
200g (7oz) plain flour
1 tsp baking powder
½ tsp salt
¼ tsp bicarbonate of soda
1 tsp ground cardamom
2 eggs, lightly beaten
200ml (7fl oz) buttermilk or soured milk (see Rachel's tip on page 24)
75ml (3fl oz) vegetable or sunflower oil
25g (1oz) shelled pistachios, roughly chopped, to serve

25cm (10in) diameter ovenproof frying pan

1 Preheat the oven to 180°C (350°F), Gas mark 4.

2 Melt the butter in the frying pan, add half the sugar and cook on a gentle heat for about 5 minutes until the sugar has dissolved and is beginning to caramelise. Tip the apricot halves into the caramelised mixture, tossing them about to coat (the sugar will harden a little, but it will melt again in the heat of the oven). Spread the apricots out in a single layer (cut side either up or down) and remove the pan from the heat.

3 Sift the flour, baking powder, salt, bicarbonate of soda and cardamom into a large bowl. Add the beaten eggs, buttermilk or soured milk, oil and the remaining sugar and whisk together well to give a smooth batter.

4 Pour the batter evenly over the apricots in the pan and transfer to the oven to bake for 30 minutes or until the cake is golden on top and feels firm when gently pressed in the middle.

5 Remove from the oven and allow to cool for about 5 minutes before inverting onto a serving plate (see tip below). Scatter with the pistachios and serve warm or at room temperature with softly whipped cream or ice cream.

Rachel's tips
* The easiest way to remove the cake from the pan is to place the serving plate face down on top of the cake and then, keeping the pan and plate firmly pressed together, carefully turn them over and lift the pan away.
* The Ginger and Syrup Ice Cream on page 241 is particularly good with this cake.

Eton mess

Eton mess is best assembled last minute, but it is quick and easy
so it won't take long, particularly if the ingredients are all prepared.
It is important to whip the cream quite softly as it will thicken a little
more as you fold in the other ingredients.

250ml (9fl oz) double
or regular cream
2 tsp caster sugar
(optional)
50g (2oz) meringue,
bought or homemade
(see page 237)
225g (8oz) strawberries,
hulled

1 In a mixing bowl, softly whip the cream with the sugar
(if using). Crumble over the meringue and fold in gently.

2 Mash the strawberries with a fork and stir into the cream and
meringue mixture (reserving some strawberries for decorating),
then spoon into a glass or bowl to serve.

Variations

Peach and raspberry: Whiz up 50g (2oz) stoned and chopped
and peeled fresh peaches (or drained tinned peaches) in a
blender or using a hand-held blender until smooth. Ripple
into the cream with 50g (2oz) mashed fresh or frozen (and
defrosted) raspberries.

Mixed berry: Stir in 50g (2oz) mashed or puréed frozen
(and defrosted) mixed berries.

Stewed apple and cinnamon: Mix a good pinch of cinnamon
with 75g (3oz) sweetened stewed apple purée (see the variations
in Fruit Crumbles, page 214) and ripple through the cream.

Meringues and cream

Making meringues is an excellent way of using up leftover egg whites. Use any broken-up meringues in Eton Mess (see page 234). Once made, the meringues keep in an airtight tin for up to two weeks or for a month if frozen.

4 egg whites
Pinch of salt
300g (11oz) caster sugar
½ tsp vanilla extract
250ml (9fl oz) double
    or regular cream
Mint sprigs, to decorate

1 Preheat the oven to 140°C (275°F), Gas mark 1. Line two baking sheets with parchment paper.

2 Place the egg whites and salt in a large, spotlessly clean bowl and whisk until soft peaks form. Gradually add the sugar, 1 tablespoon at a time, whisking between each addition, until it has all been added and the meringue is satiny and forms stiff peaks when the whisk is lifted from the mixture.

3 Using a large spatula or metal spoon, fold in the vanilla extract and your choice of flavouring from below (if using). Spoon the meringue mixture into a piping bag fitted with a 1.5cm (⅝in) nozzle and pipe a series of small mounds, each approximately 7cm (2¾in) wide, onto the prepared baking sheets. Alternatively, put dessertspoonful quantities on the baking sheets.

4 Bake in the oven for 30 minutes. Test a meringue by lifting and gently pressing the base – it should be crisp but give way with a bit of pressure. The meringues will crisp up more when cooling. For the best results, turn off the heat and allow to cool in the oven with the door slightly ajar. If possible, allow to cool completely in the oven.

5 When ready to serve, whip the cream into soft peaks and sandwich two meringues together with a little of the cream. Serve with a scattering of your favourite fruits – berries, slices of mango, peach or kiwi fruit or a spoonful of passion fruit – a fruit coulis, orange curd or chocolate or toffee sauce (see pages 336–7) and decorate.

Variations
Different flavours: Try different-flavoured meringues by adding one of these ingredients to the mixture instead of the vanilla extract: zest of 1 lemon, lime or orange; 50g (2oz) desiccated coconut; 2 tablespoons cocoa powder, sifted; 1 tablespoon coffee powder; or 50g (2oz) hazelnuts or almonds, finely chopped.
Different colours: Add a tiny dot of food colouring at the same time as the vanilla extract.

Strawberry and white chocolate tiramisu

SERVES 6—8 · VEGETARIAN

This no-cook dessert is great for entertaining as you can double and triple the quantities very easily (see tip about raw eggs). Strawberries combine very well with the creaminess of white chocolate. Serve in individual glasses so you can see the layers.

200g (7oz) caster sugar
400g (14oz) strawberries, hulled and halved
50ml (2fl oz) crème de cassis or crème de framboise
200g (7oz) white chocolate
4 eggs, separated
1 x 250g tub of mascarpone cheese
1 x 200g packet of boudoir biscuits (sponge fingers)

24 x 18cm (9½ x 7in) gratin dish with 6cm (2½in) sides, or 2.2 litre (3¾ pint) trifle bowl, or 8—10 glasses

1 First, make a syrup by placing half the sugar in a saucepan with 150ml (5fl oz) water. Bring slowly to the boil on a medium heat for 2 minutes. Turn off the heat, leave to slightly cool for 5 minutes and then add the strawberries and the crème de cassis or crème de framboise. Allow to cool completely.

2 Roughly chop 150g (5oz) of the white chocolate and melt in a small bowl over a saucepan of simmering water. Remove and allow to cool a little. Meanwhile, beat the egg yolks with the remaining sugar in a large bowl or in an electric food mixer until pale and thick. Beat in the mascarpone cheese until really smooth, then stir in the cooled melted white chocolate.

3 In a separate, spotlessly clean bowl, whisk the egg whites until they form stiff peaks. Fold them carefully into the egg and mascarpone mixture until well combined.

4 Now, strain the fruit mixture through a sieve set over a bowl to catch the syrup. Dip half the biscuits in the cooled syrup and use them to line the base of the serving glasses. Spread half the mascarpone mixture over the biscuits, followed by half the fruit. Cover the fruit with another layer of the biscuits dipped in the liquid, then spread over the remainder of the fruit, followed by the remaining mascarpone mixture.

5 Grate the remaining white chocolate over the top of each glass. Cover and chill in the fridge for a minimum of 6 hours, or ideally overnight, to allow the biscuits to absorb the juices and soften.

Rachel's tips
* You could alternatively make the tiramisu in a single glass bowl or pretty teacups, layering in the same way as the glasses above.
* Please note that this recipe contains raw eggs and so is not suitable for pregnant women, for elderly or sick people or the very young.

Ice cream

SERVES 4–6 · VEGETARIAN

This is a really good way of making ice cream without using an ice-cream machine. If covered well, it keeps for six weeks. Ice cream can be made with a huge range of different flavours, some quite unusual. Brown bread ice cream, made with caramelised breadcrumbs (see the variations below), may sound odd but it's a truly classic combination. It is important to let the ice cream freeze a little before adding your chosen flavouring, so that it doesn't sink to the bottom. (See tip about raw eggs.)

600ml (1 pint) double
  or regular cream
125g (4½oz) icing sugar,
  sifted
2 tsp vanilla extract
2 eggs, separated

1 Whip the cream, icing sugar and vanilla extract together to form soft peaks. Then, in a separate bowl, whisk the egg yolks until pale and creamy. Finally, beat the egg whites in another, spotlessly clean bowl until they form stiff peaks.

2 Stir the egg yolks into the cream mixture and then carefully fold in the egg whites. Transfer to a sealable container, place in the freezer and leave for 1½–2 hours or until just set.

3 Remove the ice cream from the freezer and add your choice of flavouring from below (if using), breaking the ice cream up and stirring in until well mixed. (For vanilla ice cream, there is no need to remove the ice cream from the freezer to add any further ingredients so simply leave in the freezer until frozen solid.) Return to the freezer for 12 hours or overnight until frozen solid. (There is no need to stir this ice cream further while it freezes.) Remove the ice cream from the freezer to soften up a little about 10 minutes before serving.

Variations

Strawberry and banana ripple: Place 700g (1½lb) hulled strawberries and 2 large bananas, peeled and roughly chopped, in a food processor and blend until they are smooth. Alternatively, mash with a fork and stir together. Pour the purée into a small saucepan on a medium heat and simmer for about 15 minutes or until thickened and reduced by half. Remove from the heat and leave to cool completely. Carefully ripple through the ice cream.
Forest fruit ripple ice cream: Place 300g (11oz) frozen (and defrosted) mixed berries, 3 tablespoons of caster sugar and the

juice of 1 lime in a food processor and blend to a smooth purée. Alternatively, purée using a hand-held blender. Pour into a small saucepan on a medium heat and simmer for 10–15 minutes until thick and jam-like. Leave to cool completely, then gently ripple through the ice cream.

Ginger and syrup ice cream: This is delicious with the Apricot and Cardamom Upside-down Cake (see page 233). Add 75g (3oz) finely chopped stem ginger to the ice cream with 100ml (3½fl oz) syrup from the stem ginger jar.

Brown bread ice cream: Preheat the oven to 200°C (400°F), Gas mark 6. Mix 175g (6oz) fresh brown bread breadcrumbs (grated by hand or in a food processor) with 110g (4oz) soft light brown sugar and spread out on a baking tray lined with parchment paper. Toast in the oven for 5–8 minutes until crisp and slightly browned. Remove and leave to cool completely before folding into the ice cream. Reserve a handful of the caramelised breadcrumbs to scatter over when serving, if you wish. You could also stir in 1 tablespoon of rum with the breadcrumbs, if you liked.

Peanut butter ice cream: Fold 250ml (9fl oz) peanut butter or homemade nut butter (see page 252) into the ice cream.

Honeycomb ice cream: Add 150g (5oz) roughly chopped pieces of honeycomb (see page 310).

Toffee, almonds and white chocolate ice cream: Ripple through 225ml (8fl oz) toffee sauce (see page 337) with 50g (2oz) toasted flaked almonds (see tip on page 50) and 75g (3oz) grated white chocolate.

Toffee and cashew nut brittle ice cream: Add 150g (5oz) roughly chopped cashew nut toffee brittle (see the variations on page 314).

Rachel's tips

* Serve any of the ice creams with the toffee or chocolate sauce (see page 337), orange curd (see page 336), or use them to make a Banana Split (see page 216).
* This recipe contains raw eggs and so is not recommended for pregnant women, for elderly or sick people or the very young.

Joshua's ice cream extravaganza

SERVES 6 · VEGETARIAN

Needless to say, this is not something to give your little ones
every day, but just once every so often. Joshua, our eldest child,
makes this for all of us — simple but certainly delicious!

1 x 1 litre tub of raspberry
   ripple or vanilla ice
   cream (see page 240 for
   homemade ice cream)
2 x 37g tubes of Smarties
1 x 37g bag of Maltesers
4 x 58g Mars bars, roughly
   chopped
2 x 40g Crunchie bars
18 large or 60 mini
   marshmallows

1 Cut the ice cream into chunks and place in a large bowl.
Leave to soften a little until easily stirred. Mix in the Smarties
and Maltesers and then divide between six small bowls or
sundae glasses. Level the tops a little and freeze for 20–30
minutes or until firm.

2 Meanwhile, melt the Mars bars in a heatproof bowl over
a pan of simmering water. Stir to blend and then remove
the bowl from the heat. Smash the Crunchie bars lightly
with a rolling pin while still in their wrappers.

3 Remove the ice-cream bowls from the freezer and scatter
the marshmallows over each bowl or sundae glass. Spoon the
melted Mars bar sauce on top and scatter with the crushed
Crunchie bars. Serve at once.

Fluffy lemon pudding

SERVES 6 · VEGETARIAN

When cooked, this delectable pudding has a layer of lemon sponge sitting on top of a pool of hot lemon curd. This has been made at Ballymaloe for years as it is a favourite of so many people.

50g (2oz) butter, softened
250g (9oz) caster sugar
3 eggs, separated
75g (3oz) plain flour
300ml (½ pint) milk
Finely grated zest and juice of 2 lemons
Icing sugar, for dusting

1.2 litre (2 pint) oval pie dish (18 x 23cm/7 x 9in) with 5cm (2in) sides

1 Preheat the oven to 180°C (350°F), Gas mark 4.

2 Beat the butter in a large bowl or in an electric food mixer until it is really soft and creamy. Add the sugar and beat with the butter until pale and fluffy. Add the egg yolks one at a time to the mixture, beating each one in before adding the next. Sift in the flour and add the milk and lemon zest and juice, and mix well together.

3 Whisk the egg whites in a large, spotlessly clean bowl until they form stiff peaks. Gently fold the egg whites into the cake mixture until well mixed. Pour the mixture into the pie dish and bake for 30–40 minutes or until golden and set on top, but not set underneath. Remove and allow to cool slightly before dredging with icing sugar and serving.

Variation

Individual puddings: Use six small–medium ramekins or ovenproof teacups arranged on a baking sheet and bake for 15–20 minutes or until just set.

Dark chocolate layered semifreddo

SERVES 6—8 · VEGETARIAN

In cooking, semifreddo (literally 'half cold') refers to certain kinds of chilled or partly frozen desserts. This particular dish is ideal for a dinner party or to serve to unexpected guests as you can prepare it in advance and take it out of the freezer shortly before serving. Simply cut into slices and serve. Feel free to add other ingredients with or in place of the dark chocolate, such as toffee brittle (see page 314) or liqueur-soaked raisins. It is fabulous served with chocolate sauce.

3 eggs, separated
150g (5oz) caster sugar
500ml (18fl oz) double
 or regular cream
200g (7oz) dark chocolate,
 finely chopped
175ml (6fl oz) dark
 chocolate sauce
 (see page 337),
 to serve

*900g (2 lb) loaf tin
(24 x 11cm/ 9½ x 4½in)
with 8cm (3in) sides*

1 Line the base of the loaf tin with parchment paper or a double layer of cling film, leaving the excess hanging out over the edges.

2 Whisk the egg yolks and sugar in a large bowl until pale and fluffy. In a second bowl, whip the cream until it forms soft peaks. Finally, in another (spotlessly clean) bowl, whisk the egg whites (with a clean whisk) until they form firm peaks. Gently fold the whipped cream into the egg yolk mixture and then carefully fold in the egg whites.

3 Sprinkle a third of the chopped chocolate evenly into the base of the prepared tin. Pour half the semifreddo mixture over the chocolate, followed by the next third of the chocolate. Finally, pour over the remaining semifreddo and top with the remaining chocolate. Cover with the excess hanging parchment or cling film and freeze for at least 6 hours until solid.

4 Once it is set, carefully remove the semifreddo from the tin, turning it upside down onto a plate, and remove the parchment or cling film. Cut into slices, using a warm knife if necessary and serve with a drizzle of chocolate sauce.

Variations
Semifreddo with nuts: Substitute some of the weight of chocolate for roughly chopped nuts, such as pecans, almonds or hazelnuts, or even candied peel.
Citrus semifreddo: Try adding the finely grated zest of 1 large orange to the semifreddo, adding it when the whipped cream is being folded into the egg yolk mixture.
White chocolate semifreddo: Substitute the 200g (7oz) dark chocolate with a good-quality white chocolate and assemble the semifreddo in the same way. Serve with toffee sauce (see page 337).

Fruity frangipane tart

This classic French tart has a moist almond sponge inside a pastry case. Experiment with different fruits, depending on the season or what is available. You can replace the fruit with nuts, such as 50g (2oz) nibbed or flaked almonds or pine nuts.

110g (4oz) butter, plus extra for greasing
350g (12oz) shortcrust pastry (see page 333)
110g (4oz) caster sugar
1 egg, beaten
1 egg yolk
110g (4oz) ground almonds
25g (1oz) plain flour
2 tbsp apricot jam, for glazing

23cm (9in) diameter, fluted, loose-bottomed tart tin with 2cm (¾in) sides

1 Preheat the oven to 180°C (350°F), Gas mark 4. Lightly grease the tart tin.

2 Prepare the pastry, line the tart tin and bake 'blind' following the instructions on page 333.

3 In the meantime, make the frangipane. Cream the softened butter in a bowl or in an electric food mixer until very soft. Add the sugar and continue beating until pale and fluffy. Add the egg and yolk, continuing to beat all the time. Tip in the ground almonds and flour, stirring well to combine.

4 Spoon the frangipane into the baked pastry case and spread evenly over the base. Arrange your chosen fruit on top (selecting from the toppings below). Either scatter the berries over evenly, arrange the apple or pear slices in an overlapping fan, or simply nestle the peaches, apricots, plums or nectarines into the frangipane, cut side up or down. Bake in the oven for 35—45 minutes or until the tart is golden in colour and feels set when you gently press the top.

5 Meanwhile, prepare the glaze. Warm the jam with 2 teaspoons of water in a small pan on a low heat. Pass the mixture through a fine sieve to give a smooth texture. Brush the glaze over the top of the tart as soon as it is removed from the oven. Serve warm or at room temperature with some softly whipped cream.

Fruit toppings
* 225g (8oz) berries, one type or mixed, such as blueberries, blackberries, strawberries or raspberries
* 3 eating apples, such as Gala, Granny Smith or Braeburn, or 2 large pears, peeled, cored, quartered and thinly sliced
* 600g (1lb 5oz) peaches, apricots, plums or nectarines, halved and stones removed

Snacks, treats and sweets

Crudités and dips

Crudités, the French word for raw vegetables served as an appetiser or hors d'oeuvre, are one of my favourite things to nibble on, especially when there is a tasty dip to indulge in. My children love them too, particularly if cut into bite-sized pieces that they can pick up easily. I find if I leave a plate of these lying around where they're playing or watching television, they eat them without really noticing. As well as the dips given here, other favourites are guacamole or tzatziki (see pages 139 and 72). You could also try baba ghanouj, hummus or spinach pesto (see pages 72, 73 and 134), or Zac's favourite, Garlic and Herb Dip (see the mayonnaise variations on page 330).

Crudités

MAKES AS MANY AS YOU LIKE
VEGETARIAN

Use a selection of vegetables that are in season.

Vegetable choices:
Tomatoes, whole if small or halved
    or quartered if large
Cauliflower, broken into florets
French beans, mangetout or sugar snap peas
Cucumber, cut into sticks
Carrots, peeled and cut into sticks
Celery, trimmed and cut into sticks
Spring onions, trimmed and cut in half
Chicory, broken into leaves
Red, green or yellow peppers,
    deseeded and cut into strips
Radishes

Prepare the vegetables and arrange them on individual plates or one big platter with small bowls of one or more dips alongside (see right and overleaf).

White bean dip

MAKES ABOUT 300G (11OZ)
VEGETARIAN

This is delicious not only as a dip but also spread on bruschetta or a piece of crispbread, or warmed up and served with a steak or lamb chops. It can be stored in the fridge for up to two days.

1 x 400g tin cannellini or butter beans,
    drained, or 125g (4½oz) dried beans,
    soaked and cooked (see page 329)
2 cloves of garlic, peeled and crushed
Juice of ½ lemon
2 tsp Dijon mustard
4 tsp extra-virgin olive oil
Salt and freshly ground black pepper

1 Place the beans in a food processor with the garlic, lemon juice and mustard and whiz until coarsely chopped. Alternatively, use a hand-held blender or mash the cooked beans with a fork before stirring in the other ingredients. Add the olive oil and blend for a few seconds more.

2 Season to taste with salt and pepper and a little more lemon juice, if you like. Pour into a serving dish to use straight away or place in the fridge to use later.

(dips continued overleaf)

Homemade nut butter

MAKES ABOUT 350G (12OZ)
VEGETARIAN

This spread is so versatile: my boys love it on a ham sandwich but it is also lovely rippled through ice cream (see the variations on page 241), great on toast and also perfect as a dip for crudités. Don't worry if it starts to look a little oily: excess oil will rise to the surface once it settles in the jar but this helps to preserve the nut butter. It should keep in your cupboard for about six weeks.

150g (5oz) salted peanuts
50g (2oz) whole hazelnuts
50g (2oz) whole almonds
100ml (3½fl oz) hazelnut or groundnut oil
1–2 tsp brown sugar (optional)

1 First check the nuts, discarding any that look dried out or darker in colour as these will have gone off, then place in a food processor with the hazelnut or groundnut oil and 1 teaspoon of brown sugar (if using).

2 Blend to a fairly smooth paste, adding the second teaspoon of brown sugar to taste, if necessary. Place in a serving bowl to use as a dip or pour into a large sterilised jar with a tight-fitting lid (see tip on page 336) if saving for later use.

Black olive tapenade

MAKES 150ML (5FL OZ)

Tapenade is great to have in your fridge at all times as it can be used as a dip or on toast, crostini or bruschetta. You can drizzle it over roasted vegetables and it is great with the Steak and Frites (see page 200–1) or with lamb chops. Thin out with olive oil to make a salad dressing. Once made, it will keep for a few months in the fridge, stored in an airtight container or jar.

110g (4oz) pitted black olives
50g (2oz) tinned anchovy fillets
1 tbsp capers, rinsed
1 tsp Dijon mustard
1 tsp lemon juice
4 tbsp extra-virgin olive oil
1 tbsp finely chopped parsley
Freshly ground black pepper

1 Place the olives, anchovy fillets, capers, mustard and lemon juice in a food processor and season with pepper. Blend for about 30 seconds until roughly chopped.

2 Add the olive oil and blend again until a little smoother. Stir in the parsley, reserving some for a garnish. Place in a bowl to use straight away or in an airtight container or sterilised jar (see tip on page 336) and place in the fridge for later use.

Potato cakes

SERVES 4–8 · VEGETARIAN (WITH NON-VEGETARIAN VARIATIONS)

Potato cakes are great as a way of using leftover cooked potato.
They make a quick and easy snack on their own, with a salad and some
relish or as part of a breakfast, brunch or supper dish.

1.1kg (2lb 6oz)
    floury potatoes
75g (3oz) butter, melted
4 tbsp plain flour
1 tbsp finely chopped
    parsley (optional)
1 tbsp single or regular
    cream
Salt and freshly ground
    black pepper
1 tbsp olive oil

1 Cook the potatoes as per the recipe for mashed potato (see page 116) and then peel and mash until really smooth (but without adding the butter and milk included in the mash recipe). Stir in 50g (2oz) of the butter, half the flour, the parsley and the cream and season with salt and pepper. Shape the mixture into eight patty shapes (about 8cm/3in wide and 2cm/¾in thick). You can place the potato cakes in the fridge at this stage for up to 24 hours or freeze them to use later. Dust with the remaining flour to lightly coat.

2 Add the olive oil and remaining butter to a large non-stick frying pan on a low–medium heat and very gently fry the potato cakes for about 5 minutes on each side until golden and warmed through, adding a little more oil or butter to the pan during cooking if necessary. Serve immediately with a crisp salad and some relish.

Variations
Stir one of the following ingredients into the potato mixture before shaping:
Cheesy potato cakes: 50g (2oz) Cheddar cheese, grated
Garlic potato cakes: 1–2 cloves of garlic, peeled and crushed
Spring onion potato cakes: 2 spring onions, trimmed and very finely chopped
Bacon or chorizo potato cakes: 50g (2oz) sliced crisp cooked bacon or chorizo

Rachel's tip
As an alternative, try serving each potato cake topped with 2–3 pieces of crispy bacon and a fried egg, or try wilted spinach and poached egg.

Crunchy cheesy melts

MAKES ABOUT 30 · VEGETARIAN

I defy anyone to not like these! You bite into the crunchy coating and
the cheesy centre just melts and oozes into your mouth. This recipe uses
a block of mozzarella cheese rather than a ball. It is firmer than a ball
and melts really well. Try serving with a tomato relish.

450ml (16fl oz) milk
225g (8oz) roux
   (see page 327)
2 egg yolks
1 x 125g block of
   mozzarella cheese,
   grated
100g (3½oz) Gruyère
   cheese, grated
1 heaped tbsp
   snipped chives
100g (3½oz) plain flour
Salt and freshly ground
   black pepper
1 egg
100g (3½oz) very fine
   and dry, toasted
   breadcrumbs
   (see tip opposite)
Sunflower oil, for
   deep-frying

1 Pour the milk into a saucepan, bring to the boil and then
reduce to a simmer. Whisk in the roux a little at a time until
it is well blended and allow the mixture to simmer and thicken
to a smooth white sauce. Remove from the heat and allow to
cool a little and then stir in the egg yolks, the two cheeses and
the chives and allow to cool completely.

2 To prepare the coating, place the flour on a plate or in a
bowl and season with salt and pepper. Beat the egg in a separate
bowl and place the breadcrumbs on another plate or in a bowl.
The cooled sauce will be putty-like, so mould into about 30
sausage shapes or round balls. Toss each one in the flour, then
in the egg and then roll in the toasted breadcrumbs to coat.
The cheese balls can be prepared to this stage and stored in
the fridge for 2–3 days for later use (bringing back up to room
temperature before deep-frying to prevent them splitting).

3 Heat a deep-fat fryer filled with sunflower oil to 170°C
(325°F). (If the oil is any hotter, the filling tends to leak out.)
The cheese balls can also be shallow-fried: pour the oil into
a deep, medium saucepan to a depth of 2cm (¾in) and heat
to the same temperature, checking with a sugar thermometer
(or see tip opposite).

4 When the oil is at the right temperature, deep-fry the cheese
balls in batches for about 8 minutes, turning round a few times
in the oil until rich golden in colour. Drain on kitchen paper
and serve immediately.

Variation
Crunchy cheese and ham melts: Add 100g (3½oz) very finely
chopped cooked ham to the cheese sauce when adding the cheeses.

Rachel's tips

* Once cooked, the cheese balls will keep uncovered in a warm oven for up to 30 minutes.

* To make really fine, dry and crispy crumbs, use stale, dry white bread. Remove the crusts and toast very lightly, then blend in a food processor to fine crumbs and push through a sieve.

* To check if the oil is hot enough, drop in a cube of bread. If it comes back up to the top relatively quickly, the oil is the perfect temperature for deep-frying. If it immediately burns, the oil is too hot.

Tuna melt

SERVES 4

The ultimate sandwich when you're feeling hungry, this makes good use of one of those store-cupboard essentials — the tin of tuna.

1 x 140g tin of tuna, drained
50ml (2fl oz) mayonnaise
1 tsp Dijon mustard
1 heaped tbsp finely chopped red or spring onion
2 tsp finely chopped tarragon or parsley
Good squeeze of lemon juice
Salt and freshly ground black pepper
50g (2oz) butter, softened
8 thick slices of bloomer bread
1 large tomato, cut into 8 thin slices (optional)
75g (3oz) Cheddar cheese, grated

1 Tip the tuna into a bowl and break up a little. Stir in the mayonnaise, mustard, red or spring onion, tarragon or parsley and the lemon juice and season to taste with salt and pepper.

2 Spread half the butter onto four of the slices of bread. Divide the tuna mix over the top and spread evenly. Arrange the tomato slices on top (if using) and scatter over the cheese. Sandwich with the remaining slices of bread and then spread on the remaining butter.

3 Put a griddle or frying pan on a medium heat. Turn the sandwich over, buttered side down, onto the heated pan and gently griddle or fry for 2–3 minutes on each side, turning carefully, until golden and the cheese has melted. If your pan is large enough, you may be able to cook two sandwiches at a time; otherwise, cook them one by one. Cut in half and serve immediately.

Toasted sandwiches

EACH RECIPE SERVES 1

A toasted-sandwich maker is the ideal way of making toasted sandwiches. If you don't have one, then simply toast one side of each slice of bread under the grill and place the slices together with the toasted sides out when assembling the sandwich. Then bake in the oven, preheated to 180°C (350°F), Gas mark 4, for 10–15 minutes to warm through (and to melt the cheese, if using). Ring the changes with different kinds of bread and have fun creating your own fillings. The bread in the recipes below and overleaf has been left to your own choice.

Toasted special

SERVES 1

1 tsp Dijon mustard
½ tsp thyme leaves
2 slices of bread (untoasted, for going in a toasted-sandwich maker, or toasted on one side)
75g (3oz) sliced ham
1 small tomato, sliced
2 thin slices from a small red onion, separated into rings
25g (1oz) Cheddar or Gruyère cheese, sliced

Mix the mustard and thyme leaves together in a small bowl and spread on one side of each slice of bread. Arrange the ham, tomato, onion and cheese on the mustard side of one slice of bread and place the other on top, mustard side down. Toast in the sandwich maker or bake in the oven (see above).

Beef and horseradish toasted sandwich

SERVES 1

1 tbsp mayonnaise
1 tsp finely grated fresh horseradish
2 tsp finely chopped tarragon
Salt and freshly ground black pepper
2 slices of bread (untoasted, for going in a toasted-sandwich maker, or toasted on one side)
50g (2oz) thinly sliced cooked beef
Small handful of spinach leaves

Mix the mayonnaise, horseradish and tarragon together in a small bowl and season with salt and pepper. Spread the mixture on each slice of bread. Arrange the beef slices on one slice of bread, pile the spinach leaves on top and then sandwich together with the other slice of bread, mayonnaise side down. Toast in the sandwich maker or bake in the oven (see above).

(toasted sandwiches continued overleaf)

Ham and cheese toasted sandwich

SERVES 1

50g (2oz) cooked ham, finely chopped
25g (1oz) Gruyère cheese (or other
   favourite cheese), coarsely grated
1 egg yolk
Salt and freshly ground black pepper
2 slices of bread (untoasted, for going
   in a toasted-sandwich maker,
   or toasted on one side)

Mix the ham, cheese and egg yolk together in
a small bowl and season with salt and pepper.
Spread on one slice of bread and top with the
other slice, then toast in the sandwich maker
or bake in the oven (see page 256). You can
also serve this as an open sandwich. Don't
top with a second slice of bread and either
grill or bake in the oven to melt the cheese.

Bacon, mushroom and egg butty

SERVES 1

2–3 rashers of back bacon, cooked
75g (3oz) mushrooms, sliced and sautéed
1 egg, fried to your liking
2 slices of bread, toasted
1 tbsp tomato relish (optional)

Arrange the bacon, mushrooms and egg
on one slice of toasted bread and drizzle
over your choice of sauce or relish (if using).
Top with the other slice of toast and serve.

Quesadillas

Quesadillas, Mexican cheese sandwiches made with tortillas instead of bread, are the perfect fast food. Some suggestions for fillings have been given below, but the possibilities are endless — choose whatever takes your fancy.

4 x 18cm (7in) flour
or corn tortillas
Sea salt and freshly ground
black pepper

1 Lay out two of the tortillas and divide the filling ingredients between them (see below), spreading them evenly to within 2cm (¾in) of the edges. Season with salt and pepper and top each tortilla with one of the remaining tortillas.

2 Select a frying pan that is wide enough to hold one quesadilla and place it on a low—medium heat. Fry the first quesadilla in the dry pan for 1—2 minutes on each side or until it is crisp and golden all over and the cheese has melted. Slide the quesadilla out of the pan onto a chopping board and repeat with the second tortilla. Cut into wedges to serve.

Fillings

Cheese, olive and basil: Mix 1 ball of grated buffalo mozzarella with 50g (2oz) grated Cheddar cheese, 25g (1oz) roughly chopped black olives (optional) and 4 shredded basil leaves. Shred a couple of extra basil leaves to sprinkle over the quesadillas when they are cooked.

Chorizo, roasted pepper and cheese: Mix together 25g (1oz) thinly sliced cooked chorizo slices, cut into thin strips, with 50g (2oz) roasted red or yellow peppers, cut or torn into thin strips, and 50g (2oz) grated Cheddar cheese.

Parma ham, sun-blushed tomatoes, mozzarella and rocket: Mix 25g (1oz) sliced Parma ham, torn into strips and the fat removed, 25g (1oz) sun-blushed tomatoes, halved if large, 1 ball of drained and sliced buffalo mozzarella and 15g (½oz) rocket leaves, with the stalks removed.

Blue cheese, onion, jam and rosemary: Mix 50g (2oz) crumbled blue cheese with 25g (1oz) cream cheese (spooned on in small blobs), 2 tablespoons of onion jam (see page 336) and ¼ teaspoon very finely chopped rosemary leaves.

Zac's oven-ready rollies

MAKES ABOUT 6 ROLLIES · VEGETARIAN
(WITH NON-VEGETARIAN VARIATIONS)

These rolled pizzas are a great ready-made snack to have in the freezer for when the children come home from school and need feeding instantly. They take a bit of time to prepare, but it's the sort of thing that kids love helping with, particularly when it comes to assembling and rolling. The convenience of being able to cook them straight from the freezer will be worth the effort beforehand. Use any toppings you like; the ideas here are just suggestions. Even leave as plain cheese and tomato, if you like.

350g (12oz) strong
   white flour
1 tsp salt
2 tsp caster sugar
50g (2oz) butter
1 x 7g sachet fast-
   acting yeast
2 tbsp olive oil, plus
   extra for brushing
175–200ml (6–7fl oz)
   lukewarm water
Plain flour, fine
   semolina or fine
   polenta, for dusting
450g (1lb) mozzarella,
   grated, or 225g (8oz)
   mozzarella and 225g
   (8oz) Gruyère
   cheese, grated

For the tomato sauce
450g (1lb) ripe
   tomatoes, halved
3 cloves of garlic, peeled
   and kept whole
5 tbsp olive oil
3 tbsp balsamic vinegar
Good pinch of caster sugar
Salt and freshly ground
   black pepper

1 Preheat the oven to 230°C (450°F), Gas mark 8.

2 Follow the method on page 149 for preparing the pizza dough and making the tomato sauce.

3 Now assemble the rollies. Place a baking sheet in the oven to heat up (if cooking straight away). Then, on a floured work surface, roll each dough ball out to a disc about 25cm (10in) in diameter. Spread about 2 tablespoons of the tomato sauce on just over half of the disc, allowing for a border of about 4cm (1½in) at the edge. (This is to help prevent the toppings from oozing out when rolling up.) Next, scatter the cheese over the sauce, followed by your choice of additional topping (if using – see opposite). Brush the dough with water and carefully roll the disc up like a Swiss roll, starting from the sauce-covered side and rolling towards the plain side. Squeeze the ends to seal closed.

4 At this stage the now oven-ready rollies can be wrapped individually and frozen or baked straight away. Transfer them onto the warmed baking sheet and bake for 10–12 minutes. When cooking from frozen allow a further 3–5 minutes. Remove from the oven and brush with a little olive oil to glaze, if wished. Leave to cool for a couple of minutes before serving. Either slice into pieces or serve whole, wrapped in a napkin, to eat on the run.

Toppings

Try adding one of the following to the tomato and cheese base:

* A sprinkling of diced cooked ham
* Thinly sliced chorizo, arranged on top, plus a scattering of thinly sliced red onion
* A little goat's cheese, crumbled over, and some slivers of roasted red or yellow pepper
* A few strips of Parma ham, arranged on top, followed by a drizzle of pesto
* A sprinkling of shredded basil and some dried chilli flakes

Croque - monsieur

The ultimate toasted cheese sandwich, this is staple fare in French cafés and is one of the first things I like to eat when I'm France. After one mouthful of it eaten at home, I am transported to a Parisian boulevard.

50g (2oz) Gruyère cheese, finely grated
150ml (5fl oz) white sauce (see page 327)
½ tsp Dijon mustard
1 tsp finely chopped chives
Tiny pinch of freshly ground nutmeg
Salt and freshly ground black pepper
4 slices of white bread
2 slices of cooked ham

1 Add 2 tablespoons of the grated cheese to the white sauce in a saucepan on a medium heat, along with the mustard, chives and nutmeg. Stir together and season with salt and pepper.

2 Lay out the slices of bread and divide the sauce equally between them, spreading to cover evenly. Lay a piece of ham on two of the bread slices and scatter the remaining cheese over all four. The slices with ham are the bottom pieces, so lift the other slices on top, sauce side up. These can be prepared up to a few hours in advance and then chilled in the fridge until needed.

3 When you are ready to eat, preheat the oven to 170°C (325°F), Gas mark 3.

4 Place the croque-monsieurs on a baking tray and bake in the oven for 10–15 minutes or until the cheese topping is golden and bubbling.

Variation
Croque-madame: To make to make a croque-madame, top each toasted croque-monsieur with a hot fried egg before serving.

Healthy root vegetable crisps

SERVES 4 · VEGETARIAN

These are fantastic! They take a bit of time to make, but the end result is so tasty and the natural sugar in the vegetables means that they brown and crisp up very nicely in the oven. You could just cook one type of vegetable or a selection. I call these 'healthy' crisps because they use relatively little oil compared to the commercial type.

1 large parsnip, carrot,
   potato, sweet potato,
   celeriac and beetroot
Extra-virgin olive oil
Sea salt and freshly ground
   black pepper

1 Preheat the oven to 220°C (425°F), Gas mark 7.

2 Using a potato peeler or mandolin, slice the vegetables into very thin, ribbon-like strips. Dry the slices well on kitchen paper (washing the potato slices, if using, in water first to remove the excess starch), then place in a large bowl and drizzle with the olive oil, tossing to coat.

3 Lay the vegetable slices out flat in a single layer on a baking sheet, season with salt and pepper and cook in the oven for 4–7 minutes until golden. Take out of the oven and carefully remove from the baking sheet with a fish slice or spatula. Place on kitchen paper before putting in shallow bowls to serve.

Rachel's tips
* I would recommend keeping any beetroot slices separate once sliced so they don't stain the other vegetables. Watch your hands too and wear rubber gloves when handling the beetroot!
* Although it's not essential to do this, I usually place each vegetable on a separate sheet as they may cook at slightly different speeds.

Healthy eating habits

We are what we eat. When we eat well, we feel better, with increased energy levels and fewer mood swings. I notice it in myself and in my children. It affects us all. Creating healthy eating habits in children is an ongoing process, but you can start as soon as your baby is ready for solids. Stick to simple fruit and vegetable purées as soon as she is ready and taking an interest in food (see pages 318–9). As your children get older, inevitably they will be exposed to all kinds of food outside your own home. I like to keep things simple by providing only healthy choices, except for special treats, and these tend to be homemade. Furthermore, if I have sweets and crisps in the house, not only will my children eat them, but I will too. I also avoid arguing about it with my children because rubbishy, processed foods are just not on the menu.

Keeping food fun

Healthy eating doesn't mean you should strip out all the flavour and enjoyment of food. Keeping food fun is so important in creating good lifelong habits as well as special memories. The odd cookie or slice of cake is fine; indeed this chapter is full of recipes for special treats. But they should be regarded precisely as that — something to have occasionally and not every day. There are lots of healthy snacks to choose from too in these pages. Instead of a bag of crisps as your TV snack, why not cut up some crudités to eat with dips (see pages 250–2)? Or if you do serve crisps, why not go for the healthier homemade option, made with a variety of root vegetables (see page 263)?

Involving your children

Getting children involved in preparing food can also really help engage their interest. Lots of parents love to bake with their children. You could try one of the recipes for biscuits or cakes in this section or, for a healthier option, go for Zac's Oven-ready Rollies (see page 260), a delicious and fun variation on pizza.

A Saturday morning or a rainy afternoon can allow for a bit more time to really relax and enjoy making food. Smoothies (see page 42) are a fantastic way to get fruit into your children, and mine love to help make them. Or, if we go out picking blackberries down the road, the children will eat loads of them straight from the bush.

If you have a garden or even just a window box for herbs, you can give your children a little education about where food comes from. Just having them help cut the parsley takes only five minutes. Even young children love washing apples, mixing flour or mashing potatoes. However you involve your children in the kitchen, make sure you do it only when you have the time and can enjoy it with them. There's no point in being stressed, especially as you may need a little extra cleaning-up time when you are finished.

Keep experimenting

Contrary to the popular notion that children prefer bland-tasting food, I find that they often love strong flavours. Pesto can be a big hit — try it on toast, pasta or broccoli. Garlic also adds loads of flavour and is so good for them. Olives can go down well, too — why not try the Black Olive Tapenade on page 252? It's delicious on toast or with roasted vegetables. If you always add herbs or spices to your food, children will get used to different flavours.

Of course, children, just like grown-ups, do have different tastes — for instance, Joshua loves bananas whereas Lucca is not so keen on them. Listen to your children but also keep experimenting with tastes and textures. Use little bowls or eggcups with carrots in one and a bit of mayonnaise for dipping in another. Cut up vegetables in a variety of shapes to make fun designs — flowers, stars, trains, animals, whatever your children fancy. (See the Crudités and Dips on pages 250–2 for some more ideas.)

How much food to give

Remember that as long as you are always providing healthy options for meals and snacks, you never need to worry about how much your children eat (within reason). With young children, you want to look at what they eat over a few days rather than at any one meal. Some days they may be absolutely starving; other days not at all. This is quite normal and as long as their intake over the period is reasonably balanced, you needn't worry. You can also help a child's eating habits by not making a fuss. My mum always did this with my sister and me and taught me to do it with my children.

I also put small amounts on their plates; they can always have more. But they're thrilled with themselves when they finish it and there is no unnecessary waste. Mealtimes should not be stressful. After all, it's an important time when the family sits together. It should be all about enjoyment of the food and each other's company.

Salmon fish fingers with a tomato and basil dip

SERVES 4

Try to buy the best-quality salmon you can afford. If it is farmed salmon, then go for organic if possible. You can easily substitute the salmon with another chunky fish such as cod, haddock or whiting. If eating the fish fingers as a meal rather than as a snack, serve with peas, Pea Purée (see page 122), boiled potatoes or chips, either chunky or as frites (see pages 176 and 200–1).

500g (1lb 2oz) centre-cut skinless salmon fillet
3 tbsp plain flour
2 eggs
110g (4oz) fresh white breadcrumbs
Salt and freshly ground black pepper
25g (1oz) butter (if shallow-frying)
2 tbsp olive oil
Lemon wedges, to serve

For the tomato and basil dip
275g (10oz) tomatoes, roughly chopped
110ml (4fl oz) crème fraîche
1 tbsp finely shredded basil

1 Preheat the oven (if using – see below) to 220°C (425°F), Gas mark 7.

2 Cut the piece of salmon in half across the width and then cut each half into six equal-sized fingers down the length. Sift the flour onto a plate or into a wide bowl, beat the eggs in another bowl and place the breadcrumbs in a third. Season each with salt and pepper. First dust the salmon fingers in the flour, then dip them in the beaten egg and finally in the breadcrumbs, to evenly coat. (The fish fingers can be prepared in advance to this stage and then stored in the fridge for up to 24 hours or freezer for up to 3 months.)

3 To shallow-fry, melt the butter with the olive oil in a large frying pan on a medium–high heat and fry the fish fingers for 3–4 minutes each side or until crisp, golden and cooked through. Drain well on kitchen paper.

4 Alternatively, drizzle the olive oil on a large baking sheet and arrange the fish fingers on the oiled sheet. Bake in the oven for 8–10 minutes, turning halfway through cooking, until crisp, golden and cooked through.

5 Meanwhile, prepare the tomato dip. Blitz the chopped tomato in a blender or using a hand-held blender until smooth. Push through a fine sieve into a small saucepan and simmer on a low heat for 4–5 minutes or until reduced and thickened. Remove and leave to cool completely before stirring into the crème fraîche with the basil and a little salt and pepper.

6 Serve the salmon fish fingers with lemon wedges for people to squeeze over together with a bowl of the tomato and basil crème fraîche to dip into.

Variations

Flavoured coatings: For a different flavour every time, try adding one of the following to the breadcrumbs before coating the fish fingers:

* 1 tsp finely grated lemon zest
* 2 tbsp finely grated Parmesan cheese
* 1 tbsp finely chopped herbs, such as parsley, chives or dill
* ½ tsp paprika, ground cumin or ground coriander

Golden chicken goujons with a homemade mayonnaise dip

SERVES 2—4

These goujons make very satisfying finger food. They are also delicious served for supper with Pea Purée (see page 122). The goujons are best eaten shortly after cooking. If keeping them warm, don't cover them up as they will go soggy. I sometimes replace the chicken with pieces of fish (any type of flat fish will work well).

Sunflower oil, for deep-frying
2 large or 3 medium skinless boneless chicken breasts (about 450g/1lb total weight)
300ml (½ pint) milk
4 tbsp plain flour
2 tbsp sesame seeds
Salt and freshly ground black pepper
100ml (3½fl oz) flavoured mayonnaise (see page 330)

1 Heat a deep-fat fryer filled with sunflower oil to 170°C (325°F). Alternatively, pour the oil into a large saucepan to a depth of 2cm (¾in) and bring to the same temperature on the hob (checking with a sugar thermometer or see tip on page 255).

2 Cut the chicken into strips each about the size of a big finger, to give goujon shapes. Pour the milk into a small bowl. Mix the flour in another bowl with the sesame seeds (or see the variations below) and season well with salt and pepper.

3 Working in batches to ensure they don't stick together, dip the chicken pieces in the milk and then in the flour to coat. Shake off any excess flour and deep-fry for 4—5 minutes or until crisp, golden and cooked through. Drain well on kitchen paper.

4 Serve the goujons with your choice of flavoured mayonnaise on the side for dipping into.

Variations
Different coatings: Substitute the sesame seeds with one of the following:
* 1 tsp medium-hot curry powder
* 1 tsp smoked paprika
* 1 tbsp finely chopped herbs, such as parsley, chives or thyme

Rachel's tip
When coating the chicken, use one hand for wet (the milk) and the other for dry (the flour) so that you don't get in a mess coating your own fingers!

Thai sticky chicken

SERVES 4—6

These sticky chicken pieces are a real treat — I love the blend of sweet,
sour and salty flavours that is characteristic of Thai cuisine.

1.3kg (3lb) chicken
drumsticks and thighs
2 red chillies, deseeded
and chopped
2.5cm (1in) piece of root
ginger, peeled and
roughly chopped
5 cloves of garlic, peeled
and roughly chopped
1 stick of lemongrass,
outer skin discarded,
roughly chopped
15g (½oz) coriander
(stalks and leaves),
roughly torn, plus a
few extra leaves to serve
2 tbsp soft light or dark
brown sugar
Juice of 2 limes (about
100ml/3½fl oz)
3 tbsp fish sauce (nam pla)

1 Using a sharp knife, cut slashes in the chicken drumsticks
and thighs and place them in a wide bowl or large food bag.
Place the remaining ingredients in a food processor and blend
to a rough paste. Alternatively, pound the chillies, ginger,
garlic, lemongrass and coriander using a pestle and mortar and
then stir in the sugar, lime juice and fish sauce and pour over
the chicken, tossing to coat. Cover the bowl with cling film or
seal the bag and leave to marinate in the fridge for a few hours,
or overnight if possible, tossing occasionally.

2 Preheat the oven to 220°C (425°F), Gas mark 7.

3 Remove the chicken from the fridge about 30—40 minutes
before cooking to bring to room temperature. Remove the
chicken pieces from the marinade (reserving the marinade)
and arrange in a single layer in a roasting tin. Roast in the
oven for 35—40 minutes or until the meat is coming away
from the bone.

4 Arrange the chicken pieces on a warm serving platter and
place the roasting tin on a medium heat on the hob. Pour in
the reserved marinade and bring to the boil. Reduce the heat
and simmer for a few minutes, stirring with a wooden spoon
and scraping the sticky bits from the bottom, until thickened
and sticky. Pour the sauce over the chicken, scatter with
coriander leaves and serve.

Chocolate and marshmallow biscuit sandwich

MAKES 1 BISCUIT SANDWICH

A variation on American s'mores (short for 'some more'), these are a real favourite. They are totally sweet and sinful and, of course, children will love them!

2 digestive biscuits
1 tbsp chopped-up pieces of milk or dark chocolate, or chocolate chips
1 marshmallow

1 Preheat the oven to 180°C (350°F), Gas mark 4.

2 Place one biscuit flat side up on a baking sheet, add the chocolate pieces and place the marshmallow on top. Bake in the oven for 5–8 minutes or until the chocolate and marshmallow have completely melted. Remove from the oven and immediately top with the remaining biscuit, flat side down. Leave to cool a little or completely before eating. You can make several at once, just increase the quantities.

Chocolate melting moments

MAKES 24 BISCUITS (12 WHEN SANDWICHED TOGETHER) · VEGETARIAN

These biscuits are intensely chocolatey and utterly moreish.

125g (4½oz) butter, softened, plus extra for greasing
50g (2oz) icing sugar
50g (2oz) cornflour
25g (1oz) cocoa powder
100g (3½oz) plain flour
About 2 tbsp chocolate hazelnut spread

1 Preheat the oven to 180°C (350°F), Gas mark 4. Lightly grease or line a baking sheet with parchment paper.

2 Cream the butter in a large bowl or in an electric food mixer, then add the icing sugar and beat until light and fluffy. Sift the cornflour, cocoa powder and flour into the butter and sugar and mix until the dough comes together.

3 Divide the dough into 24 equal parts (each about the size of a walnut in its shell). Roll into balls, place slightly apart on the prepared sheet and then flatten each biscuit a little using the back of a fork. Bake in the oven for 10–12 minutes or until slightly firm.

4 Remove from the oven and allow the biscuits to stand on the tray for 5 minutes before transferring to a wire rack to cool. Once they have completely cooled, sandwich the biscuits together with a nice thick layer of chocolate hazelnut spread.

Coffee and hazelnut cookies

MAKES 12 COOKIES · VEGETARIAN

These are ideal with a mid-morning cup of coffee. The dough can easily be refrigerated for up to two weeks or frozen for a couple of months until needed. Just be sure to roll into a sausage shape and wrap in parchment paper or cling film and cut off slices to bake the cookies as you need them.

50g (2oz) butter, cold and diced, plus extra for greasing
100g (3½oz) plain flour
1 tsp baking powder
½ tsp bicarbonate of soda
50g (2oz) soft light brown sugar
1 tbsp instant coffee powder
15g (½oz) finely chopped hazelnuts, toasted (see tip on page 50)
2 tbsp golden syrup

1 Preheat the oven to 180°C (350°F), Gas mark 4. Lightly grease 2 large baking sheets or line with parchment paper.

2 Sift the flour, baking powder and bicarbonate of soda into a bowl and rub in the butter until the mixture resembles fine breadcrumbs. Stir in the sugar, coffee powder and hazelnuts and then add the golden syrup, bringing the mixture together to form a dough (the mixture will be quite crumbly but will come together easily when pressed together).

3 Divide into 12 equal-sized pieces and roll each one into a small neat ball. Arrange the dough balls, spaced apart, on the baking sheets, flatten slightly and bake in the oven for 12–15 minutes or until the tops are golden and slightly cracked.

4 The biscuits will still be very soft so be careful not to touch them for 3–4 minutes until beginning to cool and harden a little (see tip below). Then carefully remove from the sheets with a fish slice or spatula and place on a wire rack to cool completely.

Variations
Sesame cookies: Substitute the powdered coffee and hazelnuts with 1 tablespoon of sesame seeds.
Pistachio cookies: Substitute the powdered coffee and hazelnuts with 50g (2oz) chopped pistachios.
Apricot and almond cookies: Substitute the powdered coffee and hazelnuts with 50g (2oz) very finely chopped, ready-to-eat dried apricots and 2 tablespoons of finely chopped and toasted almonds (see tip on page 50).

Rachel's tip
Always remove the cookies from the baking sheets while still warm or they'll stick. But don't remove them so soon that they fall apart!

Millionaire's shortbread

MAKES 16 SQUARES · VEGETARIAN

This is one of my all-time favourite treats. I love the fine crumbly texture
that the rice flour and cornflour give – it also means that the shortbread
is gluten-free – but you can use 175g (6oz) plain flour if you prefer.

200g (7oz) butter,
  softened
110g (4oz) caster sugar
75g (3oz) rice flour
100g (3½oz) cornflour
1 x 397g tin of condensed
  milk
200g (7oz) plain, milk
  or white chocolate,
  chopped

*20cm (8in) square cake tin
with 4cm (1½in) sides*

1 Preheat the oven to 180°C (350°F), Gas mark 4.

2 Cream half the butter and half the sugar together in a large bowl
or in an electric food mixer until pale and fluffy. Stir in the rice
flour and cornflour and bring together to make a smooth dough.
Line the cake tin with parchment paper and press the shortbread
into the tin. Bake in the oven for 15–20 minutes or until lightly
golden, then leave to cool slightly.

3 In the meantime, make the toffee to go on top of the shortbread.
Place the remaining butter and sugar and the condensed milk in
a small saucepan on a low heat and stir until the sugar dissolves.
Simmer for 10–15 minutes, continuing to stir, until the mixture
is just beginning to darken and a sugar thermometer dipped into
the mixture reads 113°C (235°F). Alternatively, check that the
soft-ball stage has been reached (see the chart on page 299).

4 Pour the toffee over the cooked shortbread base. Leave to cool
completely so that it firms up. Melt the chocolate in a small
heatproof bowl over a saucepan of simmering water. Pour over
the toffee and cool slightly before placing in the fridge for about
2 hours or until set. Cut into 16 squares and carefully remove
from the tin.

Squashed - fly biscuits

MAKES ABOUT 45—50 BISCUITS · VEGETARIAN

These shortbread biscuits (see the photographs on pages 278—9) with currants take me back to my childhood when we used to call them squashed-fly biscuits. The correct name is Garibaldi biscuits named after Giuseppe Garibaldi, the famous Italian general, who, on a visit to England in the mid nineteenth century supposedly sat on an Eccles cake and so brought about the biscuit that bears his name. They are perfect with a cup of tea.

225g (8oz) butter, softened
175g (6oz) caster sugar
2 eggs, separated
Finely grated zest of
　1 lemon
400g (14oz) plain flour,
　plus extra for dusting
1 tsp baking powder
¼ tsp salt
110g (4oz) currants

6cm (2 ½in) fluted scone cutter

1 Beat the softened butter in a large bowl or in an electric food mixer to soften a little more, then cream with 150g (5oz) of the sugar until pale and fluffy. Beat the egg yolks lightly and stir them into the mixture along with the lemon zest. Sift in the flour, baking powder and salt, add the currants and mix to give a smooth dough. Cover with cling film and place in the fridge for 20—30 minutes.

2 Preheat the oven to 180°C (350°F), Gas mark 4.

3 Roll the dough out on a floured work surface to a thickness of 5mm (¼in) and use the scone cutter (or cut into the more traditional rectangles with a knife) to stamp out the biscuits. Arrange on a couple of large baking sheets and place in the fridge for 10 minutes before baking in the oven for about 12 minutes or until just turning golden.

4 Meanwhile, lightly beat the egg whites. Remove the biscuits from the oven and, working quickly on 4—5 at a time, brush lightly with the egg whites. Sprinkle with a little of the remaining sugar and repeat until all are done. Return the biscuits to the oven to bake for a further 4—5 minutes or until golden (this gives a crunchy top). Remove and leave to cool on the baking sheets for a few minutes before transferring to a wire rack to cool completely.

Coconut and cinnamon macaroons

MAKES 12–14 MACAROONS · VEGETARIAN

These spicy macaroons make the perfect accompaniment to a cup of coffee, as does the almond and lemon variation described below. These are really easy to make and will keep for 4–5 days in an airtight container.

100g (3½oz) desiccated coconut
75g (3oz) caster sugar
½ tsp ground cinnamon
1 egg white, lightly beaten

1 Preheat the oven to 180°C (350°F), Gas mark 4. Line a large baking sheet with parchment paper.

2 Place all the ingredients in a bowl and stir together to give a firm but slightly sticky mixture. Use damp hands to divide the mixture into 12–14 even-sized pieces. The mixture will be quite crumbly, so squeeze each piece together to shape into a small nugget and place on the baking sheet.

3 Bake in the oven for 10–12 minutes or until pale golden, then transfer to a wire rack to cool.

Variation

Almond and lemon macaroons: Substitute the desiccated coconut with the same quantity of ground almonds and add the finely grated zest of 1 lemon instead of the cinnamon. This mixture will make more of a dough than a crumbly mixture, which will be easier to roll into small balls. Again, using damp hands will help. Arrange the balls on the baking sheet and flatten slightly with the back of a wet fork. Bake in the oven for 12–15 minutes.

Churros con chocolate

MAKES 18–20 CHURROS AND 300ML (½ PINT)
CHOCOLATE SAUCE · VEGETARIAN

Churros are long pieces of sweet, deep-fried dough tossed in cinnamon sugar and then dipped into a cup of rich chocolate sauce. They're fab late at night!

Sunflower oil,
   for deep-frying
50g (2oz) caster sugar
1 tsp ground cinnamon

For the churro dough
75g (3oz) butter
¼ tsp salt
100g (3½oz) plain flour
3 eggs
½ tsp vanilla extract
1 tbsp caster sugar

For the chocolate sauce
50g (2oz) dark chocolate,
   chopped
225ml (8fl oz) milk,
   plus extra if needed
50g (2oz) caster sugar
2 tsp cornflour,
   plus extra if needed

1 To make the churro dough, place the butter and salt and 225ml (8fl oz) water in a saucepan and bring to a rolling boil. Once the butter has melted, add the flour, whisking on a low heat for about a minute or until the mixture forms a smooth ball. Remove from the heat. Beat the eggs in a small bowl with the vanilla extract and sugar and gradually add to the dough, beating all the time until it comes together as a silky-smooth paste. Spoon the mixture into a bowl, cover and place in the fridge for 20–30 minutes to set a little. Remove from the fridge and spoon the dough into a piping bag with a large star nozzle.

2 Heat a deep-fat fryer filled with sunflower oil to 180°C (350°F). Alternatively, pour the oil into a large saucepan to a depth of 2cm (¾in) and bring to the same temperature on the hob (checking with a sugar thermometer, or see tip on page 255). Toss the sugar and cinnamon together in a bowl or on a plate and set aside. Preheat the oven to the lowest temperature.

3 Working in batches of about 3–4 at a time, carefully squeeze 8cm (3in) strips of dough into the preheated oil, slicing the dough from the nozzle with a knife (being careful not to burn yourself on the very hot oil). Deep-fry for about 3–4 minutes or until golden brown, turning halfway through cooking. Drain on kitchen paper briefly before rolling in the cinnamon sugar to coat, then place in the oven, uncovered, to keep warm while you make the rest.

4 Next, make the chocolate sauce. Place the chocolate and half the milk in a saucepan and gently heat, stirring, until the chocolate has melted. Mix the sugar with the cornflour and the remaining milk and whisk into the chocolate mixture. Cook on a low heat for about 5 minutes, whisking constantly, until the chocolate has thickened. (Add extra cornflour blended with milk if it doesn't start to thicken after this time.) Pour the chocolate sauce into serving cups or bowls and serve with the warm churros for dunking.

Coconut and chocolate flapjacks

MAKES 25–30 FLAPJACKS · VEGETARIAN

Flapjacks are a great sweet treat for packed lunches but the oats add good, slow-release energy. The addition of coconut gives a nice twist to the classic recipe, while the chocolate coating is just pure indulgence.

350g (12oz) butter
2 generous tbsp
   golden syrup
175g (6oz) soft light
   brown sugar
1 tsp vanilla extract
75g (3oz) plain flour
375g (13oz) rolled oats
75g (3oz) desiccated
   coconut
250g (9oz) plain or milk
   chocolate, chopped

38 x 25cm (15 x 10in)
Swiss roll tin

1 Preheat the oven to 180°C (350°F), Gas mark 4.

2 Place the butter, golden syrup, sugar and vanilla extract in a large saucepan. Bring to a simmer and stir, allowing the butter to melt and mixing to a smooth sauce. Remove from the heat and tip in the flour, oats and coconut. Stir to mix and pour into the Swiss roll tin, spreading evenly into every corner and smoothing the surface of the oats with the back of the spoon.

3 Bake in the oven (not too close to the top or it will burn) for 20–25 minutes or until golden. Remove from the oven and leave to cool in the tin.

4 Meanwhile, melt the chocolate in a small heatproof bowl over a saucepan of simmering water. Pour the melted chocolate over the cooked and cooled flapjack mixture in the tin, spreading evenly. Cut into squares or fingers and leave to cool before placing in the fridge for about an hour to set the chocolate. Carefully remove from the tin and enjoy!

Raspberry swirls

MAKES 12 SWIRLS · VEGETARIAN

I love the contrast of buttery pastry and gooey raspberry jam in these biscuits, the jam becoming lovely and sticky after being cooked in the oven. These are also delicious made with marmalade instead of jam.

75g (3oz) butter, diced, plus extra for greasing
450g (1lb) plain flour, plus extra for dusting
2 tsp baking powder
½ tsp salt
75g (3oz) caster sugar, plus extra for sprinkling
2 eggs
300ml (½ pint) milk
2 generous tbsp raspberry jam or marmalade
1 egg, beaten, for glazing
About 2 tbsp granulated sugar, for sprinkling

1 Preheat the oven to 220°C (425°F), Gas mark 7. Grease a baking sheet.

2 Sift the flour and the baking powder into a large bowl. Add the salt and caster sugar and mix together. Add the butter and, using your fingertips, rub it into the flour until the mixture resembles breadcrumbs.

3 In another bowl, whisk the eggs with the milk. Make a well in the centre of the dry ingredients and pour in most of the beaten eggs and milk. Using one hand, firmly held in a claw shape, mix in the flour from the sides of the bowl to form a soft and quite sticky dough, adding more egg and milk if necessary.

4 Place the dough on a lightly floured work surface, dust with flour and carefully roll out into a rectangle approximately 30cm (12in) long, 18cm (7in) wide and 1cm (½in) thick. Spread the raspberry jam over the top to cover the surface. With the longest side facing you, roll up the pastry away from you.

5 Cut the finished log into 12 slices and place these on the prepared baking sheet, cut side up and slightly apart. Brush with beaten egg and sprinkle with the granulated sugar. Bake in the oven for 10–15 minutes or until golden and slightly firm to the touch. Leave on the baking sheet for 5 minutes and then transfer to a wire rack to cool completely.

Rachel's tip
If using butter straight from the fridge, you can grate it into the flour and mix it without having to rub it in.

Chocolate and peanut butter cupcakes

Here is something to do on a rainy day. Bake these cupcakes and decorate them with a fudgy topping and some jelly beans or anything you like! Try chocolate buttons, dolly mixture or hundreds and thousands. Store the cupcakes in an airtight container and eat within four days — if you can resist them for that long!

150g (5oz) plain flour
25g (1oz) cocoa powder
1 tsp baking powder
Pinch of salt
125g (4½oz) caster sugar
100ml (3½fl oz) milk
75g (3oz) butter, melted and cooled
2 eggs
50g (2oz) peanut butter or homemade nut butter (see page 252)

For the topping
100g (3½oz) dark chocolate, roughly chopped
1 tbsp golden syrup
25g (1oz) butter
Your choice of decorations (see the introduction)

12-hole muffin tin

1 Preheat the oven to 180°C (350°F), Gas mark 4. Line the muffin tin with paper cases.

2 Sift the flour, cocoa powder, baking powder and salt into a large bowl and stir in the sugar. Beat together the milk, butter and eggs and add to the dry ingredients, pouring in a little at a time and stirring to give a smooth batter. Stir in the peanut butter, rippling it through rather than mixing completely.

3 Divide the cake mixture between the paper cases, filling them quite full. Bake in the oven for 20 minutes or until just firm to the touch. Remove the tin from the oven and leave to cool for about 2 minutes before transferring the cakes to a wire rack to cool completely.

4 Meanwhile, make the topping. Place the chocolate, golden syrup and butter in a small saucepan on a very low heat and stir until melted and smooth. Leave to cool for a few minutes before spooning onto the cupcakes. Top with your choice of decorations and leave to set.

Chocolate and ginger nut biscuit cake

MAKES 16 SLICES · VEGETARIAN

This is a no-cook cake that children love making — indeed, it is one of the first recipes I made when I was little. If you can keep your hands off the cake for long enough, it will store well in a tin for up to a week.

300g (11oz) good-quality dark or milk chocolate, chopped
1 tbsp golden syrup
250g (9oz) ginger nut biscuits
2 eggs, beaten

23cm (9in) diameter round cake tin or a 20cm (8in) square tin

1 Line the cake tin with parchment paper.

2 Melt the chocolate and golden syrup in a large heatproof bowl over a saucepan of simmering water. Meanwhile, roughly crush the biscuits in a bowl using your hands, or place the biscuits in a plastic bag and crush them with a rolling pin.

3 Stir the eggs and crushed biscuits into the melted chocolate mixture until they are well incorporated and pour into the prepared tin, spreading evenly and smoothing the surface with the back of the spoon.

4 Chill in the fridge for a couple of hours until well set or pop in the freezer for about 45 minutes. Remove from the fridge or freezer and cut into 16 pieces.

Variations
Boozy biscuit cake: To turn this recipe into something a little different, add 25g (1oz) raisins that have been soaked in a couple of tablespoons of warmed brandy for a few minutes — perfect for serving with coffee at the end of a meal.
Nutty biscuit cake: Add 25g (1oz) chopped pecans or hazelnuts to the mix when adding the crushed biscuits.
Biscuit cake with white chocolate icing: Melt 150g (5oz) white chocolate and either spread or drizzle over the set cake.

Dark sticky gingerbread

MAKES 1 LOAF · VEGETARIAN

This classic teatime cake can be served warm with cream as a dessert or cold, sliced and buttered at any time. It is very dark and sticky, just as the name suggests, and it keeps very well for up to a week. Made in a loaf tin, it is so easy to cut into slices.

60g (2½oz) butter
75g (3oz) golden syrup
50g (2oz) molasses or
　black treacle
110g (4oz) plain flour
25g (1oz) self-raising flour
1 tsp bicarbonate of soda
1 heaped tsp ground ginger
1 tsp ground cinnamon
1 tsp freshly grated nutmeg
1 tsp freshly ground
　black pepper
100g (3½oz) caster sugar
Pinch of salt
120ml (4½fl oz) milk
1 egg, beaten
50g (2oz) crystallised
　ginger, finely chopped

For the syrup
80g (3¼oz) caster sugar
2 tsp finely grated
　root ginger

For the topping (optional)
200g (7oz) icing sugar,
　sifted
Juice of ½ lemon

23 x 13cm (9 x 5in) loaf tin

1 Preheat the oven to 170°C (325°F), Gas mark 3. Line the loaf tin with parchment paper.

2 Melt the butter, golden syrup and molasses or treacle in a small saucepan on a low heat, then set aside.

3 Sift the two flours, the bicarbonate of soda and spices into a large bowl. Stir in the sugar and salt, then add the milk and beaten egg and mix until smooth. Gradually add the melted butter mixture, stirring until well incorporated, then fold in the crystallised ginger. The mixture will be runny.

4 Pour into the prepared loaf tin and bake in the oven for 50–55 minutes or until risen and firm to the touch and a skewer inserted into the centre comes out clean. (Wait for at least 45 minutes before opening the oven to check whether the gingerbread has cooked.) Allow the cake to stand for 10 minutes in the tin before removing to a wire rack to cool.

5 Meanwhile, make the syrup. Place the sugar and ginger in a small saucepan, pour in 75ml (3fl oz) water and simmer for 10 minutes. Prick the hot cake all over with a fine skewer, pour over the syrup and leave to cool completely.

6 If you wish, mix the icing sugar and lemon juice together in a small bowl until thick, then spread carefully over the top of the cake with a palette knife or a table knife, allowing some icing to drip over the edges.

Orange Madeira cake

MAKES 1 LOAF · VEGETARIAN

An orange-flavoured cake is perfect with a cup of tea in the afternoon. It lasts well because of the juice, which helps to retain the moisture of the sponge.

175g (6oz) butter, softened, plus extra for greasing
175g (6oz) caster sugar
1 tsp vanilla extract
3 eggs, beaten
Finely grated zest of 2 oranges
225g (8oz) plain flour
1 tsp baking powder
4 tsp freshly squeezed orange juice

For the topping
75g (3oz) icing sugar
2–3 tbsp freshly squeezed orange juice

23 x 13cm (9 x 5in) loaf tin

1 Preheat the oven to 170°C (325°F), Gas mark 3. Lightly grease the loaf tin and line with parchment paper.

2 Cream the butter in a large bowl or in an electric food mixer to soften it further. Add the sugar and vanilla extract and beat until the mixture is light and fluffy. Add the eggs in three stages, beating well between each addition, then add the orange zest.

3 Sift in the flour and baking powder and fold in with the orange juice. Stop when all the flour is incorporated. Transfer the mixture into the prepared loaf tin and smooth the top.

4 Bake in the oven for 50–55 minutes or until a skewer inserted into the centre comes out clean. Allow to stand in the tin for 5 minutes before removing to a wire rack to cool completely.

5 For the topping, sift the icing sugar into a small bowl and stir in just enough orange juice until it is soft but not runny. If you want the icing to stay just on the top of the cake, place the cooled cake back in the tin and spread the icing over the top.

Variation

Coffee Madeira cake: Follow as above, omitting the orange zest in the cake and substituting it with 1 generous tablespoon of coffee essence. For the topping, make an icing by creaming 50g (2oz) butter, then adding 100g (3½oz) sifted icing sugar and 2 teaspoons of coffee essence. Mix to combine, then spread evenly over the cake. You can scatter some toasted hazelnuts, walnuts, peanuts or almonds on top (see tip on page 50) or add 50g (2oz) to the cake mixture with the coffee essence.

Rachel's tip

You may find using a spoon or table knife dipped in boiling water makes it easier to spread the icing.

Toffee apples

MAKES 6 APPLES · VEGETARIAN

An old-fashioned fairground treat, these are great to serve at
a Hallowe'en party. Use small eating apples and make sure you
dip them very briefly in the toffee for the thinnest coating.

225g (8oz) soft light
  brown sugar
2 tbsp golden syrup
25g (1oz) butter
6 small eating apples

1 Place the sugar, golden syrup and butter in a saucepan and
pour over 110ml (4fl oz) water. Bring to the boil, stirring to
dissolve the sugar and melt the butter. Reduce the heat and leave
to simmer, without stirring, for 30–35 minutes or until a sugar
thermometer inserted into the mixture reads 138°C (280°F).
Alternatively, check whether the soft-crack stage has been
reached (see the chart on page 299).

2 Meanwhile, prepare the apples. Push a lollipop stick or
wooden skewer about halfway into the top or bottom of each
of the apples (whichever is opposite to the end that it sits flat
on). Line a baking sheet with parchment paper.

3 Once the correct temperature has been reached for the
toffee mixture, immediately remove from the heat and tilt
the pan a little so the mixture pools in one corner. Working
carefully, dip in one apple at a time, holding it by the stick
and spinning it around to completely coat in the toffee.
Allow any excess to drip off over the pan before standing the
apple on the lined baking sheet. Repeat with the remaining
apples and then leave to cool and harden before serving.

Variations

Nutty toffee apples: As soon as the apples have been dipped
in the toffee, roll them in a bowl of 75g (3oz) of toasted, very
finely chopped hazelnuts or almonds (for toasting nuts, see
tip on page 50).

Colourful toffee apples: As soon as the apples have been
dipped in the toffee, roll them in a bowl of 4 tablespoons
of hundreds and thousands.

Fruity ice pops

The zesty fruit juices make them very popular with children and they are a great stand-by for when friends come over to play.

Raspberry and yoghurt ice pops
175g (6oz) fresh raspberries
75g (3oz) icing sugar
2 tsp lemon juice
150ml (5fl oz) natural yoghurt

Melon and lime ice pops
450g (1lb) peeled and diced melon, such as Honeydew, Cantaloupe or Ogen
50ml (2fl oz) sugar syrup (see page 338)
Juice and zest of ½–1 lime

Apple ice pops
300ml (½ pint) apple juice
75ml (3fl oz) sugar syrup (see page 338)
2 tsp lemon juice

These are quite versatile; you can use fresh, frozen or tinned fruit, fruit coulis (such as the raspberry coulis on page 337) or simply fruit juice. Make up the mixture with yoghurt, water or freshly squeezed or bought fruit juices. The prepared fruit can be puréed either in a blender, food processor or using a hand-held blender. Use homemade sugar syrup (see sugar syrup on page 338), sugar, fruit juice or the syrup from tinned fruit to sweeten. Add lemon or lime juice to taste. Use special ice-lolly moulds (50–75ml/ 2–3fl oz in capacity). Or alternatively, use small glasses and lolly sticks (which you can buy from a kitchen or craft shop) or teaspoons. Pour your choice from below (or your own combination) into your chosen moulds and freeze for 5–6 hours or overnight until solid. Remove from the freezer and sit the moulds in a bowl of warm water to help release the ice pops.

Raspberry and yoghurt ice pops

Purée the raspberries, icing sugar and lemon juice together until smooth. Push the mixture through a fine sieve over a bowl. Stir the yoghurt into the mixture in the bowl until well blended.

Melon and lime ice pops

Blend the melon and sugar syrup until smooth and add enough lime juice to taste. Push the mixture through a fine sieve over a bowl and stir the lime zest into the liquid in the bowl.

Apple ice pops

Simply stir the apple juice, sugar syrup and lemon juice together.

Mixed berry ice pops
200g (7oz) mixed frozen
    (and defrosted) berries
50g (2oz) icing sugar
150ml (5fl oz) fruit juice
    or water

Mango ice pops
250g (9oz) peeled and
    chopped mango
200ml (7fl oz) sugar syrup
    (see page 338)

Mixed berry ice pops

Purée the berries and icing sugar until smooth and push
through a fine sieve over a bowl. Stir the fruit juice or water
into the liquid in the bowl.

Mango ice pops

Blend the mango and sugar syrup until smooth and push
through a fine sieve over a bowl.

Hot chocolate

SERVES 1 · VEGETARIAN

This is made with real chocolate so is very luxurious.
Increase the quantities as necessary for more people.

200ml (7fl oz) milk
50g (2oz) good-quality
    dark, milk or white
    chocolate, chopped
Splash of single or
    regular cream
1–2 tsp caster sugar
    (optional)

1 Pour the milk into a saucepan and add the chopped chocolate
and cream. Bring to a gentle simmer, stirring continuously,
and cook for 3–4 minutes or until the chocolate is melted and
completely smooth.

2 Check for taste and stir in a little sugar if necessary. Pour
into a cup or mug to serve.

Variations
Boozy hot chocolate: Add a splash of brandy, whiskey or Baileys.
Chocolate and orange: Add the finely grated zest of 1 small
orange to the saucepan with the milk and chocolate.
Hot chocolate with cinnamon or nutmeg: Blend a good pinch
of ground cinnamon or freshly grated nutmeg into the saucepan
with the milk and chocolate.

Soft drinks

MAKES 4–6 GLASSES · VEGETARIAN

The flavoured syrups can be made in advance and stored in the fridge or frozen in small portions. Serve the drinks within a few hours of adding still water; if using sparkling water, they should be served at once. In each case, add ice when serving.

Lemonade

Mix the juice of 3 lemons (about 150ml/5fl oz) and 200ml (7fl oz) sugar syrup (see page 338) together in a large serving jug. Stir in 500ml (18fl oz) still or sparkling water (adjust the amount of water to suit your taste).

Lime and gingerade

Mix the juice of 5 limes (about 150ml/5fl oz) and 1 tbsp finely grated root ginger together in a large serving jug. Stir in 200ml (7fl oz) sugar syrup (see page 338) and 500ml (18fl oz) still or sparkling water (adjust the amount of water to suit your taste).

Cherryade

1 Place 500g (1lb 2oz) stoned cherries, 50g (2oz) caster sugar and 1 split vanilla pod in a small saucepan and pour over 200ml (7fl oz) cold water from the tap. Bring slowly to the boil, stirring until the sugar dissolves. Reduce the heat and simmer for about 10 minutes or until the cherries have softened.

2 Remove from the heat, discard the vanilla pod and then blitz in a blender or using a hand-held blender until smooth. Push the mixture through a sieve into a small bowl and allow to cool. To serve, pour the syrup into a large serving jug or glasses and top up with 500ml (18fl oz) still or sparkling water (adjusting to taste).

Choc ices

Surprisingly easy to put together, these choc-ice balls are tremendous fun both to make and to eat. Although an ice-cream scoop works best for creating the balls, you could just use a large spoon instead. Use any flavour of ice cream you like, either shop bought or one of the homemade ice creams on page 240–1. They will keep in the freezer for a few days if covered.

300ml (½ pint) ice cream
100g (3½oz) milk, dark
  or white chocolate,
  chopped, or
  chocolate chips
1 tsp sunflower oil

1 Scoop the ice cream into six even-sized balls. Push an ice-lolly stick halfway into each ball, arrange on a baking tray lined with parchment paper and place in the freezer for 15–20 minutes or until they have set hard.

2 In the meantime, melt the chocolate with the sunflower oil in a small heatproof bowl over a pan of simmering water. Once melted, remove and allow to cool for a few minutes until tepid. Scatter your choice of additional ingredients (if using – see below) into a small bowl.

3 Once the ice-cream balls have hardened, dip into the melted chocolate, allowing the excess to drip into the bowl before quickly dipping into the additional ingredients (if using), to coat. Allow the chocolate to set (about 30 seconds) and eat immediately or return to the freezer on the lined baking tray until ready to enjoy.

Additions
Dip the choc ices into one of the following, if you like:
* 100g (3½oz) finely chopped nuts, such as hazelnuts, almonds or pistachios
* 4 tablespoons of hundreds and thousands

Cold-water test for sweet making

The following sweets recipes refer to a few different stages of cooking a sugar syrup. This table explains what the stages mean.

Stage of cooking the syrup	What happens to a small amount of syrup dropped into a bowl of very cold water
Thread stage 110–113°C (230–235°F)	Forms a liquid thread that won't ball up
Soft-ball stage 113–116°C (235–240°F)	Forms a soft, squidgy ball; removed from the water, it will flatten in your hand
Hard-ball stage 121–130°C (250–265°F)	Syrup forms thick, ropy threads when dropped into the water; these can be gathered into a hard ball that won't flatten when removed from the water; although hard, you can still change its shape by squashing it
Soft-crack stage 132–143°C (270–290°F)	Solidifies into flexible threads that bend a little before breaking
Hard-crack stage 149–154°C (300–310°F)	Solidifies into hard, brittle threads that immediately break when you bend them. NB: The syrup is now very hot and can easily burn; allow it to cool in the water for a few moments before touching it

Liquorice toffees

MAKES ABOUT 1.1KG (2LB 6OZ) OR 128 PIECES · VEGETARIAN

These are up there as one of my favourite sweets. Ground aniseed is not easily available in supermarkets but you will find it in health-food stores or specialist food shops.

450g (1lb) caster sugar
350g (12oz) glucose syrup (available from a chemist)
1 x 395g tin of condensed milk
100g (3½oz) butter
4 tbsp ground aniseed
Black food colouring

23cm (9in) square cake tin

1 Line the cake tin with parchment paper.

2 Place the sugar, glucose syrup, condensed milk, butter and ground aniseed in a saucepan and cook on a medium heat, stirring until the sugar dissolves and the butter melts. Bring to the boil over a high heat, then reduce the heat to low and simmer gently for 35–40 minutes, stirring frequently to avoid sticking, until a sugar thermometer dipped into the mixture reads 115°C (240°F). Alternatively, check that the soft-ball stage has been reached (see the chart on page 299). The mixture will be reduced and thickened and rich golden brown in colour.

3 Immediately remove the pan from the heat and stir in enough food colouring (adding bit by bit) to give a strong black colour. Working quickly, carefully pour the mixture into the prepared tin, swirling the tin around to spread the mixture evenly. Leave in a cool place for a couple of hours or until cool and set (the toffee will become even harder after this time, so it's best to score out the pieces at this stage).

4 Remove from the tin and peel off the paper. Cut the slab of toffee into 64 pieces (eight cuts down and eight cuts across) with a sharp knife and then cut each piece in half again to give 128 pieces in total. Layer the liquorice toffees spaced apart between sheets of parchment paper to prevent them sticking together or wrap each toffee individually in a small piece of parchment paper and store in an airtight container.

Nougat

MAKES ABOUT 800G (1¾LB) OR ABOUT 36 PIECES · VEGETARIAN

Delicious on its own, nougat also makes a lovely petit four, served with a strong cup of coffee at the end of a meal. It keeps very well and any leftover pieces can be chopped up and added to ice cream (see pages 240–1).

450g (1lb) caster sugar

225g (8oz) powdered glucose (found in the baking section of some supermarkets or at your local chemist)

2 egg whites

8 sheets of rice paper measuring 6 x 15cm (2½ x 6in)

150g (2oz) hazelnuts or pistachios, roughly chopped and toasted (see tip on page 50)

25 x 15cm (10 x 6in) cake tin with 2.5cm (1in) sides

1 Place the sugar, powdered glucose and 150ml (5fl oz) water in a large, heavy-based saucepan on a medium heat and bring slowly to the boil, stirring all the time until the sugar dissolves. Reduce the heat to low and simmer for 10–15 minutes, without stirring, until a sugar thermometer dipped into the mixture reads 121°C (250°F). Alternatively, check whether it has reached the hard-ball stage (see the chart on page 299).

2 Place the egg whites in a large bowl and once the sugar syrup temperature reaches about 110°C (230°F) (or the soft-thread stage – see chart page 299) begin whisking them to stiff peaks in an electric food mixer on a low setting. Once the syrup reaches its final temperature, pour about a quarter of it, in a slow, steady stream, into the egg whites, continuing to whisk.

3 Immediately return the remaining syrup to the heat and continue to cook, without stirring, for about 5 minutes or until the thermometer reads 149°C (300°F) or the hard-crack stage has been reached (see chart page 299), all the while continuing to whisk the egg whites on a slow speed. Again, once the syrup reaches the right temperature, pour it carefully and in a slow, steady stream into the whisking egg whites.

4 Continue to whisk the egg whites for about 30 minutes until stiff and halved in volume. Scrape down the sides of the bowl every so often with a palette knife or spatula dipped in boiling water.

5 Meanwhile, cover the bottom of the cake tin with half the rice paper. Stir the nuts into the fully whisked nougat mixture, mix well and pour into the prepared tin. Working quickly, spread evenly using a palette knife or spatula dipped in boiling water. Place the remaining sheets of rice paper on top to cover, pressing down to stick. Allow to cool and then place in the fridge for 4–6 hours or overnight until set. Remove the slab of nougat from the baking tin and cut into about 36 fingers. Store in the fridge, wrapped individually in parchment paper or cling film.

Fruity lollipops

MAKES ABOUT 30–35 LOLLIPOPS · VEGETARIAN

Not the kind of thing you give your children every day, but when making your own sweets you at least know there are no preservatives in them. Lollipop sticks can be bought in any good craft or cookware shop. It is worth investing in a sugar thermometer if you're planning on making sweets because a specific temperature is often called for. If you don't have one, however, you can try the cold-water test (see the chart on page 299) at various stages of cooking.

450g (1lb) caster sugar
⅛ tsp cream of tartar
4 tbsp undiluted fruit cordial, such as blackcurrant, orange or lime

1 Arrange 30–35 lollipop sticks (or wooden skewers which have been cut down to size) spaced apart on several large, non-stick baking sheets.

2 Place the sugar, cream of tartar and 150ml (5fl oz) water in a heavy-based saucepan on a medium heat and bring to a gentle boil while stirring all the time. Reduce the heat to low and simmer for 20–25 minutes without stirring, until the temperature on a sugar thermometer dipped into the mixture reads 143°C (290°F). Alternatively, check whether the soft-crack stage has been reached (see the chart on page 299). Stir in the cordial just before the syrup reaches this temperature (after 15–20 minutes). The mixture will bubble up, so be careful as it is very hot.

3 Once the correct temperature has been reached, remove the pan from the heat and, working quickly, spoon small pools of the syrup onto one end of each lollipop stick and allow to set for about 5 minutes, until hardened.

4 If you wish, wrap the lollipops in cellophane and tie with string as soon as they have cooled and hardened, to prevent them from absorbing moisture. Store them in an airtight container in a cool, dry place for up to a week.

Variations
Peppermint lollipops: In place of the cordial add ½ teaspoon of peppermint extract and a few drops of green food colouring to the syrup.
Speckled lollipops: Instead of or in addition to the cordial, add 1 tablespoon of candied sprinkles, such as hundreds and thousands or edible glitter, as soon as the syrup is taken off the heat.

Turkish delight

This recipe is the smooth rosewater version, but if you like Turkish delight with pistachios, feel free to chop up a handful and stir into the mixture. It keeps for ages and makes a particularly lovely gift — one batch will fill quite a few boxes.

850g (1lb 14oz) caster sugar
3 x 7g sachets gelatine powder
125g (4½oz) cornflour
1 tsp cream of tartar
2 tbsp lemon juice
1 tbsp sunflower oil
2 tsp rosewater
Few drops of red food colouring
75g (3oz) icing sugar

20cm (8in) square non-stick cake tin

1 Place the sugar and 500ml (18fl oz) water in a large, heavy-based saucepan on a medium heat and bring to the boil, stirring until the sugar dissolves. Reduce the heat to low and simmer for about 25 minutes without stirring, until a sugar thermometer dipped into the mixture reads 125°C (257°F). Alternatively, check that the hard-ball stage has been reached (see chart on page 299).

2 In the meantime, stir the gelatine, cornflour and cream of tartar together in another large pan. Measure out another 500ml (18fl oz) water and gradually whisk it into the mixture, beating well after each addition, to form a smooth paste. Be sure to break up any lumps as the gelatine may cause the mixture to stick together a little. Place the pan on a medium heat and simmer, whisking all the time, for 3–5 minutes or until the mixture thickens. Remove from the heat.

3 Stir the lemon juice into the sugar syrup as soon as it reaches the correct temperature (standing back as it will sizzle up a little). Working carefully, gradually pour the sugar syrup into the gelatine and cornflour mixture, whisking constantly.

4 Place the pan on a low heat and simmer the mixture gently for about 1 hour until it reaches 110°C (230°F) in temperature or the thread stage (see the chart on page 299). Stir frequently to prevent the mixture sticking to the pan, particularly towards the end of cooking. Grease the cake tin with the sunflower oil.

5 As soon as the mixture reaches the correct temperature (it should be a deep golden colour), add the rosewater and food colouring and stir until well combined. Pour the mixture into the prepared tin, spreading out evenly. Set aside to cool to room temperature before placing in the fridge for 4 hours or overnight until firm.

6 Spoon the icing sugar into a fine sieve and dust half of it onto a clean work surface. Turn the Turkish delight out of the tin and use a lightly oiled knife to cut it into about 48 pieces. Dust with the remaining icing sugar and toss the pieces about to coat generously. Store in an airtight container in a cool, dry place.

Marshmallows

These are very popular in our house and are perfect with hot chocolate (see page 295). It's a great rainy afternoon recipe: there's a lot of whisking and temperature checking, but the end result is scrumptious and well worth the effort.

450g (1lb) caster sugar
2 x 7g sachets powdered gelatine
2 tsp vanilla extract
1 tbsp sunflower oil
2 tbsp icing sugar
2 tbsp cornflour

20cm (8in) square, deep-sided cake tin

1 Pour the sugar and 175ml (6fl oz) cold water into a heavy-based saucepan, place on a medium–high heat and bring to a rolling boil, stirring all the time until the sugar dissolves. Reduce the heat to low and allow to simmer for about 15–20 minutes without stirring, until a sugar thermometer dipped into the mixture reads 113°C (235°F). Alternatively, check that the soft-ball stage has been reached (see the chart on page 299).

2 Meanwhile, pour the gelatine and 100ml (3½fl oz) cold water into the bowl of an electric food mixer and leave for about 10 minutes to soften before stirring to loosen up.

3 As soon as the sugar syrup reaches the correct temperature, begin to whisk the gelatine in the food mixer on a very low setting and then carefully pour in the syrup in a slow, steady stream, whisking all the while until it is fully incorporated. Add the vanilla extract, increase the whisking speed and leave to beat for about 20 minutes until thick, cool and beginning to set.

4 Meanwhile, grease the cake tin with some of the sunflower oil, line with parchment paper and grease again. Toss the icing sugar and cornflour together and place in a sieve. Dust a little into the tin to evenly coat the base and sides, reserving the rest for later.

5 Pour the creamy marshmallow mixture into the prepared tin, spreading it evenly and smoothing the surface. (A palette knife or spatula that has been dipped in boiling water is perfect for this.) Dust with a little more of the icing sugar and cornflour mixture, cover with cling film and allow to set in a cool, dry place (not the fridge) for 1–2 hours or overnight.

6 Once the marshmallow mixture has set, dust a clean work surface with the remaining icing sugar and cornflour mixture and turn the marshmallow slab out of the tin. Peel off the parchment paper and cut the marshmallows into about 36 squares. Toss them around to coat evenly in the icing sugar and cornflour. Store in an airtight container in a cool, dry place for up to three weeks.

White chocolate fudge

I find it hard to resist anything that contains white chocolate —
and when combined with fudge … well! The white chocolate chips
give texture to the traditional fudge mixture. Presented in a
decorative box, it makes a wonderful present.

1 tbsp sunflower oil
1 x 397g tin of condensed
    milk
100g (3½oz) butter
450g (1lb) caster or soft
    light brown sugar
50g (2oz) white chocolate
    chips

*18cm (7in) square cake tin
with 2.5cm (1in) sides*

1 Grease the cake tin with a little of the sunflower oil, line with
parchment paper and grease again.

2 Place the condensed milk, butter and sugar in a saucepan on
medium heat, stir together and bring to the boil, stirring frequently
to prevent the sugar from sticking and burning on the bottom.
Reduce the heat to low and simmer for 10–15 minutes, stirring
regularly, until a sugar thermometer dipped into the mixture reads
113°C (235°F). Alternatively, check whether the soft-ball stage
has been reached (see the chart on page 299). The fudge will also
have darkened in colour to a rich golden brown.

3 Immediately remove the pan from the heat and sit the bottom
of the saucepan in a bowl of cold water that comes a few centimetres
up the sides of the pan. Whisk the mixture vigorously for 7–10
minutes until it cools down and goes from being smooth, shiny
and toffeeish to matt, thick and grainy in appearance (as well as
becoming quite thick and difficult to stir). Whisking the mixture
like this is important for ensuring that the fudge has a good
crumbly texture.

4 Pour half the mixture into the prepared tin. Scatter with the
white chocolate chips and then pour over the remaining mixture,
spreading evenly. (A palette knife or spatula that has been dipped
in boiling water is perfect for this.) Allow to cool and then place
in the fridge for 2–3 hours or overnight to set before cutting
into about 36 squares.

Variation
Hazelnut fudge: Omit the white chocolate and stir 50g (2oz)
roughly chopped and lightly toasted hazelnuts into the fudge
before pouring the mixture into the tin in one go. (For toasting
nuts, see tip on page 50.)

Honeycomb

MAKES 500G (1LB 2OZ) · VEGETARIAN

This great recipe comes from our friend, chef Andrew Nutter. Delicious on its own, it is divine tossed in melted chocolate and allowed to set, stirred into ice cream (see the variations on page 241) or sprinkled on top. The cream of tartar causes the mixture to bubble and fizz up, giving it the characteristic air bubbles that are associated with honeycomb.

1 tsp sunflower oil
325g (11½oz) caster sugar
50g (2oz) honey
125g (4½oz) glucose syrup (available from a chemist)
1 tbsp bicarbonate of soda

1 Line a large baking tray with parchment paper and grease lightly with the oil. Alternatively, line the tray with a non-stick mat (there is no need to grease this).

2 Place the sugar, honey and glucose syrup in a large saucepan and add 4 tablespoons of water. Bring to the boil over a high heat, stirring until the sugar dissolves, then reduce the heat to medium and simmer without stirring for 5–10 minutes or until the syrup turns a light golden colour and a sugar thermometer dipped into the mixture reads 149°C (300°F). Alternatively, check whether it has reached the hard-crack stage (see the chart on page 299).

3 Immediately remove from the heat and quickly whisk in the bicarbonate of soda. The mixture will grow, trebling in size very quickly, so be careful it doesn't spill over. Pour into the prepared baking tray, swirling the tray to spread the mixture evenly. Leave to completely cool and harden before breaking into chunks. Cut with a knife or break with your hands and store in an airtight container.

Fruit jellies

In this recipe fruit juices have been used to make these jellies, but you could substitute these with fruit cordials diluted with water according to taste.

250ml (9fl oz) fruit juice, such as orange, cranberry, pomegranate or apple
50g (2oz) caster sugar
2 x 12g sachets powdered gelatine
3 tbsp cornflour

1 Place half the juice and the sugar in a small saucepan and cook on a gentle heat, stirring until the sugar dissolves. Bring just to the boil and then remove from the heat and stir in the powdered gelatine for a few minutes or until completely dissolved. It is really important that all of the gelatine is dissolved or you'll get lumps in the finished jellies. If you're having trouble dissolving the last few lumps, then strain the liquid through a fine sieve. Once the gelatine is dissolved, whisk in the remaining juice.

2 Pour the mixture into small moulds (that will take 2−3 teaspoons of the liquid). Mini-muffin tins or ice-cube trays are ideal for this. Leave to cool and then place in the fridge for about 1 hour or until completely set.

3 Sift the cornflour onto a large plate or into a bowl. Remove the set jellies from the moulds by running a small knife around the edge of them to loosen. Toss the jellies in the cornflour to lightly coat. Arrange in a single layer on a plate or baking sheet lined with parchment paper, cover with cling film and store in the fridge for 4−5 days.

Candy canes

Make these either with a hook at the top for hanging on the Christmas tree or keep them as straight sticks of rock. These are definitely a bit more tricky than the average recipe but are very rewarding and great fun. It is best for two people to be involved, particularly for folding and twisting the sugar mixture, as one person can work on each colour before it sets hard. Make sure you are working in a warm environment to help prevent the sugar mixture hardening too quickly.

225g (8oz) caster sugar
100g (3½oz) glucose syrup (available from a chemist)
⅛ tsp cream of tartar
3 tsp vegetable or sunflower oil
½ tsp peppermint extract
Red, blue or green food colouring

1 Place the sugar, glucose syrup and cream of tartar in a heavy-based saucepan, add 100ml (3½fl oz) cold water and bring to the boil over a high heat, stirring until the sugar dissolves. Reduce the heat to low–medium and simmer for about 15 minutes or until the temperature on a sugar thermometer dipped into the mixture reads 150°C (302°F). Alternatively, check whether the hard-crack stage has been reached (see the chart on page 299).

2 Meanwhile, grease two non-stick baking trays with 1 teaspoon of the vegetable or sunflower oil. As soon as the correct temperature has been reached, remove the pan from the heat and add the peppermint extract, stirring briefly. Working quickly, carefully pour about two-thirds of the mixture onto one of the prepared trays. Stir a few drops of your chosen food colouring into the remaining mixture and pour onto the second tray.

3 Once the bubbling sugar settles, leave for about 1 minute to set a little. This is where you will need a hand. Both cooks should wear gloves to protect them from the hot sugar mixture (heavy washing-up gloves are ideal). Rub the remaining oil over the gloves, rubbing off any excess with kitchen paper. Using a separate metal spatula for each tray, flip each slightly set edge inwards, continuing to do so for about 2 minutes until the mixture gathers into a stiff mound that is cool enough to handle (while still wearing gloves).

4 Each person should gather up a ball of mixture and roll this between their gloved hands into a long sausage shape about 15cm (6in) long. Fold in half, twist a little and then pull into the sausage shape again. Continue to do this until both pieces have cooled, begun to stiffen and the piece from the uncoloured mixture turns white. This will take 5–8 minutes in total.

5 Pull each piece into a sausage shape about 15cm (6in) long, lay them on top of each other on a clean work surface and twist together. Each person can work from opposite ends. Pull and twist the end of the mixture until it is about 5mm (¼in) thick and then cut off 18cm (7in) long sections and quickly bend one end to give the cane shape (or leave straight if sticks of rock are preferred). Continuing to work quickly, repeat with the rest of the mixture until it is all used up.

6 Place the candy canes or sticks of rock on the greased baking sheets for about 5 minutes to completely cool and harden. Be careful not to snap the candy when removing it from the trays. Wrap individually in parchment paper and store in a cool dry place.

Butterscotch

MAKES ABOUT 600G (1LB 5OZ) · VEGETARIAN

Keep some of this in the car for a long journey. Your dentist will definitely not approve of it – be careful taking a bite if you have any loose fillings!

1 tsp lemon juice
500g (1lb 2oz) demerara sugar
75g (3oz) butter
¼ tsp cream of tartar
¼ tsp vanilla extract

25 x 17cm (10 x 6½in) baking tray

1 Line the baking tray with parchment paper.

2 Pour 150ml (5fl oz) water into a saucepan, place on a medium–high heat, add the lemon juice and bring almost to the boil. Add the sugar and butter and simmer on a gentle heat for 4–5 minutes, stirring all the time, until the sugar dissolves and the butter melts.

3 Whisk in the cream of tartar and allow to simmer on a low–medium heat, without stirring, for about 35–40 minutes or until a sugar thermometer dipped into the mixture reads 138°C (280°F). Alternatively, check that the soft-crack stage has been reached (see the chart on page 299).

4 Immediately remove from the heat and add the vanilla extract. Working quickly but carefully, pour the mixture into the prepared tin. Leave in a cool place for about 1 hour or until completely set before cutting into squares and individually wrapping in pieces of parchment paper. Store in an airtight container.

Toffee brittle

MAKES 400G (14OZ) · VEGETARIAN

This is divine as it is or covered in chocolate (see the variations below).

225g (8oz) butter, diced
225g (8oz) caster sugar
½ tsp salt

1 Place the butter, sugar, salt and 50ml (2fl oz) water in a heavy-based saucepan, place on a medium heat and bring slowly to the boil, stirring until the sugar has dissolved. Reduce the heat to low and simmer for 20–25 minutes without stirring until a sugar thermometer dipped into the mixture reads 150°C (302°F). Below this temperature and the toffee will not set; above and the toffees will taste burnt. If you don't have a sugar thermometer, check that the hard-crack stage has been reached (see the chart on page 299).

2 Immediately (and taking great care as it is very hot), pour the syrup onto a large, non-stick baking tray (or one lined with parchment paper) and swirl the tray around to spread evenly. It will begin to set almost straight away, so you do need to work quickly.

3 Once completely hardened, after 5–10 minutes, slam the baking tray on the counter to break into small pieces. Place the toffee pieces in an airtight container and store somewhere cool and dry.

Variations

Salted cashew nut toffee brittle: Roughly chop 150g (5oz) salted cashews and scatter them evenly over the baking tray before pouring over the toffee.

Chocolate-coated toffee brittle: Once the toffee has been spread evenly on the baking tray, scatter with 100g (3½oz) chopped dark chocolate or chocolate drops and leave for a few minutes to soften in the toffee's heat. Once melted, spread evenly with a palette knife or spatula and place somewhere cool to set.

Toffee brittle cups: Arrange 35–40 foil mini cupcake cases on a large baking sheet and carefully pour in the toffee. Scatter with hundreds and thousands or chopped toasted nuts (for toasting nuts, see tip on page 50), if you wish, and leave to cool and set.

Chocolate and almond toffee brittle: Follow the steps for chocolate-coated toffee brittle above and scatter with 25g (1oz) toasted flaked almonds before placing in the fridge to set.

Baby purées

Baby purées suitable from six months old

Below are a few ideas for some purées for your baby. Two of them — the Avocado and Banana Mash and Banana and Mango Purée (see opposite) — are ultra-easy and require no cooking, only a fork for mashing. All the recipes contain more than one fruit or vegetable, but do remember to try your baby out on individual foods first, before you mix them together, to make sure there are no adverse reactions. Once your baby is used to a purée on its own, simply stir it into baby rice, porridge or yoghurt.

Pea, spinach and carrot purée

MAKES ABOUT 400ML (14FL OZ)
VEGETARIAN

75g (3oz) peeled carrot,
    chopped into 1cm (½in) cubes
150g (5oz) fresh or frozen peas
75g (3oz) baby spinach

Put the carrot in a saucepan with 250ml (9fl oz) water and bring to the boil. Reduce the heat and simmer, uncovered, for 10–12 minutes or until tender. Add the peas and spinach and continue to simmer for a further 4 minutes. Purée until really smooth and allow to cool a little before serving.

Carrot, butternut squash and red split lentil purée

MAKES ABOUT 400ML (14FL OZ)
VEGETARIAN

50g (2oz) peeled carrot,
    chopped into 1cm (½in) cubes
150g (5oz) peeled butternut squash,
    chopped into 1cm (½in) cubes
25g (1oz) red split lentils

Put the carrot and butternut squash in a saucepan with 175ml (6fl oz) water and bring to the boil. Reduce the heat, cover with a lid and simmer for 10 minutes until tender. Add the lentils and another 175ml (6fl oz) water and continue to simmer for 25 minutes. At this point the lentils should be nice and mushy (if they are a little dry, add 1–2 tablespoons of water). Purée until really smooth and allow to cool a little before serving.

Apricot, prune and raisin compote

MAKES ABOUT 300ML (1/2 PINT)
VEGETARIAN

3 tbsp finely chopped dried apricots
3 tbsp finely chopped pitted prunes
4 tbsp raisins

Place all the dried fruit in a bowl and add 250ml (9fl oz) just boiled water. Cover with cling film and leave to soak in a cool place for at least 4 hours or overnight. Purée until really smooth.

Rachel's tips
* This is ideal for your baby if he or she is a little uncomfortable in the bowel department!
* Stored in an airtight container, this mixture will keep for at least a week in the fridge.

Avocado and banana mash

MAKES 1 PORTION · VEGETARIAN

½ ripe avocado, peeled and chopped
½ banana, peeled and sliced

Mash the avocado and banana together until as smooth as possible and serve immediately (both the avocado and the banana will go brown very quickly).

Banana and mango purée

MAKES 1 PORTION · VEGETARIAN

½ banana, peeled and sliced
¼ ripe mango, peeled and chopped

Mash the banana and mango together until as smooth as possible and serve immediately before the banana goes brown.

Variation
Substitute the mango with 1 small ripe peach.

Pear and apple purée

MAKES ABOUT 400ML (14FL OZ)
VEGETARIAN

2 ripe pears, peeled, cored and
  chopped into 1cm (½in) cubes
3 eating apples, peeled, cored and
  chopped into 1cm (½in) cubes

Put the pears and apples in a saucepan and add 200ml (7fl oz) water. Bring to the boil, reduce the heat and simmer, uncovered, on a low heat for 8–10 minutes. Purée until really smooth and then allow to cool a little before serving.

Variations
* Try adding a pinch of ground cinnamon during cooking.
* Mix the purée with ½ mashed banana.

Baby food

Making food for your baby is easier than you may think and certainly more economical than buying it ready made. From about six months of age your baby will be ready to move on to solid food and that's when you can get going with some tasty purées. By trying out a number of different recipes, you will soon discover which are favourites and which to avoid … for now. Though do try them again periodically, as you'll find your baby's tastes will change over time.

What foods to choose

Starting with naturally sweet-tasting fruit and vegetables can be easier, but do make sure to introduce the more savoury-tasting ones, too, or you may have a struggle to do this later. You may also be encouraging your child to develop a sweet tooth.

I always like to think of how food looks as well as tastes, so do bear this in mind with your baby meals. For a little one getting used to solid foods, a bright green or fun orange colour will look so much more appealing than just white or beige. As well as taste, texture is really important, and certain fruit and vegetables (carrots, peas, sweet potato, parsnip, butternut squash, apples and pears) purée to a smoother consistency than others. You will soon discover your baby's preferences. As your baby grows older, it is good to make a more textured purée or mash to encourage chewing and using new teeth!

Remember that her kidneys aren't sufficiently developed to cope with too much salt and giving sugar may encourage a sweet tooth, as well as damaging young teeth. So there's no need to add these to your baby's first foods.

When it comes to teething, a good tip is to keep some pieces of fruit and vegetables (such as melon, blueberries, banana, carrot or apple) in the fridge or freezer for those sore gums. They are both cooling on the gums and fun to munch on and play with — providing a welcome distraction from the pain.

When to introduce different foods

When introducing foods for the first time, do take things slowly. As your baby tries new foods, keep an eye out for any allergic reactions or digestive problems. It's best to introduce only one new food at a time and stick to that food for a few days to make sure your baby is happy with it. In this way, you can spot a problem straight away and remove any food that may be causing discomfort.

Up until 12 months of age, the 'nightshade' family of vegetables (potatoes, aubergines, peppers and tomatoes) are best avoided because they contain toxic elements to which a young child could be sensitive. Sweet potato and butternut squash make excellent alternatives until then. Dairy foods such as cheese, cow's milk and yoghurt should also be introduced very carefully in case your baby reacts to them. If there is a family history of cow's milk allergy, it's best not to give dairy products to her until after her first birthday.

From nine months is a good age to introduce citrus fruit and berries to your baby's diet. Some experts, however, recommend waiting until your baby is a year old before introducing them, as any earlier the acidity could cause tummy trouble or trigger an allergic reaction. The seeds from the berries are great for an older baby's digestive system and is particularly good for constipation. Or you could try adding mashed kiwi fruit, a little freshly squeezed orange juice or a light sprinkling of linseeds. It is also best to avoid wheat until your baby is at least one year old.

Preparing the purées

All these recipes have been tried and tested on some willing and hungry babies and all were very happy with the results, including the mums and dads preparing them. The ingredients for the purées can be blended in a food processor, blender or hand-held blender, whatever is most convenient for you. I always suggest making the full recipe and freezing some in ice-cube trays or small sealable containers, ensuring a ready stock of instant meals for when time is limited. Any purée not being eaten straight away should be allowed to cool completely before being placed in the fridge or freezer. Stored in an airtight container, all purées keep fresh in the fridge for a couple of days.

As a guide, I find 1oz (25g) of either fish or chicken is perfect for one serving, which can be mixed with 2–3 tablespoons of purée depending, of course, on your child's appetite. You can cook a little more of either, as they can be frozen in convenient portions for later use.

The recipes in this chapter use the cooking water so you keep as much of the vitamin and mineral content as possible. From 12 months you can substitute the water in the recipe with homemade chicken or vegetable stock (see page 326), making sure that you do not add any salt while making it for your baby.

Getting into the habit of making purées can benefit the whole family. You can use the sweet purées as a base for smoothies for older children and adults, and any of the vegetable purées would make a delicious and quick soup for everyone. Simply add a little more stock and season to taste with salt and pepper.

Baby purées suitable from nine months old

In these recipes I've moved from simple fruit and vegetables to introduce a bit of chicken and fish as your baby's digestive system will now be able to cope with the high level of protein. The fish is so soft that it doesn't need to be puréed — you can simply mash it, taking great care to ensure there are no bones. The two sweet purées included here (see page 322) both include berries, which are suitable to give to your child from this age — any earlier and it may be difficult to digest the seeds. If your baby doesn't like the seeds you can push the purée through a fine sieve to remove them. My boys loved eating berry purées at this age, but introduce them to your baby slowly or wait until 12 months (see pages 323–4).

Chicken, leek, sweet potato and parsnip purée

MAKES ABOUT 500ML (18FL OZ)

10g (½oz) butter
25g (1oz) trimmed leek, thinly sliced
175g (6oz) peeled sweet potato,
    chopped into 1cm (½in) cubes
25g (1oz) peeled parsnip,
    chopped into 1cm (½in) cubes
50g (2oz) cooked chicken, finely chopped

Melt the butter in a small saucepan and gently sauté the leek on a low heat for 2–3 minutes. Add the sweet potato and parsnip and pour over 275ml (9½fl oz) water. Bring to the boil and then reduce the heat, cover with a lid and simmer for 10 minutes or until almost tender. Add the chicken and continue to simmer, still covered, for 4 minutes. Purée until the mixture is really smooth and then leave to cool a little before serving.

Plaice with spinach and pea purée

PURÉE MAKES 400ML (14FL OZ)
VEGETARIAN (PURÉE ONLY)
PLAICE MAKES 1 PORTION

175g (6oz) fresh or frozen peas
150g (5oz) baby spinach
25g (1oz) skinned and trimmed plaice
2 tbsp milk

To make the purée, bring 200ml (7fl oz) water to the boil in a large saucepan. Add the peas, return to the boil and then reduce the heat and simmer, uncovered, for 5 minutes. Add the spinach and continue to simmer for a further 3 minutes. Purée until really smooth and then allow to cool a little before serving. Meanwhile, cook the fish. Put the plaice in a small saucepan and pour over the milk. Poach on a low heat, uncovered, for 3–4 minutes until the fish flakes easily. Remove the plaice with a slotted spoon, straining off the milk. Mash with a fork, ensuring no bones remain. To serve, combine the mashed plaice with 2–3 tablespoons of purée (depending on your baby's appetite).

Chicken, sweetcorn and butternut squash purée

MAKES ABOUT 400ML (14FL OZ)

225g (8oz) peeled butternut squash,
  chopped into 1cm (½in) cubes
5 tbsp drained sweetcorn
  (tinned or frozen and defrosted)
50g (2oz) cooked chicken breast,
  finely chopped

Put the butternut squash in a saucepan
and add 250ml (9fl oz) water. Bring to the
boil and then reduce the heat and simmer,
uncovered, for 12 minutes or until just soft.
Add the sweetcorn and chicken and continue
to simmer for a further 5 minutes. Purée
until really smooth and then allow to cool
a little before serving.

Broccoli, cauliflower and sweet potato purée

MAKES ABOUT 400ML (14FL OZ)

VEGETARIAN

75g (3oz) broccoli, cut into small pieces
110g (4oz) cauliflower, cut into small pieces
110g (4oz) peeled sweet potato,
  chopped into 1cm (½in) cubes

Put all the vegetables in a saucepan, pour in
350ml (12fl oz) water and bring to the boil.
Reduce the heat, cover with a lid and simmer
for 15 minutes or until tender. Purée until
really smooth and then allow to cool a little
before serving.

Blackberry and apple purée

MAKES ABOUT 250ML (9FL OZ)
VEGETARIAN

1 eating apple, peeled,
  cored and cut into small pieces
150g (5oz) blackberries

Put the apple and blackberries into a small
saucepan and pour over 175ml (6fl oz) water.
Cover with a lid and cook on a low heat for
5 minutes. Remove the lid and continue to
simmer for a further 5 minutes until really
soft. Purée until really smooth and then
leave to cool a little before serving.

Raspberry and strawberry purée

MAKES ABOUT 250ML (9FL OZ)

VEGETARIAN

150g (5oz) fresh or frozen
  (and defrosted) raspberries
150g (5oz) strawberries, hulled
½ banana, chopped (optional)

Place the raspberries and strawberries together
with the banana (if using) in a blender or food
processor and purée until smooth. You can
serve this purée added to semolina, porridge,
baby rice or yoghurt.

Baby purées suitable from 12 months old

As your baby gets older, you can try puréeing to a coarser texture to help make the transition to more solid food. You can also introduce tomatoes from 12 months. Eggs are such an easy food to prepare for your baby and highly nutritious too; just make sure that they are thoroughly cooked.

Minced beef with courgette, leek, tomato and parsnip

MAKES ABOUT 400ML (14FL OZ)

2 tsp olive oil
150g (5oz) minced beef
25g (1oz) trimmed leek, thinly sliced
25g (1oz) peeled parsnip,
   chopped into 1cm (½in) cubes
50g (2oz) courgette, sliced
1 clove of garlic, peeled and thinly sliced
½ x 400g tin of plum tomatoes

Heat the olive oil in a small saucepan and fry the minced beef for 3–4 minutes. Add the leek and cook for a further 2 minutes. Add the remaining ingredients, cover with a lid and simmer on a low heat for 10 minutes or until tender. Purée to the right texture for your baby. Serve with some cooked mini pasta shapes and some grated (mild) Cheddar cheese.

Cheesy scrambled egg

MAKES 1 PORTION · VEGETARIAN

1 egg
2 tbsp milk
½ tsp butter
1 tbsp mild Cheddar cheese, finely grated

Beat the egg and milk together in a small bowl. Melt the butter in a small saucepan on a low heat. Add the egg mixture and stir for 2–3 minutes until completely cooked. Remove from the heat and stir in the grated cheese. Allow to cool a little before serving.

Salmon with butternut squash, sweet potato and garlic mash

MAKES ABOUT 400ML (14FL OZ)
VEGETARIAN (PURÉE ONLY)

For the mash
175g (6oz) peeled sweet potato,
   chopped into 1cm (½in) cubes
175g (6oz) peeled butternut squash,
   chopped into 1cm (½in) cubes
1 clove of garlic, peeled and thinly sliced
125ml (4½fl oz) chicken or vegetable stock
   (see page 326) or water

For the fish
25g (1oz) trimmed salmon fillet,
   skinned and deboned
3 tbsp milk

1 First make the mash. Put the all the prepared vegetables in a saucepan, add the stock or water and bring to the boil. Reduce the heat, cover with a lid and simmer for 15 minutes or until tender. Mash (or purée if a finer texture is required) and then leave to cool a little.

2 To cook the fish, place the salmon in a small saucepan with the milk. Gently poach on a low heat, uncovered, for 4–5 minutes or until the fish flakes easily. Remove the fish from the milk with a slotted spoon and then flake the fish, checking again for any bones and discarding any you find.

3 To serve, combine the flaked salmon with 2–3 tablespoons of mash (depending on your baby's appetite).

Chicken with potato, carrot and garlic mash

MAKES ABOUT 400ML (14FL OZ)
VEGETARIAN (PURÉE ONLY)

For the mash
225g (8oz) peeled floury potato,
   chopped into 1cm (½in) cubes
175g (6oz) peeled carrot,
   chopped into 1cm (½in) cubes
1 clove of garlic, peeled and thinly sliced
125ml (4½fl oz) chicken or vegetable stock
   (see page 326) or water
1 tsp butter, softened

For the chicken
1 tsp butter, plus extra to dot over the chicken
25g (1oz) raw chicken breast, trimmed of any fat
2 tsp chicken or vegetable stock or water

1 Preheat the oven to 180°C (350°F), Gas
mark 4.

2 First make the mash. Put the potato, carrot,
garlic and stock or water into a saucepan and
bring to the boil. Reduce the heat, cover with
a lid and simmer for 15 minutes until tender.
Leave to cool for about 10 minutes and then
add the butter and mash until smooth (or
purée if a smoother texture is required).

3 Meanwhile, to cook the chicken, lightly
grease the base of a small ovenproof dish
with some of the butter and place the chicken
in. Dot the remaining butter on top of the
chicken and add the stock or water. Cover
with foil and bake in the oven for 15 minutes.
Allow the chicken to cool a little and then
finely dice.

4 To serve, combine the diced chicken with
2–3 tablespoons of the mash (depending on
your baby's appetite).

Apricot and pear semolina

MAKES ABOUT 400ML (14FL OZ)
VEGETARIAN

225g (8oz) ready-to-eat dried apricots,
   finely chopped
110g (4oz) peeled and cored ripe pear,
   finely chopped
25g (1oz) fine semolina
125ml (4½fl oz) milk

1 Put the apricots and pear in a saucepan and
pour over 175ml (6fl oz) water. Bring to the
boil, reduce the heat and simmer, uncovered,
for 12–15 minutes or until soft. Purée until
the right texture for your baby.

2 Meanwhile, cook the semolina. Place the
semolina and milk in a small saucepan and,
stirring constantly, bring almost to the boil.
Reduce the heat to low and, continuing to stir,
cook for 3–4 minutes or until it thickens.
Remove from the heat and allow to cool a little.

3 To serve, place the semolina in a bowl and
make a well in the centre. Spoon in 2–3
tablespoons of the purée.

Custard with plum and apple

MAKES ABOUT 250ML (9FL OZ)
VEGETARIAN

1 eating apple, peeled, cored and finely diced
200g (7oz) stoned ripe plums, finely chopped
½ tsp caster sugar
2 tsp custard powder
125ml (4½oz) milk

1 Place the apple and plums in a small saucepan
with 4 tablespoons of water, cover with a lid and
cook on a low heat for 12 minutes or until soft.
Purée until the right texture for your baby.

2 Meanwhile, make the custard. Put the sugar
and powder in a small pan and blend in the
milk until smooth. Cook on a low heat for 3–4
minutes, stirring constantly, until the custard
thickens. Pour into a bowl and allow to cool.

3 Put 2–3 tablespoons of the purée into the
centre of the custard and serve immediately.

Basics

Chicken stock

MAKES ABOUT 2 LITRES (3 1/2 PINTS)

Chicken stock is invaluable, forming the basis for so many stews, sauces and soups. Homemade stock, with its intense, fresh flavour, is best of all. Indeed, making stock is a very good way of using up ingredients that might otherwise be thrown away — onion peel, carrot and celery trimmings and, of course, chicken bones. Get into the habit of making stock whenever you have a chicken carcass to hand — whether cooked or raw. If you're not using the stock straight away, it will store in the fridge for 2–3 days or you can pour it into several small containers to freeze.

1 chicken carcass (either raw or cooked)
1 onion, unpeeled and halved (or 1 leek, split and halved)
1–2 carrots, peeled and halved lengthways
1 stick of celery
1 small bay leaf
1 sprig of parsley
1 sprig of thyme
4 peppercorns
Salt and freshly ground black pepper

1 Place all the ingredients in a large saucepan and then pour over about 3 litres (5 pints) water. Bring to the boil, reduce the heat and simmer, covered but with a wooden spoon between the lid and the pan to allow the steam to escape, on a medium heat for 1–2 hours or until you have a well-flavoured stock.

2 Season to taste with salt and pepper and then strain the stock through a fine sieve into a large bowl or jug, discarding the bits in the sieve. Allow to cool, skimming off any fat from the surface of the stock as it cools.

Variation
Vegetable stock: Prepare and cook as above, simply omitting the chicken carcass.

Beef stock

MAKES ABOUT 1.8 LITRES (3 PINTS)

This involves a little more work than the chicken stock (see left) as you have to roast the bones first. Use the stock straight away; otherwise store in the fridge for 2–3 days or freeze in batches.

900g–1.3kg (2–3lb) beef bones, raw or cooked
1 onion, unpeeled and halved
1 large carrot, peeled and halved lengthways
1 stick of celery
1 bay leaf
2 sprigs of thyme
4 peppercorns
1 clove
½ tsp tomato purée
Salt and freshly ground black pepper

1 Preheat the oven to 230°C (450°F), Gas mark 8.

2 Put the beef bones in a roasting tin and roast in the oven for about 40 minutes or until well browned. Add the onion, carrot and celery for the last 15 minutes of cooking.

3 Tip everything in the tin into a large pan, add the remaining ingredients and top with 2.2 litres (3¾ pints) water. Pour away any fat in the roasting tin and put the tin on a high heat and deglaze with a good dash of water, stirring with a wooden spoon and scraping any sediment from the bottom.

4 Add the deglazed cooking juices to the pan with the beef bones and vegetables and bring slowly to the boil. Reduce the heat and simmer, covered but with a wooden spoon between the lid and the pan to allow the steam to escape, for 4–5 hours or until you are happy you have a strong-flavoured stock. During cooking, skim off any fat or impurities that rise to the surface.

5 Season to taste with salt and pepper. Strain the finished stock through a fine sieve into a large bowl or jug, discarding the bits in the sieve. Allow to cool, again skimming off any fat that rises to the top while cooling.

Roux

Roux is a basic and simple sauce thickener made with equal quantities of butter and plain flour. Hence, for example, 100g (3½oz) butter and 100g (3½oz) flour makes 200g (7oz) of roux. If you find yourself using quite a lot, make a big batch as it keeps for up to a month in the fridge.

1 Melt the butter in a small saucepan on a low to medium heat and add the flour.

2 Allow to cook for 2 minutes, stirring regularly, and then either use straight away or leave to cool and place in the fridge.

Basic white sauce

MAKES ABOUT 300ML (½ PINT)
VEGETARIAN

This makes a sauce thick enough to coat the back of a spoon. If you would like a thicker sauce, add more roux or start with less milk, and if you would like a thinner sauce, then use less roux or start with more milk.

300ml (½ pint) whole milk
Few slices of carrot
Few slices of onion
1 sprig of parsley
1 sprig of thyme
3 peppercorns
25g (1oz) roux (see above)
Salt and freshly ground black pepper

1 Pour the milk into a small saucepan and add the carrot, onion, parsley, thyme and peppercorns. Bring to the boil, reduce the heat and simmer for 4–5 minutes. Remove from the heat and leave to infuse for about 10 minutes.

2 Strain the milk through a sieve placed over a small saucepan and bring the milk back to the boil. Whisk in the roux, a little at a time, until well blended and leave to simmer gently for 4–5 minutes or until thickened to the desired consistency. Season to taste and use as a plain white sauce or add your choice of flavouring.

Rachel's tip
For a speedier version, melt the butter in a large saucepan on a medium heat and add the flour, stirring for a few seconds. Take off the heat and gradually add the milk, stirring continuously until the milk is fully incorporated and the sauce is lump free. Return the pan to a gentle heat and cook the sauce for 6–8 minutes, stirring constantly, until thickened and smooth.

Herb butters

EACH RECIPE MAKES 85G (3½OZ)
VEGETARIAN

Herb butter is easy to make, using whatever herbs are to hand. To store, spoon it onto some greaseproof paper, roll into a sausage shape, securing the ends, and pop in the fridge or freezer. Slice the butter off as you need it.

Dill butter
75g (3oz) butter
1 heaped tbsp finely chopped dill
Squeeze of lemon juice
Salt and freshly ground black pepper

Mash the butter with a fork in a small bowl to soften. Stir in the dill along with a good squeeze of lemon juice and a little salt and pepper and place in the fridge or freezer until ready to use.

Garlic and herb butter
75g (3oz) butter
3 cloves of garlic, peeled and crushed
1 heaped tbsp finely chopped mixed herbs
Salt and freshly ground black pepper

Mash the butter with a fork in a small bowl to soften. Stir in the garlic, herbs and a little salt and pepper and place in the fridge or freezer until ready to use.

Horseradish sauce

MAKES 400ML (14FL OZ) VEGETARIAN

This sauce, which is perfect with roast beef (see page 103), will keep in the fridge in a jar or bowl for 2–3 days.

5 tbsp finely grated fresh horseradish
2 tsp white wine vinegar
1 tsp lemon juice
1 tsp Dijon mustard
1 tsp caster sugar
300ml (½ pint) crème fraîche
Salt and freshly ground black pepper

Place 3 tablespoons of the grated horseradish in a bowl and add the vinegar, lemon juice, mustard and sugar. Fold in the crème fraîche and then taste, adding the remaining horseradish if you wish. Season with salt and pepper and serve the sauce straight away or store in the fridge.

Tartare sauce

MAKES 200ML (7FL OZ) · VEGETARIAN

The classic sauce for fish and chips (see page 176), it keeps in the fridge for 3–4 days.

125ml (4½fl oz) mayonnaise (see page 330)
1 hard-boiled egg (see page 25),
    cold and finely chopped
3 tsp capers, rinsed and chopped
25g (1oz) gherkins, chopped
2 tsp chopped chives or spring onions
2 tsp chopped flat-leaf parsley
1 tsp Dijon mustard
Salt and freshly ground black pepper
Squeeze of lemon juice

Spoon the mayonnaise into a bowl and stir in the egg, capers, gherkins, chives or spring onions, parsley and mustard. Season with salt and pepper and add a little lemon juice to the sauce if necessary.

Redcurrant jelly

MAKES 2 X 400G (14OZ) JARS
VEGETARIAN

Delicious with roast meat, especially lamb (see page 106), this will keep for months in sterilised jars in the fridge. Use frozen redcurrants instead of fresh if necessary.

500g (1lb 2oz) fresh or frozen (and defrosted)
    redcurrants, stalks removed
500g (1lb 2oz) caster or granulated sugar

1 Place the redcurrants and sugar in a large, heavy-based saucepan and stir on a medium heat until the sugar dissolves and the mixture comes to the boil. Turn up the heat and boil for 6 minutes, stirring every now and then to prevent it from sticking to the bottom of the pan.

2 Spoon off any froth that has come to the top and then pour the mixture into a sieve (not an aluminium one as the acidity of the heated fruit juice can react with this metal). Allow it to drip through without pushing it with a spoon (which will cause the jelly to become cloudy) and then place in clean, sterilised jars (see Rachel's tip on page 336).

Mint sauce

75ML (3FL OZ) · VEGETARIAN

The classic accompaniment to roast lamb (see page 106), mint sauce is best made on the day – up to a couple of hours before serving.

3 tbsp chopped mint
1 heaped tbsp caster or granulated sugar
50ml (2fl oz) boiling water
1 tbsp lemon juice or white wine vinegar

Simply put the mint and sugar in a small bowl and pour over the boiling water. Stir to dissolve the sugar and then stir in the lemon juice or vinegar. Leave to stand for at least 10 minutes before serving.

Rachel's ketchup

MAKES ABOUT 200ML (7FL OZ)
VEGETARIAN

If your children regularly eat ketchup, then
you might want to try them with this delicious
and much healthier homemade version.
If you think they won't take to it, ease them
into it by mixing some into their usual brand
and gradually adjusting their taste. This is
definitely best made in the summer with
lovely ripe red tomatoes. It keeps for many
weeks in the fridge because of the spice and
sugar. It's possible to freeze the sauce —
perhaps as ice cubes for speedy thawing.

2 tbsp olive oil
225g (8oz) onions, peeled and roughly chopped
650g (1lb 7oz) (about 6 small–medium)
    tomatoes, roughly chopped (no need to peel)
2 cloves of garlic, peeled and crushed or
    finely grated
75ml (3fl oz) white wine vinegar
75g (3oz) caster sugar
2 tsp Dijon mustard
Pinch of ground allspice
Pinch of ground cloves
½ level tsp salt
½ level tsp freshly ground black pepper

1 Heat the olive oil in a saucepan, add the
onions and sauté on a medium heat for 8–10
minutes or until softened and a little golden.
Add the rest of the ingredients, cover with a
lid and leave to simmer for about 30 minutes
or until very soft.

2 Remove from the heat and purée in a
blender or food processor or using a hand-
held blender. Pour through a sieve into a
clean saucepan and simmer, uncovered and
stirring regularly, for another 30 minutes
or until the mixture is thick.

3 Pour into sterilised jars or bottles (see tip
on page 336) and cover with lids to seal.

Dried beans and peas

VEGETARIAN

These are cheap, nutritious and very filling.
They are also very versatile and can be added to
soups, stews and salads, mashed and made into
purées, such as hummus (see page 73). Stored
in airtight containers in a cool, dry place, dried
beans and peas should keep for up to two years.

1 To work out what quantity to start with,
it is useful to know that dried beans more
or less double in weight when soaked in water
and cooked. So if a recipe asks for a 400g tin
of beans (giving about 250g/9oz beans once
drained), then you would start with 125g (4½oz)
dried beans. Also, for when not following a
specific recipe, it's handy to know you should
allow about 50g (2oz) dried beans per person.
If you are going to take the time to prepare a
batch, then soak and cook more than required
as the leftover beans will keep perfectly in the
fridge, for up to 3 days, or freezer.

How to cook dried beans or peas
1 Rinse the beans and then soak them in
2–3 times their volume of water for 6–8
hours or overnight. Discard any that rise to
the top of the water during soaking or that are
discoloured or shrivelled. Drain and then place
in a large saucepan with again 2–3 times their
volume of fresh water. Do not salt the water as
this will toughen their skins during cooking.

2 Boil rapidly for about 15 minutes (this is
particularly important for red kidney beans
to destroy their toxins), then simmer for
30 minutes to 1 hour, depending on the
type of bean, until tender (soya beans will
take about 3 hours). Drain well and reserve
the cooking water to use as a vegetable stock,
if wished. Use the beans or peas in your
chosen recipe or leave to cool and place
in the fridge or freezer.

Rice

Many people believe they can't cook rice, but this is a pretty much foolproof recipe that should work every time.

450g (1lb) white rice, such as basmati
1 tsp salt
15g (½oz) butter (optional)

1 Preheat the oven to 140°C (275°F), Gas mark 1.

2 Bring a large saucepan of water to the boil. Add the rice and salt, give the pan a stir, cover with a lid and boil for 4–5 minutes or until the rice is nearly cooked but still has a tiny bite.

3 Drain the rice and place in a serving dish. Stir in the butter (if using), cover and put in the oven for at least 15 minutes. When ready to eat, fluff up the rice with a fork and serve.

Rachel's tips

* If you want to get the rice into the oven 30 minutes before you eat, just preheat it to 100°C (200°F), the lowest gas mark.
* Sometimes I add whole spices to the water, such as a small cinnamon stick or 2–3 star anise and a few green cardamom pods, and serve them on top of the rice.

Mayonnaise

MAKES 300ML (½ PINT) · VEGETARIAN

Great on its own, mayonnaise is also delicious with other ingredients added to it – see the suggested variations to the right and the photograph on page 268. It will keep in the fridge for at least a week.

2 egg yolks
1 tsp Dijon mustard
2 tsp white wine vinegar
Salt and freshly ground black pepper
225ml (8fl oz) oil (I like to use 200ml/7fl oz
    sunflower oil and 25ml/1fl oz olive oil)

1 Put the egg yolks into a bowl with the mustard, vinegar and a pinch of salt and mix together.

2 Very gradually add the oil, drop by drop, whisking all the time. You should start to see the mixture thickening. Keep adding the oil as you whisk until it is all used up and you have a thick mayonnaise. Season to taste.

Variations

Relish mayonnaise: Stir together three times as much mayonnaise as tomato relish for a slightly sweet dip: for example, 75ml (3fl oz) mayonnaise and 25ml (1fl oz) relish.

Garlic and herb dip: Using a hand-held blender or by hand, mix 100ml (3½fl oz) mayonnaise with 1 small, finely chopped garlic clove and 4 tablespoons of chopped mixed herbs (or just use a single herb) such as parsley and chives.

Sweet chilli mayonnaise: Add 2 tablespoons of sweet chilli sauce to 100ml (3½fl oz) mayonnaise for a sweet and spicy mix.

Roast tomato and lime mayonnaise: Arrange 12 halved cherry tomatoes on a baking tray, drizzle over 1 teaspoon of balsamic vinegar and season with salt, pepper and a pinch of caster sugar. Roast in an oven preheated to 200°C (400°F), Gas mark 6 for about 10–15 minutes or until softened. Allow to completely cool and then place in a blender, add 100ml (3½fl oz) mayonnaise and blitz for a few seconds. Alternatively, use a hand-held blender for blitzing the tomatoes with the mayonnaise. Add 1 teaspoon of basil and 1 teaspoon of lime juice and blend a little more until smooth. Taste and adjust the seasoning if necessary. It should taste quite zingy, so add more lime juice if you wish.

Rachel's tip

I often make the mayonnaise using a hand-held blender with a whisk attachment, adding the oil a little at a time. That way it takes only a minute to make.

Hollandaise sauce

MAKES ABOUT 150ML (5FL OZ)
VEGETARIAN

There are two ways of making hollandaise sauce and this is the simpler method. It is fantastic served with fish, and in particular it transforms poached salmon into a feast. Add any leftover sauce to some mashed potato for a luxuriously creamy dish. This sauce can also be made directly in a small saucepan, but be careful that it doesn't get too hot or the eggs will scramble.

2 egg yolks
110g (4oz) butter, diced
Salt and freshly ground black pepper
Squeeze of lemon juice

1 Place a heatproof bowl over a saucepan of simmering water on a medium heat. Add the egg yolks and 1 tablespoon of cold water and whisk together. Gradually add the butter, bit by bit, until each addition has melted and emulsified as it is whisked in, before adding the next.

2 Once all the butter had been added, cook for a few minutes more, stirring regularly, until the sauce has thickened enough to coat the back of a spoon. Taste and season with salt, pepper and lemon juice.

3 Remove from the heat, and keep warm if necessary, by covering with cling film and leaving to sit over the warm water, until you're ready to serve.

French dressing

MAKES 75ML (3FL OZ) · VEGETARIAN

Here is a recipe for a basic and delicious everyday vinaigrette for dressing salad. Use a good extra-virgin olive oil for the best flavour. The vinaigrette will keep in the fridge for around 3–4 days.

3 tbsp extra-virgin olive oil
1 tbsp white wine vinegar
1 tsp Dijon mustard
1 tsp caster sugar
1 large clove of garlic, peeled and crushed
2 tsp finely chopped chives
Salt and freshly ground black pepper

1 Place all the ingredients in a jar with a lid, season with salt and pepper and give it a good shake to mix. Taste for seasoning and adjust if necessary.

2 When ready to serve, drizzle sparingly over a selection of your prepared salad ingredients in a bowl and toss to coat.

Bread rolls

MAKES ABOUT 24–30 ROLLS
VEGETARIAN

These bread rolls are fun to make as well as good to have stored in the freezer as an instant accompaniment for soups or salads or just enjoyed smeared with a knob of herb butter (see page 327). If you are intending to freeze them, split the rolls in half after you have made them: that way, they can be toasted straight from the freezer.

2 tsp caster sugar
425ml (15fl oz) warm water
2½ tsp dried yeast or 20g (¾oz) fresh yeast
**   or 1½ x 7g sachets fast-acting yeast**
750g (1lb 10oz) strong white flour,
**   plus extra for dusting**
2 tsp salt
40g (1½oz) butter or 4 tbsp olive oil,
**   plus extra oil for greasing**
1 egg, beaten, and poppy or sesame seeds,
**   for the top of the loaf (optional)**

1 In a measuring jug, mix the sugar with 150ml (5fl oz) of the warm water and the yeast and allow to stand in a warm place for 5 minutes until frothy. If using fast-acting yeast, there is no need to let the mixture stand.

(continued overleaf)

2 Sift the flour and salt into a large bowl. Rub in the butter and make a well in the centre. (If using olive oil instead of butter, pour the olive oil into the remaining water.) Pour in the yeast mixture and most of the remaining water (and the olive oil, if using). Mix to a loose dough, adding the remaining water if needed, plus extra if necessary.

3 Knead for about 10 minutes or until the dough is smooth and springy to the touch. (If kneading in an electric food mixer with a dough hook, 5 minutes is usually long enough.) Put the dough into a large oiled bowl. Cover the top tightly with cling film and place somewhere warm (such as beside a radiator or Aga or in the airing cupboard) to rise until doubled in size. This may take up to 2 or even (on a cold day) 3 hours.

4 When the dough has more than doubled in size, knock back, punching the dough to let out any trapped air in the dough, and knead again for 2–3 minutes. Leave to relax for 10 minutes before you begin to shape the rolls.

5 Meanwhile, preheat the oven to 220°C (425°F), Gas mark 7.

6 Divide the dough in two and, working on a lightly floured surface, roll each piece into a log shape about 4–5cm (1½–2in) thick. Cut each piece into 12–15 equal-sized pieces and mould to you choice of shape (see right).

7 Once shaped (and placed on baking sheets or in muffin tins – see right) cover with a clean tea towel. Allow to rise again in a warm place for 20–30 minutes until the shaped dough has once again doubled in size. When fully risen, it should leave a dent when you gently press the dough with your finger.

8 Carefully (as the bread is full of air at this point and therefore very fragile) brush with the beaten egg and sprinkle with poppy or sesame seeds (if using), or dust lightly with flour for more rustic-looking rolls.

9 Bake in the oven for about 15 minutes or until golden and cooked through. When cooked they will feel light and sound hollow when tapped on the base. Transfer to a wire rack to cool.

Roll shapes

Plain rolls: Roll each dough piece into a ball and flatten slightly and place on a lightly floured baking sheet.

Clover leaf rolls: Divide a dough piece into three and shape each one into a small ball. Place all three balls into a section of a lightly greased muffin tin, so that they join together during cooking, and repeat with the remaining dough.

Snail or spiral rolls: Roll each dough piece into a sausage shape about 15cm (6in) long. Coil each one up separately and place in a section of a lightly greased muffin tin.

Flower rolls: Roll each dough piece into a ball and flatten into a circle. Place on a lightly floured baking sheet and use a sharp knife to make 5–6 slits from the outside almost to the inside, right around the circle.

Knots: Roll and twist each dough piece into a sausage shape about 15cm (6in) long. Tie into a loose knot and place on a lightly floured baking sheet.

Variation

Loaves of bread: To make two loaves instead of rolls: after knocking back and relaxing the dough, divide it in half. Mould into round or oval loaf shapes and place on a floured baking sheet to rise again, as described in step 7 to the left. Top with the beaten egg and seeds or dust with flour, as in step 9 above, and bake in the oven at 220°C (425°F), Gas mark 7 for 15 minutes before reducing the temperature to 200°C (400°F), Gas mark 6 for a further 15–30 minutes. When cooked, the bread should sound hollow when tapped on the base.

Soda bread

This traditional Irish loaf is one of the fastest bread recipes to make.

450g (1lb) plain flour, plus extra for dusting
1 tsp caster sugar
1 level tsp bicarbonate of soda
1 tsp salt
350–425ml (12–15fl oz) buttermilk or soured milk (see tip on page 24)

1 Preheat the oven to 230°C (450°F), Gas mark 8.

2 Sift the dry ingredients into a large bowl and make a well in the centre. Pour in most of the buttermilk or soured milk (leaving about 50ml/2fl oz in the measuring jug). Using one hand with your fingers outstretched like a claw, bring the flour and liquid together, adding more buttermilk if necessary. Don't knead the mixture or it will become heavy. The dough should be softish, but not too wet and sticky.

3 When it comes together, turn onto a floured work surface and bring together a little more. Pat the dough into a round about 4cm (1½in) deep and cut a deep cross in it.

4 Place on a baking sheet and bake in the oven for 15 minutes, then turn down the heat to 200°C (400°F), Gas mark 6 and cook for 30 minutes more. When cooked, the loaf will sound slightly hollow when tapped on the base and be golden in colour. I often turn it upside down for the last 5 minutes of cooking. Allow to cool on a wire rack.

Shortcrust pastry

MAKES 350G (12OZ) · VEGETARIAN

It's always worth making your own shortcrust pastry as it is so quick to make and tastes meltingly delicious with a whole range of sweet and savoury fillings.

110g (4oz) cold butter, diced, plus extra for greasing
200g (7oz) plain flour
1 tbsp icing sugar
1 egg yolk

23cm (9in) diameter, fluted, loose-bottomed tart tin with 2cm (¾in) sides

1 Preheat the oven to 180°C (350°F), Gas mark 4. Lightly grease the tart tin.

2 Sift the flour and sugar into a bowl and rub in the butter until the mixture resembles fine breadcrumbs. Mix the egg yolk with 2 tablespoons of cold water and add just enough of this to bring the pastry together to a firm dough. Shape the dough into a ball and flatten slightly, then cover with cling film and chill in the fridge for at least 30 minutes.

3 Roll the pastry out between two sheets of cling film (each sheet larger than the tin) to a thickness of about 5mm (¼in). Keep the pastry in a round shape as you roll it out, making sure you have a large enough piece to line the base and sides of the tin.

4 Remove the cling film (keeping the top layer to help shape the pastry, if you wish) and carefully lift the pastry into the tart tin. It will be very soft and may break in places but simply patch it back together. Press the pastry into the edges and, using your thumb, 'cut' it along the edge of the tin for a neat finish. Remove the top layer of cling film (if not already removed) and prick over the base with a fork. Place in the freezer for 2 minutes to chill.

5 To bake 'blind', place a disc or square of parchment paper in the tart case, large enough to cover the base and sides plus a bit extra, and fill with baking beans or dried pulses. Bake in the oven for 15–20 minutes or until the pastry feels slightly dry on the base and looks light golden around the edges. Remove the foil or paper and the beans and leave to cool a little before adding your choice of filling.

Stocking the larder

There will always be times when you don't seem to have a moment to do any shopping. If your larder is well stocked with a good selection of basics, it will tide you over until your next supermarket run, making your life so much easier. Of course, you'll need to stock up on fresh fruit and vegetables and other perishables every week or every few days but with a full larder you'll always be ready for the unexpected.

Staple supplies

These are the things I always keep in my larder so I never need to worry that I have the wherewithal for rustling up a meal if I don't have time to get to the shops. I make sure to keep tins of tomatoes and beans such as chickpeas and haricot beans as well as packets of dried beans for soaking and cooking (see page 329). Different kinds of dried lentils – Puy lentils or red lentils – cook quickly and can be used in a variety of delicious soups and salads. Pasta of various shapes and different types of rice, such as multi-purpose basmati or long-grain and Arborio for risottos (see page 146), are all essential. In addition, a good stock of eggs, potatoes, onions and cloves of garlic is invaluable.

I'll also stock a wide selection of vinegars – red, white, sherry, balsamic, rice and cider vinegar – as well as a selection of oils. Extra-virgin olive oil and a good neutral oil such as sunflower oil are essential, while seed or nut oils such as walnut oil and hazelnut oil are wonderful in salad dressings. Nut oils tend to go off quite quickly, so I buy them in small quantities and keep them in the fridge. Soy sauce, fish sauce (nam pla) and sweet chilli sauce keep forever and are a must for stir-fries.

When it comes to what to store your groceries in, you can buy all kinds of ziplock bags and airtight boxes. These work well and will keep your food fresher for longer. However, you don't have to spend money on these – old ice cream containers, jam jars, sweet or biscuits tins and even plastic bags work well, too.

Baking basics

For baking, I make sure the larder is well stocked with plain, self-raising and wholemeal flour, together with cornflour, rice flour and baking powder, bicarbonate of soda and cream of tartar. And I keep all the different sugars I may need – caster, icing, soft brown and demerara sugar – as well as golden syrup and honey. A good-quality vanilla extract is also important for baking.

Whenever possible, I like to buy whole dried spices as their flavour lasts a lot longer than ground spices. Spices start to lose flavour as soon as they are ground and after a couple of months they become very dull-tasting. I always have jars of black peppercorns, cumin, coriander and mustard seeds, cinnamon sticks, green cardamom pods and nutmeg kernels. As some spices such as turmeric, ginger and cayenne pepper are only available ready-ground, I buy them in slightly smaller quantities. As well as spices, I always have a fine salt for baking and a coarse sea salt for the table and for seasoning.

I love adding seeds to bread or rolls (see page 331–2) or sprinkling them into smoothies and salads. I keep all kinds of seeds in the larder: golden linseed, pumpkin, sesame, flax, poppy and sunflower. Rolled oats are another essential – for porridge, granola and flapjacks (see pages 12, 11 and 284). I also like to keep a variety of nuts, such as pecans, hazelnuts and almonds. These I buy in small quantities to ensure I always have fresh ones to hand.

Basics for the freezer and fridge

My freezer is stocked with raw meat and fish, which I rotate according to freshness to make sure everything gets used. I also keep stock in the freezer (see page 326) and breadcrumbs – for adding to burgers or sausages or coating meat or fish. I freeze any slices of bread left over from a loaf and when there's a sufficiently large batch, defrost them and whiz into breadcrumbs in the food processor, then pop them in a sealed food bag or covered container in the freezer. I keep pine nuts for making pesto (see page 62) or adding to salads and scattering over pizza. Good-quality frozen peas are just excellent as an instant vegetable and for adding to soup, kedgeree (see page 36) or pasta and

other rice dishes. If you have a glut of tomatoes in the summer, you can freeze these to use in cooking throughout the year. (For more on the benefits of home freezing, see pages 170-1.)

Like the freezer, the fridge is a vital adjunct to the larder. I make sure I keep it well stocked with butter, cream, milk, natural yoghurt and a variety of cheeses as well as fruit and vegetables. I also love chorizo, which I keep on hand to add a spicy touch to sauces, soup and pizza (see page 149).

Onion jam

MAKES ABOUT 500G (1LB 2OZ)
VEGETARIAN

This is just divine and very versatile, a perfect accompaniment to cheese, cold meats, sausages, steak, lamb chops or roast pork. It will keep for about year in the fridge because of all the sugar and alcohol it contains. If you don't have crème de cassis, use blackcurrant cordial instead.

25g (1oz) butter
675g (1½lb) onions, peeled and thinly sliced
150g (5oz) caster or granulated sugar
Salt and freshly ground black pepper
100ml (3½fl oz) sherry vinegar
    or balsamic vinegar
250ml (9fl oz) full-bodied red wine
2 tbsp crème de cassis

1 Melt the butter in a large saucepan and stir in the onions, sugar and some salt and pepper. Cover with a tight-fitting lid and cook on a gentle heat for 30 minutes, stirring occasionally, until the onions are softened but not browned.

2 Add the vinegar, wine and crème de cassis and cook, uncovered, for another 30–35 minutes, stirring occasionally, until slightly thickened. Remove and leave to cool (it will thicken more once cool) and then store in the fridge in an airtight container.

Orange curd

MAKES 400ML (14FL OZ)
VEGETARIAN

This variation on the classic lemon curd is wonderful with yoghurt (see page 10), on pancakes, toast or freshly baked bread. It will successfully keep in a sealed jar in the fridge for a couple of weeks.

75g (3oz) butter
150g (5oz) caster sugar
Finely grated zest and juice of 2 oranges
2 whole eggs and 1 egg yolk, beaten

1 Place the butter, sugar and orange zest in a large saucepan and strain the orange juice in through a fine sieve. Gently warm the mixture through on a low heat until the sugar has dissolved.

2 Remove the saucepan from the heat and stir in the beaten eggs. (It is important to stir the mixture vigorously to prevent the eggs from scrambling.) Return to a very low heat and continue stirring for 10–15 minutes or until the curd has thickened enough to coat the back of the wooden spoon.

3 Remove from the heat, pour into a bowl or sterilised jars (see Rachel's tips below) and leave to cool.

Rachel's tips
* Use the leftover egg white to make Eton Mess or meringues (see pages 234 and 237).
* To sterilise jars, either put them through a dishwasher cycle, boil in a saucepan filled with water for 5 minutes or place in a preheated oven (150°C/300°F/Gas mark 2) for 10 minutes.

Toffee sauce

MAKES ABOUT 700ML (1 1/4 PINTS)
VEGETARIAN

This is the best recipe, and it keeps for ages; weeks, even months! It is great to have some in a jar in the fridge for reheating. Wonderful over ice cream, crumbles, meringues (see pages 240, 214 and 237), inside a meringue roulade or simply over chopped-up bananas and cream.

110g (4oz) butter, diced
250g (9oz) soft light brown sugar
  (or half brown and half caster sugar)
275g (10oz) golden syrup
225ml (8fl oz) single or regular cream
½ tsp vanilla extract

Place all the ingredients in a saucepan on a high heat. Stir until the butter has melted and the sugar dissolves. Bring to the boil and cook for about 4–5 minutes, stirring regularly, until thickened and smooth. Serve warm.

Dark chocolate sauce

MAKES 175ML (6FL OZ)
VEGETARIAN

Very quick to make, this hot chocolate sauce is the ultimate in sinfulness — perfect drizzled over ice cream or with the Dark Chocolate Layered Semifreddo (see page 246). Although it keeps in the fridge for several weeks, I challenge you to leave it there for that long.

75g (3fl oz) dark chocolate, chopped
100ml (3½fl oz) double or regular cream

Melt the chocolate in a heatproof bowl sitting over a saucepan of gently simmering water. Whisk in the cream to give a smooth melted sauce and then keep warm in the bowl until ready to serve.

Raspberry coulis

MAKES ABOUT 225ML (8FL OZ)
VEGETARIAN

A fresh-tasting, summery sauce for serving with fresh fruits and ice cream, this also makes a terrific base for a cocktail.

250g (9oz) fresh or frozen
  (and defrosted) raspberries
1 tbsp icing sugar
2 tbsp lime juice

1 Place all the ingredients in a blender or use a hand-held blender and blitz until really smooth. Taste and add a little more sugar or lime juice if wished.

2 Push through a fine sieve over a small bowl and serve or place in the fridge (for up to two days) until ready to use. This can also be frozen.

Variation
Other berry coulis: Use strawberries or mixed berries instead of the raspberries.

Mocha sauce

MAKES ABOUT 200ML (7FL OZ)
VEGETARIAN

The term 'mocha', referring to the delicious drink in which coffee and chocolate are combined, is believed to derive from the port of Mocha, in Yemen, through which coffee was exported. This sauce is wonderful with ice cream and keeps in the fridge for several weeks.

100g (3½oz) dark chocolate, chopped
100ml (3½fl oz) good strong coffee
  (use leftovers)
1 tbsp coffee liqueur, such as Tia Maria
  or Kahlúa (optional)

Melt the chocolate in a heatproof bowl sitting over a saucepan of gently simmering water. Take off the heat and whisk in the coffee and liqueur (if using). The sauce will thicken a little as it cools. Serve warm or cold.

Custard

MAKES 700ML (1 1/4 PINTS)
VEGETARIAN

Custard is the perfect accompaniment for
a fruit tart or crumble (see pages 210 and
214). This recipe takes me right back to
my childhood and is lovely either plain
or flavoured (see the variations below).
Cinnamon custard goes beautifully with
either apple tart or crumble (see pages 210
and 214), for instance, while vanilla custard
is yummy with plum or rhubarb crumble
and orange custard goes especially well with
Dark and White Chocolate Fudge Pudding
and apple and raspberry crumble (see pages
229 and 214).

500ml (18fl oz) milk
5 egg yolks
100g (3½oz) caster sugar

1 Pour the milk into a large saucepan and
slowly bring to the boil. Meanwhile, beat the
egg yolks and sugar together in a large bowl
until pale and thick. Gradually whisk the hot
milk into the beaten eggs and sugar and pour
the whole mixture back into the saucepan.

2 Return to a low heat and cook gently for
5–8 minutes, stirring all the time, until the
custard thickens slightly (it should just coat
the back of the spoon). Pour into a warm
jug to serve. If reheating, do so very gently
on a low heat so that the eggs don't scramble.

Variations
Vanilla custard: Add 1 vanilla pod, split,
to the milk when bringing to the boil in
the pan. Remove the pod from the custard
before pouring it into the jug to serve.
Orange custard: Add 1 strip of orange zest
to the milk when bringing to the boil in the
pan. Remove the zest from the custard before
pouring it into the jug to serve.

Cinnamon custard: Add ½ teaspoon
of cinnamon to the milk when bringing
to the boil in the pan.

Rachel's tip
When finished with, the vanilla pod can be
reused. Store it in a jar of sugar to add flavour
– perfect for baking.

Sugar syrup

VEGETARIAN

Sugar syrup is very useful to have to hand
for such things as making soft drinks and
poaching fruit (see pages 296 and 212),
or for making sorbet (such as the Blueberry
and Buttermilk Sherbet, see page 221).
Stored in a jar or bottle with a lid in a
cool place, it keeps indefinitely.

Makes about 150ml (5fl oz)
100g (3½oz) caster sugar
100ml (3½fl oz) water

Makes about 225ml (8fl oz)
150g (5oz) caster sugar
150ml (5fl oz) water

Makes about 375ml (13fl oz)
200g (7oz) caster sugar
200ml (7fl oz) water

To make the sugar syrup, place the sugar and
water in a small saucepan and bring slowly to
the boil, stirring to dissolve the sugar. Boil
for 2 minutes and leave to cool.

Index

A
aioli, tomato 175
almonds: almond and lemon
    macaroons 280
  apricot and almond cookies
    275
  chocolate and almond toffee
    brittle 314
  fruity frangipane tart 248
  poached dried fruits 44
  toffee, almonds and white
    chocolate ice cream 241
alphabet soup 59
Alpine breakfast omelette 20
American buttermilk
    pancakes 16–17
apples: apple and cinnamon
    muesli 17
  apple and raspberry
    crumble 214
  apple and sweet geranium
    yoghurt 10
  apple and sweet mincemeat
    crumble 214
  apple, blackberry and
    pecan nut muesli 17
  apple ice pops 294
  apple tart 210
  blackberry and apple
    fool 220
  blackberry and apple
    purée 323
  Bramley sauce 100–2
  custard with plum and
    apple 324
  fresh apple muesli 17
  fruity frangipane tart 248
  grated apple and Dijon
    mustard sausages 188
  kiwi fruit and apple
    juice 43

pear and apple purée 317
pear, apple and ginger
    smoothie 42
spicy prune and apple
    muffins 24
stewed apple and cinnamon
    Eton mess 234
toffee apples 292
apricots: apricot and almond
    cookies 275
  apricot and cardamom
    upside-down cake 233
  apricot and pear
    semolina 324
  apricot, prune and raisin
    compote 317
  fruit and nut stuffing 96
  poached dried fruits 44
  poached fruits 212
Asian noodle broth with
    chicken dumplings 51
asparagus: boiled eggs with
    soldiers 25
  creamy asparagus and
    Parmesan sauce 134
aubergine and tahini dip 72
avocados: avocado and
    banana mash 317
  guacamole 137–9

B
baba ghanouj 72
baby purées 315–24
bacon: bacon and cabbage
    with parsley sauce 190
  bacon and maple syrup
    waffles 19
  bacon and mushroom
    omelette 21
  bacon, mushroom and
    egg butty 258

bacon potato cakes 253
cabbage with bacon and
    cream 125
carbonara sauce 135
creamy bacon and mushroom
    sauce 136
crumbed bacon chops with
    sweet whiskey sauce 186
pork and egg picnic pie 80
potato, leek and smoked
    bacon soup 60
scrambled eggs with crispy
    bacon and Gruyère
    cheese 29
smoked bacon stuffing 96
weekend fry-up 38–9
bananas: avocado and banana
    mash 317
  baked banana split 216
  banana and cumin lassi 204
  banana and mango
    purée 317
  banana pancakes 17
  banana split 216
  fried bananas 39
  strawberry and banana
    ripple ice cream 240
  strawberry, banana and
    yoghurt smoothie 42
basil: tomato and basil
    dip 266–7
  tomato and basil sauce 191
beans (dried) 329, 334
  lamb, bean, olive and feta
    salad 79
beansprouts: fragrant sugar
    snap and beansprout
    noodle laksa 65
beef 104, 201
  beef and horseradish toasted
    sandwich 256

beef, oyster mushroom and
Savoy cabbage stir-fry 156
beefburgers with gherkin
relish 198–9
blue cheese burgers 199
Bolognese sauce 136
chilli con carne 202
individual steak and
mushroom pies 194–6
meatloaf with tomato and
basil sauce 191
minced beef with courgette,
leek, tomato and parsnip
323
oxtail soup 57
steak and frites 200–1
steak and kidney pie 196
steak and onion baked
potatoes 164
stock 326
traditional roast rib of
beef 103–5
berry pancakes 17
biscuit cakes 288
biscuits: almond and lemon
macaroons 280
apricot and almond
cookies 275
chocolate and marshmallow
biscuit sandwich 272
chocolate melting
moments 272
coconut and cinnamon
macaroons 280
coffee and hazelnut
cookies 275
pistachio cookies 275
raspberry swirls 285
sesame cookies 275
shortbread biscuits 220
squashed-fly biscuits 277

blackberries: blackberry
and apple fool 220
blackberry and apple
purée 323
blueberries: blueberry and
buttermilk sherbet 221
blueberry blush 43
Bolognese sauce 136
boozy biscuit cake 288
boozy hot chocolate 295
bread: bread and butter
pudding 226
bread rolls 331–2
bread sauce 96
brown bread ice cream 241
French toast 21
loaves 332
soda bread 333
spicy pitta wedges 73
spotted dog 32
toasted sandwiches
256–8, 262
tuna melt 255
broad beans: broad bean,
mint and feta sauce 132
minted broad beans 124
broccoli: broccoli, cauliflower
and sweet potato purée 322
broccoli, olive and Parmesan
salad 66
broccoli with nutty buttered
crumbs 126
brown bread ice cream 241
Brussels sprout soup 50
buffalo mozzarella and crisp
pancetta topping 199
burgers: beefburgers 198–9
blue cheese burgers 199
family chicken burgers 178
butter: herb butters 88, 327
sage and pine nut butter 141–2

buttermilk: American
buttermilk pancakes 16–17
blueberry and buttermilk
sherbet 221
butternut squash: butternut
squash ravioli 141–2
butternut squash risotto 148
carrot, butternut squash
and red split lentil
purée 316
chicken, sweetcorn and
butternut squash purée 322
creamy gratin of butternut
squash 122
salmon with butternut
squash, sweet potato
and garlic mash 323
butterscotch 313

C

cabbage: bacon and cabbage
with parsley sauce 190
beef, oyster mushroom and
Savoy cabbage stir-fry 156
buttered cabbage 125
cabbage with bacon and
cream 125
cakes: apricot and cardamom
upside-down cake 233
biscuit cakes 288
chocolate and peanut butter
cupcakes 286
chocolate and raspberry
Swiss roll 213
coffee Madeira cake 290
dark sticky gingerbread 289
orange Madeira cake 290
tomato salsa 137–9
candy canes 312–13
cannellini beans: white
bean dip 250

smoked salmon and goat's
cheese omelette 21
wild mushroom and goat's
cheese baked potatoes 165
gooseberry sponge tart 228
granola, crunchy 12
grape, melon and grapefruit
salad 14
grapefruit: grape, melon
and grapefruit salad 14
pink grapefruit and
pomegranate salad 14
gratins: cheese and garlic
potato 121
creamy gratin of butternut
squash 122
crunchy-topped parsnip 120
gravy 97, 100—6
green beans with garlic, chilli
and mustard seeds 124
guacamole 137—9
Mexican-style baked
potatoes 164

H
haddock see smoked haddock
ham: croque-monsieur 262
crunchy cheese and ham
melts 254
eggs Benedict 30
ham and cheese macaroni 143
ham and cheese toasted
sandwich 258
Mum's chicken and ham
lasagne 183
turkey and ham potato pie 189
see also Parma ham
hazelnuts: coffee and
hazelnut cookies 275
crunchy granola 12
hazelnut fudge 408

nougat 301
nutty toffee apples 292
healthy eating 264—5
herbs: green-speckled
pasta 131
herb butters 88, 327
summer herb dressing 184
traditional herb stuffing 96
hollandaise sauce 331
honeycomb 310
honeycomb ice cream 241
horseradish sauce 328
hot chocolate 295
hot water crust pastry 80, 194
huevos revueltos 29
hummus 73

I
ice cream 240—1
banana split 216
choc ices 298
Joshua's ice cream
extravaganza 242
see also semifreddo
ice pops, fruity 294—5
ingredients 334—5
Ivan Allen's dressed crab 90—2

J
jam: raspberry swirls 285
jellies, fruit 311
jelly, redcurrant 328
Joshua's ice cream
extravaganza 242
juices 42—3

K
kedgeree 36—7
ketchup, Rachel's 329
kidney beans: chilli con
carne 202

refried beans 137—9
kidneys: steak and kidney
pie 196
Kinoith pork casserole 187
kippers with dill butter 40
kiwi fruit: kiwi fruit and
apple juice 43
kiwi fruit and raspberry
waffles 19

L
laksa 65
lamb: coconut lamb curry 208
lamb and tomato curry 208
lamb, bean, olive and feta
salad 79
lamb cutlets with chickpea,
caramelised onion and
smoked paprika mash 197
Middle Eastern spiced lamb
koftas 70
mild lamb curry with
coriander rice 205—8
roast leg of lamb with mint
sauce and redcurrant
jelly 106
shepherd's pie 193
larders 334—5
lasagne, Mum's chicken
and ham 183
lassi 204
leeks: chicken, leek, sweet
potato and parsnip purée 320
leek and cheese baked
potatoes 164
leek, chorizo and potato
pie 114
minced beef with courgette,
leek, tomato and parsnip 323
potato, leek and smoked
bacon soup 60

shortbread biscuits 220
shortcrust pastry 333
shrimps: egg-fried rice 179
  fish cakes 86—8
  linguini with shrimps,
    garlic and herbs 83
  see also prawns
smoked haddock: kedgeree 36—7
smoked mackerel: nettle soup
    with smoked mackerel
    crostini 55
  scrambled eggs with smoked
    mackerel, chives and
    parsley 28
smoked salmon: smoked
    salmon and goat's cheese
    omelette 21
  smoked salmon, leek and
    potato pie 114
  tagliatelle with smoked salmon,
    watercress and peas 84
smoothies 42
soda bread 333
soft drinks 296
sole à la meunière 167
soups: alphabet soup 59
  Asian noodle broth with
    chicken dumplings 51
  Brussels sprout 50
  chicken and garlic 56
  chicken noodle laksa 65
  fragrant sugar snap and
    beansprout noodle laksa 65
  gazpacho 48
  Molly Malone's cockle and
    mussel chowder 52
  mushroom 47
  nettle 55
  oxtail 57
  potato, leek and smoked
    bacon 60

roast tomato 46
Zac's chicken and
    sweetcorn 60
spaghetti with herby pork
    meatballs 144
spices 334—5
spinach: green-speckled
    pasta 131
  pea, spinach and carrot
    purée 316
  plaice with spinach and
    pea purée 320
  spinach, garlic and walnut
    pesto 134, 148
  vegetarian eggs Benedict 30
spotted dog 32
spotted dog scones 32
spring onions: spring onion
    potato cakes 253
spring vegetable risotto 148
squash see butternut squash
squashed-fly biscuits 277
squid with tomato aioli 175
steak, frying times 201
steak and frites 200—1
steak and kidney pie 196
steak and mushroom
    pies 194—6
steak and onion baked
    potatoes 164
steamed puddings: date and
    orange syrup pudding 222
  steamed ginger treacle
    pudding 223
stock 326
strawberries: Eton mess 234
  poached fruits 212
  raspberry and strawberry
    purée 323
  strawberry and banana
    ripple ice cream 240

strawberry and rhubarb
    crumble 214
strawberry and white
    chocolate tiramisu 238
strawberry, banana and
    yoghurt smoothie 42
strawberry tart 210
stuffings 96—9
sugar 334
sugar snap and beansprout
    noodle laksa 65
sugar syrup 338
  cold-water test 299
summer garden salad 68
sunflower seeds: crunchy
    granola 12
sweet potatoes: baked sweet
    potato chips 118
  broccoli, cauliflower and
    sweet potato purée 322
  celeriac and sweet potato
    mash 117
  chicken, leek, sweet potato
    and parsnip purée 320
  salmon with butternut squash,
    sweet potato and garlic
    mash 323
sweet and sticky pork noodle
    stir-fry 154
sweetcorn: chicken, sweetcorn
    and butternut squash
    purée 322
  Zac's chicken and sweetcorn
    soup 60
sweets: butterscotch 313
  candy canes 312—13
  fruit jellies 311
  fruity lollipops 303
  honeycomb 310
  liquorice toffees 300
  marshmallows 307

nougat 301
toffee brittle 314
Turkish delight 304
white chocolate fudge 408
Swiss roll, chocolate and
    raspberry 213
syrup, sugar 299, 338

T

tagliatelle with smoked salmon,
    watercress and peas 84
tahini: aubergine and tahini
    dip 72
tapenade, black olive 252
tarragon: tarragon cream
    sauce 97
    tarragon, wholegrain mustard
    and honey sausages 188
tartare sauce 328
tarts: fruit tarts 210
    fruity frangipane tart 248
    gooseberry sponge tart 228
Thai peanut, vegetable and
    coconut noodles 158
Thai sticky chicken 270
tiramisu, strawberry and
    white chocolate 238
toasted sandwiches 256–8, 262
toffee: butterscotch 313
    hazelnut fudge 408
    liquorice toffees 300
    millionaire's shortbread 276
    toffee, almonds and white
    chocolate ice cream 241
    toffee and cashew nut brittle
    ice cream 241
    toffee apples 292
    toffee brittle 314
    toffee sauce 337
    white chocolate fudge 408
tomatoes: alphabet soup 59

Bolognese sauce 136
chilli con carne 202
fried squid with tomato
    aioli 175
gazpacho 48
lamb and tomato curry 208
meatloaf with tomato and
    basil sauce 191
Mexican scrambled eggs 29
minced beef with courgette,
    leek, tomato and parsnip 323
Parma ham, sun-blushed
    tomatoes, mozzarella and
    rocket quesadillas 259
Rachel's ketchup 329
roast tomato and lime
    mayonnaise 330
roast tomato soup 46
skinning 144
spaghetti with herby pork
    meatballs 144
tomato and basil dip 266–7
tomato and basil salad 90–2
tomato and cream sauce 135
tomato, garlic and basil
    sauce 132
tomato pasta 131
tomato salsa 137–9, 208
tomato sauce 149–51, 260
tortillas: quesadillas 259
tostados 137–9
treacle pudding, steamed
    ginger 223
tropical fruit mix 14
trout with herb butter 165
tuna melt 255
turkey and ham potato pie 189
Turkish delight 304
turmeric lassi 204
tzatziki 72
    spiced chicken salad with 76

V

vanilla custard 338
vegetables: crudités and
    dips 250–2
    healthy root vegetable
    crisps 263
    pecan and vegetable loaf 112
    Thai peanut, vegetable and
    coconut noodles 158
    see also carrots, tomatoes etc
vegetarian eggs Benedict 30
vinegars 334
waffles 19
walnuts: spinach, garlic and
    walnut pesto 134
watercress: mushroom and
    watercress sauce 97
    tagliatelle with smoked
    salmon, watercress and
    peas 84
weekend fry-up 38–9
whiskey sauce 186
white bean dip 250
white sauce 327
wine: red wine risotto 148

yoghurt: homemade yoghurt 10
    lassi 204
    raita 73
    raspberry and yoghurt ice
    pops 294
    smoothies 42
    tzatziki 72
Yorkshire puddings 103–5

Zac's chicken and sweetcorn
    soup 60
Zac's oven-ready rollies 260–1

Acknowledgements

It has been lots of fun making this book as, fortunately, two of my favourite pastimes are cooking and eating!

Firstly, I would like to thank everyone at Collins who has been involved in my last four books – you are all super: Katie Fulford, Denise Bates, Jenny Heller (who has the remarkable talent of treating all her authors like they are her only one); Lizzy Gray and Emma Callery (who are both an example in patience when trying to gently tie me down to meet my deadlines while I tend to run around like a headless chicken); Ione Walder and Kate Parker.

Fab photographer David Loftus, stylists Abigail Fawcett and Liz Belton, and designers Smith & Gilmour have all helped to make this book look so great, while Sharon Hearne-Smith, who worked so hard on this book with me, was brilliant at keeping me on the straight and narrow with her gentle but firm requests for more recipes every week.

A big thanks to my lovely sister Simone with the help of her husband Dodo for double-testing all the baby recipes, and my delicious nieces, Lola and Rosa, who gave them the seal of approval.

I am so grateful to my parents-in-law Tim and Darina and also to all the rest of the family at Ballymaloe for never minding when I bring teams of photographers, cameramen and goodness knows who else to Ballymaloe.

Thank you Susan Mannion for all the typing, Liz McCarthy, Melissa Evans, Gillian Beamish and Tina Young for making me look somewhat decent, and Eddie O'Neill at Teagasc for helping to get the yoghurt recipe perfected. Thanks also to Connor Pyne and Diarmaid Falvey.

I am greatly indebted to my wonderful parents who babysit time and time again. Thanks Mum for being supernanny!

To my agents at Limelight: Fiona, Mary, Alison and Maclean – thanks all for sorting out my life in such an efficient manner!

Finally, a huge thanks to my three gorgeous children, Joshua, Lucca and Scarlett, and my husband Isaac (I couldn't do it all without you). I dedicate this book to you because without you home cooking would be no fun at all.